Teaching and Learning Religion

Also Available from Bloomsbury:

All Religion Is Inter-Religion: Engaging the Work of Steven M. Wasserstrom,
Edited by Kambiz GhaneaBassiri and Paul Robertson
Fieldnotes in the Critical Study of Religion: Revisiting Classical Theorists,
Edited by Richard Newton and Vaia Touna
Teaching Critical Religious Studies: Pedagogy and Critique in the Classroom,
Edited by Jenna Gray-Hildenbrand, Beverley McGuire and Hussein Rashid

Teaching and Learning Religion

Engaging the Work of Eugene V. Gallagher and Patricia O'Connell Killen

Edited by
Davina C. Lopez and Thomas Pearson

BLOOMSBURY ACADEMIC
LONDON • NEW YORK • OXFORD • NEW DELHI • SYDNEY

BLOOMSBURY ACADEMIC

Bloomsbury Publishing Plc, 50 Bedford Square, London, WC1B 3DP, UK
Bloomsbury Publishing Inc, 1385 Broadway, New York, NY 10018, USA
Bloomsbury Publishing Ireland, 29 Earlsfort Terrace, Dublin 2, D02 AY28, Ireland

BLOOMSBURY, BLOOMSBURY ACADEMIC and the Diana logo are
trademarks of Bloomsbury Publishing Plc

First published in Great Britain 2023
Paperback edition published 2025

Copyright © Davina C. Lopez, Thomas Pearson, and contributors, 2023

Davina C. Lopez and Thomas Pearson have asserted their rights under the Copyright, Designs and Patents Act, 1988, to be identified as Editors of this work.

Cover image © Jacob Lund / Alamy

All rights reserved. No part of this publication may be: i) reproduced or transmitted in any form, electronic or mechanical, including photocopying, recording or by means of any information storage or retrieval system without prior permission in writing from the publishers; or ii) used or reproduced in any way for the training, development or operation of artificial intelligence (AI) technologies, including generative AI technologies. The rights holders expressly reserve this publication from the text and data mining exception as per Article 4(3) of the Digital Single Market Directive (EU) 2019/790.

Bloomsbury Publishing Plc does not have any control over, or responsibility for, any third-party websites referred to or in this book. All internet addresses given in this book were correct at the time of going to press. The author and publisher regret any inconvenience caused if addresses have changed or sites have ceased to exist, but can accept no responsibility for any such changes.

A catalogue record for this book is available from the British Library.

Library of Congress Control Number: 2023934706

ISBN: HB: 978-1-3502-7868-4
       PB: 978-1-3502-7872-1
       ePDF: 978-1-3502-7869-1
       eBook: 978-1-3502-7870-7

Typeset by Integra Software Services Pvt. Ltd.

For product safety related questions contact productsafety@bloomsbury.com.

To find out more about our authors and books visit www.bloomsbury.com
and sign up for our newsletters.

For those who teach and learn about theology and religion—past, present, future

Contents

Introduction: A Teaching *Festschrift* for Gene and Patricia *Thomas Pearson* 1

Part One Plan

1. Midrange Reflection for the Climate Rebellion: How the Scholarship of Teaching and Learning Can Inform Activism *Kevin J. O'Brien* 15
2. Paschal Pedagogy *Mara Brecht* 27
3. Art and the Unexpected *Alicia J. Batten* 39
4. Laughter in the Temple: Hermeneutics and Humor in Teaching Religion *Anita Houck* 49
5. Planning for Playfulness *Richard S. Ascough* 71
6. The Tao of the Post-It: Empowering Student Engagement in Gene Gallagher's Classroom *Lydia Willsky-Ciollo* 83
7. Taking the General Education Student Seriously *Bruce David Forbes* 91
8. The Challenges of Teaching as Racial and Ethnic Minority Scholars *Kwok Pui-lan* 103
9. The Magic or Midrange Reflection *Molly H. Bassett* 117

Part Two Persona

10. Overcoming Fears of a Normative Valence *Susan Marks* 129
11. A Vulnerable Persona: Wrestling with the Legacy of Jean Vanier *Reid B. Locklin and Andrea Nicole Carandang* 137
12. "Ungrading" and the Unmaking of Professorial Persona *Kathryn D. Blanchard* 153
13. Tennis, Anyone? *Joanne Maguire* 165

Part Three Place

14. Who Is in the Chair? The Professor Faces the Classroom *Arthur M. Sutherland* 179
15. Finding Your Place on the Map *Rebekka King* 187

16 Mise en Place: Efficiency and Ethics in the Practice of Teaching
    Tina Pippin   197
17 Teaching about Religion and/at/as the Edge: From What to
    How to Why *Davina C. Lopez*   209

List of Contributors   219
Index   220

Introduction

A Teaching *Festschrift* for Gene and Patricia

Thomas Pearson
Nielsen Center for the Liberal Arts at Eckerd College

Eugene V. Gallagher and Patricia O'Connell Killen are consummate teachers of teachers. For nearly twenty years, they were among several dozen faculty who were invited to lead summer teaching workshops at the Wabash Center for Teaching and Learning in Theology and Religion.[1] They mentored a generation of religious studies faculty teaching now at colleges and universities across North America. This volume is a testament to their impact. The essays collected here provide testimony from seventeen former workshop participants—their "students," in a sense. It is a *festschrift*, demonstrating the power of their mentorship and the clarity of their insights about college teaching and faculty life.

The word *festschrift* carries antiquated overtones of its emergence in nineteenth-century German-language academic traditions. It is the name for a collection of essays presented as a tribute to a scholar, typically by his or her students, demonstrating their influence in a field of inquiry. Cognately, it is a "feast-script," a celebration-writing, a banquet. This is a *teaching festschrift* for Gene and Patricia, presented by their workshop "students," demonstrating and celebrating the fruit of their critical reflection on teaching religion and theology in colleges and universities. Each essay is a demonstration and application of the fruitful field Gene and Patricia opened for us, and each is a tribute and celebration of them—individually and together—as teachers and mentors.

My colleague, Davina C. Lopez, first approached me with this idea several years ago, and she has exercised primary leadership throughout. I know Davina from several Wabash Center workshops, where I was Associate Director for nearly two decades. She has contributed the final essay in this volume, written from her position as Professor of Religious Studies at Eckerd College. My contribution to the volume is this Introduction, written from the perspective of Associate Director of the Wabash Center, where I worked with Gene and Patricia on many workshop leadership teams. Since the commencement of this writing project, I have taken a new position as Director of the Nielsen Center for the Liberal Arts at Eckerd College.

Although this is a teaching *festschrift*, the research and scholarship of Gene and Patricia are clearly deserving of a companion, traditional, *festschrift*. Gene Gallagher is an historian of religions, publishing widely in new religious movements in the United States, originally trained at the University of Chicago in religions in the Greco-Roman world. Patricia O'Connell Killen (Ph.D., Stanford University) publishes on Catholicism in North America, and religion and spirituality in the Pacific Northwest. Gene taught religious studies for thirty-seven years at Connecticut College, retiring as the Rosemary Park Professor of Religious Studies *Emeritus*. Patricia served as Academic Vice President at Gonzaga University for nearly a decade before retiring as Professor of Religion, *Emerita* and Faculty Research Fellow at Pacific Lutheran University, where she had taught for years and served as Provost.

This teaching *festschrift* is organized around three themes that have been central to Gene and Patricia's teaching about teaching: Place, Plan, and Persona.

Place is the institutional context in which we teach: the actual students enrolled in our courses (maybe not the students we *wish* we had), the institutional history and curriculum in which our courses fit, and the relationship we have with our colleagues and the administration.

Plan is the intentions we bring to the classroom: the design that creates a learning experience for students. It is the lesson plan—what we intend to say and do, and ask the students to say and do, to facilitate their learning.

Persona is the identity of the teacher: the personality we inhabit at the front of the classroom, and the identity that structures our most fundamental purposes and passions in teaching.

As teachers, we are each a persona, with a plan, in a particular place. This is the structure that Gene and Patricia proposed in their teaching workshops. A Wabash Center teaching workshop is itself a teaching and learning environment shaped by place, plan, and persona. And thus these categories appropriately structure my thoughts about Gene and Patricia as teachers and as teachers of teachers.

I offer these comments and introduce this volume in the generous and generative spirit of Wabash Center workshop hospitality—as though at a feast, a festival, celebrating and honoring their accomplishment, offering warm and intimate reflections that betray my feelings and no doubt some personal projections. It is less scholarly than impressionistic. Bear with me. As teachers, Patricia and Gene inhabit quite different approaches to place, plan, and persona. I think this is what has made them such good friends and such an effective workshop leadership team.

Plan

Gene describes teaching as a triangle connecting the teacher, the students, and the subject matter. That triangle has a lot of energy for him. I've also heard him describe teaching as a basketball game. Sure, there's a play that has been designed, but there are so many moving parts (moving players) with motivations and responses that you can't predict, so you have to intuit how the play is unfolding in real time and make adjustments on the fly. All the players are doing this, simultaneously. It's a creative dance, with a goal, and a plan, that falls apart and then falls into new patterns again in unanticipated ways. And then, Gene likes to say, you walk out of the classroom covered in sweat and chalk and wonder what the hell just happened.

Famously, Gene fits his plan for class on a single Post-It note, but he has a lot more in mind that is left unsaid. His teaching plan is an interpersonal experience. He teaches through dialogue, scribbling phrases and shapes on the board to represent students' contributions, and drawing arrows and lines between their ideas. He asks them follow-up questions to help them see the implications of their ideas. The plan is enacted organically.

In contrast, for Patricia, teaching is the "design of the intellectual experience." Teaching is a significant academic pursuit because the design of students' intellectual experience is a significant academic challenge. Design is the outcome or application of rigorous analysis of student learning through evidence and reflection on teaching practice.

And in workshops, Patricia designed prompts to help participants describe their classroom experience: what were your intentions, what did you expect would happen, what actually occurred, and how do you account for the difference? Her carefully planned incremental steps made teachers' self-reflection on teaching visible to themselves.

It is her interest in the design of the intellectual experience that leads to Patricia's interest in the scholarship of teaching. There, the goal is for an author to surface their pedagogical intentions, describe and analyze a design for learning, place it in the context of student learning goals, reflect on the evidence of success or failure, and then draw the implications of this concrete example to a more generally pervasive aspect or issue in higher education.

This is what she calls "midrange reflection."[2] It is a space or level of analysis of teaching that is grounded in careful description and reflection on specific teaching occasions, with the aim of drawing more generalized insights transferable to other specific teaching occasions, forestalling the leap to broad principles of teaching philosophy. Midrange reflection remains productive as it holds to the middle ground between low-level description of teaching and high-level abstractions.

Midrange reflection is the method of Gene and Patricia's Wabash Center teaching workshops, and many of the essays collected in this volume invoke this concept and then illustrate this process of analysis and writing. This is the method of writing about teaching that Gene and Patricia recommend in their influential essay, "Sketching the Contours of the Scholarship of Teaching and Learning in Theology and Religion,"[3] and many of the contributors to this volume explicitly place their contribution within the categories established in that essay.

Alicia Batten's essay, "Art and the Unexpected," is a classic statement of midrange reflection applied to the experience of revising a course for online learning. Molly H. Bassett's essay, "The Magic or Midrange Reflection," narrates an introductory course, rethought through midrange reflection at her Wabash workshop, in which she was writing an article on using multiple-choice exams. The essay from Anita Houck, "Laughter in the Temple," is an extended use of midrange reflection, analyzing the role of humor in the classroom. Mara Brecht's contribution, "Paschal Pedagogy," calls attention to the importance of the arc of learning in Patricia's conception of design. The essay in this volume contributed by Tina Pippin, "*Mise en Place*: Efficiency and Ethics in the Practice of Teaching," responds to Gene and Patricia's "Sketching the Contours" essay by asking what a scholarship of teaching would look like if developed in a lineage from Paulo Freire. It would critique the teacher-centric model of "research on student learning" that advances the neoliberal educational structures. And the essay by Kevin J. O'Brien, "Midrange Reflection for the Climate Rebellion," makes the case for religious studies and the humanities, through an imagined conversation between Patricia Killen and Greta Thunberg. He invokes critical reflection for theology, for life, and for thinking about your teaching and what your students most need to learn. Richard Ascough's essay develops the notion of plan and design all the way to its logical opposite—planning for spontaneity, for the unexpected, for play.

Place

If plan is central to how Gene and Patricia conceptualize teaching, and teach teaching, then reflection on the place in which this plan is devised and executed is the natural corollary and the inevitable complement. The first question of teaching is: who are my students, and how do they learn? This question is prior even to the question of what I should teach them. The latter, according to Gene and Patricia, is a question too readily formulated by the academic disciplines in which we have been trained as scholars.

Many times I heard Patricia voice concern that whereas previous generations of faculty were embedded in the institution where they taught, the new generation is much more likely to remain answerable primarily to the guild—to the academic discipline that formed them as scholars, gathering at national conferences and sharing new research questions and results. She encourages new faculty to think of themselves not as independent contractors or intellectual entrepreneurs, but as teammates in an educational mission, a broadly conceived academic project shaped by faculty governance and institutional traditions. She urges faculty to recognize that they pursue the rigor of their research within a particular organizational context and that teaching is an equally rigorous academic project, with its own questions, purposes, and concerns.

Gene was an early advocate of the need to refocus a department's concerns onto the general education curriculum. The now well-recognized nationwide decline in the number of religious studies majors, and in humanities majors more generally, is for Gene a moment of opportunity to ask what is most important for undergraduates to learn in their one and only college religion course. Less is clearly more in this situation, and the selections and emphases must be informed by careful, highly trained academic discernment of the dynamics and rhetorics of religion, in contemporary societies, as well as the goals and purposes of liberal arts education.

More than one essayist in this collection explores this element of Gene's reflection on teaching. The essays by Lydia Willsky-Ciollo, Rebekka King, and Bruce Forbes respond to this question in different ways in their essays. The essay by Davina C. Lopez, "Teaching about Religion and/at/as the Edge," analyzes her students and the history of Eckerd College in order to reflect on the what, how and why of teaching religion. It is an egregious intellectual error (and missed opportunity) to think about the students you *wish* you had, or to resent and withdraw from the institutional context in which you do your work. Gene is fond of quoting the hook to the Stephen Stills song from the 1960s: you have to "love the one you're with."

Surfacing and analyzing the dynamics that shape institutions was often a key moment in Gene and Patricia's Wabash Center teaching workshops. They developed the "Institutional Profile Form" to help workshop participants find and list for each other the significant characteristics of their institutions. What's the size of your institution (the number of faculty and students) and the distribution of majors? What's the size of your department? How does it compare to other academic units on campus? What is your institution's endowment? The acceptance rate? The tuition, and the tuition discount rate? How many courses do you teach each year? What is the percentage of tenured and tenure track positions? All of this contributes to new teachers' grasp of the wide variety of higher educational contexts (putting their own in comparative perspective) and the variety of teaching contexts represented in the room from which the workshop participants speak. This is the first crucial step in analyzing how context does and should impact teaching practice.

Persona

Gene loves to poke fun at Parker Palmer, the widely read philosopher of teaching who famously wrote that "you teach who you are"—becoming in Gene's mind an avatar for the idea of teaching as a vocation.[4] Gene is skeptical that there is a true and authentic deep self that great teachers (according to Palmer), reach down to and teach from. Gene found his most effective retort to Parker Palmer in Jay Parini's short essay on the mask of the teacher.[5] For Gene, agreeing with Parini, the identity of the teacher is a crafted persona, a mask, a personality you learn to adopt as you become comfortable and live into your performance on a teaching stage. Teaching is a role that you play. There's nothing inauthentic or false about this. It's inevitable and necessary. And, Gene insists, it is helpful to be aware of it and intentional about it. I have seen Gene and Patricia in workshops pose Parker Palmer's formulation as a question, or one pole of an alternative, with Parini's mask on the other extreme. It's a helpful puzzle for a new teacher to consider, as they transition from an identity as graduate student researcher and embark on a career as a teacher of students. Reid B. Locklin and his co-author Andrea Nicole Carandang explore the issue of masks at considerable length in their essay, "A Vulnerable Persona: Wrestling with the Legacy of Jean Vanier"—remarking on the masks that empower us, hide us, or reveal our most telling secrets. Susan

Marks' essay, "Overcoming Fears of a Normative Valence," configures course redesign through teaching persona, as does the essay by Kathryn D. Blanchard, "'Ungrading' and the Unmaking of Professorial Persona."

Another workshop exercise I've seen Gene and Patricia deploy asks workshop participants to consider for themselves the implicit metaphor they have for themselves as a teacher and draw it on a sheet of flipchart paper. Are you a guide? A camp counselor? The conductor of an orchestra? Or perhaps a juggler or magician, an acrobat, lifeguard, window washer or manicurist. The image you articulate can tell you a lot about your teaching practice and give you insight into quandaries and successes. See Arthur Sutherland's essay, "Who Is in the Chair?" for an exploration of various *student* personas—characterizations that might be understood as metaphors for *students*. Kwok Pui-lan's essay, "The Challenge of Teaching as Racial and Ethnic Minority Scholars," centers the person of the teacher (as delineated in Killen and Gallagher's "Sketching the Contours"), highlighting the intersection of race and gender in course design and content, as well as the assessment of students Tina Pippin's essay, "*Mise en* Place," explores a metaphor not of the teacher but of the plan or design of the teaching experience—that is, putting everything in its place.

In addition to what Gene and Patricia teach about the importance of reflecting on your teaching persona, there is also the actual teaching personas that each of them inhabit in the classroom and workshop environment. And their personas are quite different from each other. Here my reflections get particularly personal.

I think Gene teaches because he wants to share his astonishment at the bizarre phenomenon of religion, but fundamentally because he loves the social interaction of teaching. It is the sociability of teaching that gets him started and keeps him going. He gets to the classroom early and greets each student as they arrive, making small talk as they are able, referencing previous conversations, some event he knows they've experienced since their last class session, or an inside joke they share.

Patricia, on the other hand, teaches to reenact and vicariously relive her awakening as an undergraduate to the intellectual thrill of the rigorously posed academic question. I've heard her recount her childhood growing up on a marginal farm in the Pacific Northwest, and how the world opened up for her when she entered Gonzaga University, a Jesuit school that would one day hire her as Academic Vice-President. She describes the thrill when she discovered that there is such a thing as an academic question to which one could apply sustained research and analysis. It's been the passion and purpose of her life ever since.[6] She loves teaching in no small part because she loves trying to stage that experience for newcomers to this academic world. Rebecca King's essay, "Finding Your Place on the Map," puts Patricia's arrival story to somewhat different use, noting that our students may not share the awakening we experienced in our encounter with the academic world.

Gene grew up in an urban Philadelphia neighborhood, an only child, whose mother suffered health issues. For both of them, their childhood worlds could not contemplate the academic life. College provided a new way to be, a new person to be, and an escape into something bigger and more interesting. For both of them, the academic world is liberation. I think this moment informs the rest of Patricia's academic life and purposes. I'm not sure how it stands or breathes for Gene. His Parini-mask is pretty secure now. He finds Parker Palmer's language of vocation pious and alienating. "I don't have a calling, I have a job," he likes to quip. It's an important part of his mask. But I think teachers often want to see themselves in their students.

See the essay by Joanne Maguire, "Tennis, Anyone?" for a thorough exploration of the language of vocation, which she also finds problematic. The essay explores tennis as a metaphor for teaching—also appropriate for Gene, because reminiscent of his basketball metaphor but more pertinent to his actual current pastime on actual tennis courts. Joanne was first Gene's student before continuing on into the field and becoming his colleague and co-author—a testimony to his mentorship. Lydia Willsky-Ciollo too was Gene's student as an undergraduate and even taught a course with him for a semester before landing a permanent position at Fairfield University. And it should be added that both Alicia J. Batten and Kevin J. O'Brien learned to teach with Patricia as chair of their department and later Provost at Pacific Lutheran University.

Together, at the front of a teaching workshop, the personas of Gene and Patricia feed each other in fruitful contrasts. Patricia has a sure hand on the tiller, but she is disarmed by his casual jocular demeanor. And Gene is challenged by Patricia's intense analytic focus, her seriousness, and her careful preparation. He is challenged by her, and ups his game—having learned that her responses will push him further. And she seems to check to see whether what she's just articulated is confirmed by his own experience. He likes to say that his goal is to make her laugh so hard she snorts, and Patricia is not one who seeks to laugh quickly or build frivolity. They are an odd couple, polar opposites in many ways, making a very dynamic duo.

Patricia loves to craft precise sentences, carefully choosing words to exactly articulate her idea in as few words as possible. Her phrase, "the design of the intellectual experience," is a good example of this. I've heard her say: "judgement is the process that slows down the jump from an idea to a conclusion." And: "Thinking about teaching is a compositional act. Consider how this contributes to your authority, your agency, your artistry, and audacity, in building a bridge or scaffolding between students and the material."

Gene, on the other hand, enjoys interjecting clever slogans cast in a casual vernacular—almost like bumper stickers or tweets that succinctly sum up his view on a topic. "You have to throw the ball so they can catch it." And: "It's the students, stupid." He's good at repeating back to his conversation partner what he's just heard them say, distilling it into a pithy bumper sticker or witticism. "You don't want to send your students down a mountainside without guardrails." And when you have left the exalted heights of your doctoral institution and find yourself teaching marginal students in a failing college in rural Arkansas, it doesn't do you any good to blame your students—"you gotta love the one you're with."

I've seen them working together trying to articulate a workshop question or assignment—and then Gene will suddenly pick up a phrase from Patricia and start to slowly build, methodically, word by word, as though dictating to himself, crystalizing their thinking in a short declarative, plainly spoken sentence or question—as Patricia quickly types it down.

Patricia is rigorously analytical. She takes the idea apart and gives each part a name. Gene, on the other hand, is a great synthesizer, categorizer, simplifier, and distiller into lucid sound bites. Thus, he writes fluidly, quickly, cogently, and persuasively. And thus he is a clear and persuasive teacher. Together they are a powerful team.

A teaching workshop led by Gene and Patricia is all about making teaching visible through midrange reflection—critical reflection on specific teaching occasions, to form more general understandings transferable to other contexts. To do this, you must be a careful observer, and you need to denaturalize the act of teaching. You must become conscious of your intentions and judgments, so you can analyze them and improve them.

Plan, place, and persona are helpful categories for thinking about teaching. Each of our authors has taken up one of these categories to reflect on their own teaching, as formed by their Wabash Center workshop experience with Gene and Patricia.

A Wabash Center workshop is itself an exercise in plan, place, and persona. The plan is to denaturalize the practice of teaching and open it up for critical self-reflection. The Wabash Center provides a hospitable place for reflection, sharing, and exploration. And the personas of Gene and Patricia, diverging and yet complementary personalities and teaching styles, inspire and encourage the feast. Gene and Patricia teach about plan, place, and persona in their teaching workshops. And their workshops are a manifestation of their particular plan, place, and personas.

And hence, the feast, and now the *festschrift*, as a tribute that honors and extends the critical reflection on teaching of plan, place, and persona embodied in Gene and Patricia and passed on to their students.

Notes

1. The Wabash Center for Teaching and Learning in Theology and Religion is funded by Lilly Endowment, Inc. Since the mid-1990s it has been supporting faculty teaching religious and theological studies through workshops, grants, resources, and other programs. https://www.wabashcenter.wabash.edu/.
2. Patricia O'Connell Killen, "Midrange Reflection: The Underlying Practice of Wabash Center Workshops, Colloquies, and Consultations," *Teaching Theology & Religion* 10 (2007): 143–9.
3. Patricia O'Connell Killen and Eugene V. Gallagher, "Sketching the Contours of the Scholarship of Teaching and Learning in Theology and Religion," *Teaching Theology & Religion* 16 (2013): 115–22.
4. Parker J. Palmer, *The Courage to Teach: Exploring the Inner Landscape of a Teacher's Life*, 20th Anniversary Edition. 1st edn. (San Francisco, CA: Jossey-Bass, 2007).
5. Jay Parini, "Point of View: Cultivating a Teaching Persona," *The Chronicle of Higher Education*, September 5, 1997.
6. See her use of this story in Patricia O'Connell Killen, "Gracious Play: Discipline, Insight, and the Common Good," *Teaching Theology & Religion* 4 (2001): 2–8.

Bibliography

Gallagher, Eugene V. *Divine Man or Magician? Celsus and Origen on Jesus*. Chico, CA: Scholars Press, 1982.

Gallagher, Eugene V. *Expectation and Experience: Explaining Religious Conversion*. Atlanta, GA: Scholars Press, 1990.

Gallagher, Eugene V. *The New Religious Movements Experience in America*. Westport, CT: Greenwood Press, 2004.

Gallagher, Eugene V. "Welcoming the Stranger." *Teaching Theology & Religion* 10 (2007): 137–42.

Gallagher, Eugene V. "Teaching for Religious Literacy." *Teaching Theology & Religion* 12, no. 3 (2009): 208–21.

Gallagher, Eugene V. "The AAR Teaching Series." *Teaching Theology & Religion* 12, no. 1 (2009): 24–36.

Gallagher, Eugene V. "'Discussion Starter' Papers." *Teaching Theology & Religion* 13, no. 3 (2010): 241–2.

Gallagher, Eugene V. *Reading and Writing Scripture in New Religious Movements: New Bibles and New Revelations*. London, UK: Palgrave/Macmillan, 2014.

Gallagher, Eugene V. "Is the 'New Culture of Learning' All That New?" *Teaching Theology & Religion* 17 (2014): 232–8.

Gallagher, Eugene V., and James D. Tabor. *Why Waco? Cults and the Battle for Religious Freedom in America*. Berkeley, CA: University of California Press, 1995.

Gallagher, Eugene V., and Benjamin E Zeller. "Teaching New and Alternative Religious Movements." *Spotlight on Teaching* (2015).

Gallagher, Eugene V., and Joanne Maguire Robinson. *The Religious Studies Skills Book: Close Reading, Critical Thinking, and Comparison*. London: Bloomsbury, 2018.

Gallagher, Eugene V., and Joanne Maguire. "Teaching Religion to Undergraduates in the 2020s: A Preliminary Reconnaissance." *The Wabash Center Journal on Teaching* 1, no. 1 (2020): 9–21.

Gallagher, Eugene V., and Lydia Willsky-Ciollo. *New Religions: Emerging Faiths and Religious Cultures in the Modern World*. Santa Barbara, CA: ABC-CLIO, 2021.

Killen, Patricia O'Connell. "Gaps and Gifts." *Prism: A Publication of the Division of Humanities at Pacific Lutheran University* 12 (1999): 6–8.

Killen, Patricia O'Connell. "Students' Inner Conflicts: A Pedagogical Resource." *Teaching and Learning Forum*, Pacific Lutheran University (Spring 2000): 1–2.

Killen, Patricia O'Connell. "Gracious Play: Discipline, Insight, and the Common Good." *Teaching Theology & Religion* 4 (2001): 2–8.

Killen, Patricia O'Connell. "Making Thinking Real Enough to Make It Better: Using Posters to Develop Skills for Constructing Disciplinary Arguments." *Teaching Theology & Religion* 5, no. 4 (2002): 221–2.

Killen, Patricia O'Connell. "Midrange Reflection: The Underlying Practice of Wabash Center Workshops, Colloquies, and Consultations." *Teaching Theology & Religion* 10, no. 3 (2007): 143–9.

Killen, Patricia O'Connell, Madeline Duntley, Constance Furey, W. Clark Gilpin, and Horace E. Six-Means. "Teaching the History of Christianity: Critical Themes and Challenges." *Teaching Theology & Religion* 12, no. 3 (2009): 258–86.

Killen, Patricia O'Connell. "Building Questioning Strategies: Or, Why Am I Asking These Questions and Where Are They Taking Us?" *Teaching Theology & Religion* 13, no. 3 (2010): 251–3.

Killen, Patricia O'Connell, and John De Beer. *The Art of Theological Reflection*. New York: Crossroad Publishing Company, 1994.

Killen, Patricia O'Connell, and Eugene V. Gallagher. "Sketching the Contours of the Scholarship of Teaching and Learning in Theology and Religion." *Teaching Theology & Religion* 16, no. 2 (2013): 107–24.

Killen, Patricia O'Connell. Editor's Note. *Teaching Theology & Religion* [inclusive dates] 10:2 (2007)—15: 2(2012).

Palmer, Parker J. *The Courage to Teach: Exploring the Inner Landscape of a Teacher's Life.* San Francisco, California: Jossey-Bass, 2007.

Parini, Jay. "Point of View: Cultivating a Teaching Persona." *The Chronicle of Higher Education*, September 5, 1997.

Pearson, Thomas, Kwok Pui-lan and Eugene V. Gallagher. "Conversation on the Scholarship of Teaching." *The Wabash Center Journal on Teaching* 1, no. 2 (2020): 63–78.

Part One

Plan

Midrange Reflection for the Climate Rebellion: How the Scholarship of Teaching and Learning Can Inform Activism

Kevin J. O'Brien
Pacific Lutheran University

Introduction

Anyone who ever sees Eugene Gallagher and Patricia Killen together gets a lesson in how to have an intellectual conversation. They listen to each other, learn from each other, and challenge each other. They frequently cite their teachers, mentors, and extensive reading but provide enough context so that even those of us who have read and learned far less remain fully engaged. They invite and inspire everyone else in the room to join in, finding wisdom in every comment while continuously pushing for deeper thinking and exploration. They model active engagement and learning in community.

The example of such conversation inspires me to imagine one of them in dialogue with another partner. What would happen if Patricia Killen had a conversation with climate activist Greta Thunberg? I'm nowhere near smart enough to put words in either woman's mouth, but I am confident that they would find a lot to talk about and learn from one another. They come from different generations and different parts of the world, and their styles of discourse are widely distinct. But both are principled, thoughtful people who combine deep commitment with profound intelligence.

That imagined conversation inspires the argument of this essay: those of us who teach about religion and the environment should seek to foster what Killen calls "midrange reflection" in our students in order to equip them for a world in which climate change is and will increasingly be a prominent and disturbing fact of life.

Inspired by Killen's work with Eugene Gallagher, I want to be as transparent and thoughtful as I can about this argument. They write that a good essay in the scholarship of teaching and learning requires, "A clear statement of the problem or issue to be addressed, comprehensible organization, an accessible form and style, and critical engagement with the evidence make for persuasive argumentative writing across contexts."[1] The issue I am addressing is: Why should teaching about religion matter to our students in an age of climate change? My answer develops in two steps: First, I use Thunberg's work to reflect on the contemporary cultural context and argue that climate change is a vital part of the context through which students enter our courses. Second, I argue that Killen's work on midrange reflection is a helpful way to articulate the goal of teaching about religion and its relevance to that context. My primary evidence is the work of Thunberg and Killen, supplemented by my own experience and other literature on teaching and climate activism.

This argument fits into the genre that Gallagher and Killen call "unified field theory" because I articulate a pedagogical goal that I hope will influence others who teach religion. I aspire to a "coherent vision of a community" of professors who share a political and pedagogical project.[2] In other words, this essay aims to inspire others to join in the project of training students to engage and teach midrange reflection on climate change and religion.[3]

Greta Thunberg and Contemporary College Students

Greta Thunberg has, to my knowledge, said very little publicly about religion. But those of us who teach religion have much to learn about our students from her. As I write this in fall of 2021, she is the same age as the traditional-age students who are beginning their college career. Like many of these students, she struggles openly with depression, anxiety, and eating disorders. She and her family have written about this extensively in *Our House Is on Fire: Scenes of a Family and a Planet in Crisis*.[4] The book discloses that, while Thunberg is famous for the school strike she began at the age of fifteen, she first stopped regular school attendance at the age of eleven when she was admitted to the hospital after barely eating for 2 months due to her anxiety.

This experience is sadly not unique. The *Chronicle of Higher Education* reported in 2018 that more than 25 percent of college students in the United States report symptoms of anxiety and noted in 2021 that campus counseling centers were overwhelmed even before the Covid-19 pandemic drastically increased needs for mental health care.[5] Like Greta Thunberg, our students are processing a great deal of stress within and around themselves, and they want to talk about it. So those of us who teach need to think about how we shape our classrooms to allow them to process their anxiety rather than be paralyzed or marginalized by it. A good place to start is embracing the principles of universal design.[6]

Thunberg also speaks for many of our students in feeling betrayed by her elders, and on this issue she is perhaps the most recognized spokesperson of her generation. In *Our House Is on Fire,* she attributes part of her early struggles to a governmental and school system that was not designed to help her or her family understand that she is on the autism spectrum. Even more emphatically, her public career has emphasized that previous generations created the climate crisis and continue to refuse to treat it with the seriousness it deserves. For example, she told the European Union's Economic and Social Committee: "You are acting like spoiled, irresponsible children [and have] wasted decades through denial and inaction."[7]

Again, I believe Thunberg speaks for many of her peers. While my evidence is anecdotal, it is extensive. In recent years, my students are more and more skeptical of older people and distrustful of authority that comes from the past. They frequently attribute this to a disappointment about the state of the world, seeing their elders as having degraded the world they inherit. So, when we teach about the past and received traditions, we need to work with students' distrust and acknowledge that this distrust is reasonable while helping them to critically analyze received wisdom.

A third way Thunberg represents her generation is her resolutely intersectional understanding of how the world needs to change. For example, while previous generations of climate activists made frequent distinctions between their cause and others,[8] Thunberg mentions issues of equity and justice in every speech she gives. Throughout 2020, she insisted that climate concerns intersect with widespread protests about farm policy in India and police violence in the United States. She writes that feminism, anti-racism, anti-poverty, animal rights movement, advocacy for refugees and people with mental illness, and many other causes all intersect with environmental degradation, asserting that "the climate movement has a key that fits all the doors" to these issues.[9]

Like Thunberg, our students are increasingly embracing intersectional approaches to the issues they care about. They are passionate about being recognized for their identities and their moral commitments, and they reject firm distinctions between the two.[10] As educators, we need to help them use this intersectional impulse to think more deeply about climate change and other challenges. A good place to start is the activist style of teaching advocated by Todd LeVasseur, who encourages professors of religion to "help students create a critical consciousness so they can learn to perceive the social, political, and economic contradictions within which they have been raised and that permeate higher education."[11]

College professors also need to respond to a fourth aspect of Thunberg's example that connects the previous three. Anxious about the future, disappointed in authority, and insisting on intersectionality, many of our students have a deep suspicion that education is not a key or relevant project for their lives or our times.

Thunberg exemplified this most powerfully by her refusal to go to school. Inspired partly by the students who went on strike after the Parkland, Florida shooting, fifteen-year-old Thunberg sat outside Swedish parliament in 2018 and declared that she would not attend school until her nation took more meaningful political action on climate change. Later that year, she told a group of activists about her disillusionment with traditional education: "why should I be studying for a future that soon will be no more, when no one is doing anything whatsoever to save that future?" She called, instead, for civil disobedience and protest: "Everything needs to change. And it has to start today …. It's time to rebel."[12]

Thunberg suggests that the reality of crisis calls for immediate rebellion rather than the traditional, measured, and systemic work of formal learning. Disillusioned with the educational institutions built by her untrustworthy elders, Thunberg addressed her anxiety by taking action on climate change and other issues that intersect with it. Since traveling the world on a speaking tour, Thunberg has returned to school, but she continues to strike every Friday. So the questions posed by her activism remain: In these times, what is the point of education? If a rebellion is called for, is there time to slowly, thoughtfully study and learn? If previous generations have fundamentally failed to build a sustainable world, can their educational institutions be trusted?

The Value of Humanistic Reflection

Before defending a qualified "yes" in answer to each of those questions, I need to narrow them to a manageable scope. While Thunberg went on strike from high school in Sweden, I teach college in the United States, and so I will speak from my own context and address the value of higher rather than secondary education. Furthermore, while there is much that can be studied in college,

I teach religion and will focus on defending that enterprise, arguing that the study of religion—if done thoughtfully and well—remains vitally important and even urgent in these times. The best justification of this argument I know of comes from Patricia Killen, who helpfully articulates the value of education out of a tradition while also leaving room for the urgent truth that the world cries out for urgent change.

More specifically, Killen argues that students continue to benefit from teaching that helps them to reflect. Reflection is central both to Killen's contributions to the scholarship of teaching and learning and her introductory text in theology, *The Art of Theological Reflection*. In the latter, Killen and her co-author John de Beer define reflection as "the act of deliberately slowing down our habitual processes of interpreting our lives to take a closer look at the experience and at our frameworks for interpretation."[13] While much of life is lived instinctually and habitually, reflection examines events and experiences with an openness to learning from them. For Killen and de Beer, it is vitally important for reflective Christians to put their individual experiences into exploratory dialogue with religious communities and traditions.

The first requirement of such reflection is to slow down, to separate oneself from the regular pace of life and thought. As Killen writes elsewhere, "reflection begins when one pauses and ponders. Pausing gathers and refocuses attention."[14] The second requirement is a dialogue with tradition, with a body of knowledge or experience outside oneself. Killen and de Beer insist that traditions bring us beyond the limits of ourselves and our times. When we engage in conversation with the past "we can be surprised and transformed by new angles of vision on our experience and acquire a deepened understanding and appreciation of our tradition."[15]

Killen develops this perspective in an essay about the nature of Humanistic teaching called "Gaps and Gifts," which again articulates the importance of slowing down and entering into dialogue with the past. She suggests that the "fundamental human drama involved in learning," is only possible if learners slow down enough to examine the world and find challenging conversation partners from traditions that will help them question their own assumptions.

This kind of reflection is fundamental to the teaching of religion. When we train students to look closely at religious practices and texts, to use precise interpretive methods, and/or to explore new cultural and historical contexts for ideas, we ask them to slow down their thinking. We ask them to re-examine assumptions and prejudices they have learned about religion and religious people and to test and develop what Killen refers to as "frameworks for interpretation."

Western, industrialized culture too often discourages reflection, limiting peoples' capacity to raise and ponder necessary and important questions about the systems in which we live. College offers—or at least should offer—space and time for deliberate thought, for slow examination of ideas. The academic study of religion offers—or at least should offer—an engagement with tradition open to the possibility that there is something to learn from those who have come before us.

So, if a college course on religion emphasizes reflection, it can develop alternatives to the anxiety-producing pace of contemporary life and the intractability of existing systems. Our students have good reason to fear the future ahead of them. But learning reflection in dialogue with traditions can offer some hope when we attend to the ways such traditions have inspired fundamental cultural changes in the past and can inform those who wish to do so again. Careful study of religion can also offer some relief from fear simply by stirring curiosity and engagement in students. Killen writes that one aspiration of her teaching is for students to become so engaged in the learning process that they "become fascinated. Fascination overcomes fear. Insight arises, capacity for discrimination develops. Students begin to notice themselves perceiving and thinking and relating differently."[16]

While I noted above that Thunberg rhetorically contrasted education with the urgency of rebellion, this discussion demonstrates that she is calling for *more* rather than less critical thinking. When she critiques her elders for behaving like "spoiled, irresponsible children," she is calling out political leaders for failing to think and relate to the world differently, for failing to re-examine the interpretive frameworks that led to the climate crisis. In Killen's terms, Thunberg is critiquing politicians' lack of reflection. And while she is dismissive of simplistic appeals to conventional wisdom, Thunberg is clearly open to learning from traditions. While speaking to the United States Congress, for example, she cited the courage of soldiers in the Second World War, the commitment of the civil rights movement, and the boldness of Kennedy's promise to send human beings to the moon.[17] The past and its wisdom have a place in Thunberg's rebellion, as would a course that emphasizes reflection in dialogue with tradition.

Our students come to our classes anxious about the state of the world; distrustful of traditions; and concerned about climate change, violence, and prejudice. Out of these reasonable perspectives comes a suspicion that slowing down to read in dialogue with tradition might be a waste of time. But if we give them space to articulate and examine their anxieties, their distrusts, and their concerns, we can teach them to slow down and reflect in dialogue with others who have struggled and continue to struggle in other contexts. Our teaching matters because students desperately need such reflection.

Teaching Midrange Reflection in a Changing Climate

More specifically, Killen articulates a type of reflection particularly relevant to preparing students for a world of climatic change: midrange reflection. She has most fully developed this concept in her work on the scholarship of teaching and learning, and she suggest that it is a quintessential goal of the Wabash Center workshops that she and Eugene Gallagher played a key role in shaping.

Midrange reflection is broader than any one person's experience but remains specific enough to be useful in particular circumstances. The "mid" range is a "horizon of interpretation" in which it is possible for professors to look at a specific event in our teaching with "intellectual space for free-flowing or directed pondering," allowing for "generalization without premature leaps to universal claims." Midrange reflection "lifts out from the particularities of a concrete teaching incident" and seeks to develop insight "of general relevance in other situations of teaching and learning."[18]

The present essay is an attempt at such midrange reflection. I begin from a specific observation from my own teaching, which is that Greta Thunberg and her questioning of traditional schooling powerfully represents much of what students in my classrooms are going through. I have argued that this is more broadly relevant and built to a suggestion that applies to other teachers of religion: we should train our students to reflect on climate change at a middle range.

Midrange reflection is a way to take something that challenges us, learn from it, and help others do the same. This is, I think, what students most need when seeking to make sense of a problem as enormous and intractable as climate change. They already have specific experiences of this phenomenon. Some are personal, including students whose family's livelihood are changing with changing weather patterns. Some are more abstract, including students who are increasingly aware of extreme weather events around the world and regularly exposed to frightening news reports about what might happen or stop happening in the future. This can all be terrifying. But reflection helps: when presented with a set of tools to learn from them, such experiences can be a catalyst for learning and action.

Midrange reflection also discourages students from making overly simplistic generalizations about a problem like climate change. Generalizations are tempting, ranging from "We are all doomed" to "The real problem is capitalism" to "The real problem is fear-mongering" to "Technology will solve everything." But such broad claims are impossible if students take time to think through their experience and understanding of climate change and are open to the kinds of critical questions that come from traditions of critical thought.

Learning about our students from Greta Thunberg, we should aim to teach them about the intersection between climate change and religion by helping them explore their own experiences of climate change and patiently articulate their feelings and experience of the issue. We should then encourage them to reflect on what can be learned by bringing those experiences into conversation with religious figures and communities who are responding to the issue today[19] and those who responded to serious threats and crises in the past.[20] This will help students to make sense of the world and make arguments about it beyond their own experience, using midrange reflection to gain perspective on the state of the world and their own responsibilities within it.

Killen writes, "Design for midrange reflection involves composing a context for discovery."[21] If we design our religion courses as training grounds for midrange reflection on climate change, then we are inviting students to discover the complexity of the issue, the relevance of religion and other systems of meaning-making, and the importance of thoughtful action in response. We are inviting them to be curious about something that is too often only terrifying, to think critically about something that is too often only shouted or chanted about.

Conclusion

Greta Thunberg decided for a year that protesting climate change was more important than high school. While I have yet to have students as willing to put their education on hold, I do worry that many in my classroom similarly doubt the usefulness of college given their fears about the future. I worry that others have disengaged from the humanistic aspect of college given the understandable impulse to secure as much financial security as possible in an unstable world. And I worry that many students never enroll at my or any other college because of increasing suspicion that what we do does not matter. For all these reasons, I believe that we need to explain to students and prospective students why our classes matter, why they have enduring value and importance to each learner and to the wider society.

I've suggested here that the ability to nurture reflection, and more specifically midrange reflection on climate change, is an important way to explain what we are doing to our students and to organize it for ourselves. I look forward to continued conversation with anyone sympathetic to my argument about how it could shape our pedagogy. I am also interested to hear from those who are unconvinced, with other proposals for how we should explain what we are doing and why.

I find one option utterly unacceptable: to simply continue the status quo and expect students to learn what we are teaching just like previous generations did. That would ignore the fact that they have come of age in a world of rampant and dangerous change. We must reflect on where we are and what is going on and we must re-examine our assumptions and received practices as necessary. This is the way to engage our students in our ongoing conversations about the complexities of their world and the work to be done within it.

Notes

1. Patricia O'Connell Killen, and Eugene V. Gallagher, "Sketching the Contours of the Scholarship of Teaching and Learning in Theology and Religion," *Teaching Theology & Religion* 16, no. 2 (2013): 120.
2. Ibid., 116–17.
3. I develop the latter argument more fully in Kevin J. O'Brien, "Approaching Crisis in a Subjunctive Mode," *Worldviews: Global Religions, Culture, and Ecology* 25, no. 1 (2021). That essay focuses on the power of religious studies and theology to help students to think critically about the narratives being used in public debates; this essay seeks to make a prior argument about why students should be in our classrooms in the first place.
4. Greta Thunberg, et al., *Our House Is on Fire* (New York: Penguin Books, 2020).
5. Sara Lipka, "'I Didn't Know How to Ask for Help': Stories of Students with Anxiety." February 4 (2018): accessed August 11, 2021, https://www.chronicle.com/article/i-didnt-know-how-to-ask-for-help-stories-of-students-with-anxiety/. In a May, 2021 survey co-sponsored by *Inside Higher Ed*, 50 percent of students cited mental health as a significant concern about the 2021–22 academic year.
6. Brenda Llewellyn Ihssen, "Learning with Lessened Limitations: Choose Your Own Adventure," *The Wabash Center Journal on Teaching* 21, no. 1 (2021).

7   Thunberg, *Our House Is on Fire*, 38.
8   For example, in a 2005 book Bill McKibben wrote that other important causes like racism and poverty are important and urgent, but "will be around for the next generation to solve." By contrast, "the environmental crisis is not an historic and eternal crisis. It is new, and it is a timed exam—a hundred years from now, our descendants will not be trying to solve the greenhouse effect. We will solve it, or it will be too late." Bill McKibben, *The Comforting Whirlwind: God, Job, and the Scale of Creation* (Grand Rapids, MI: W.B. Eerdmans Pub. Co., 1994), 15. It is important to note that McKibben's own activism has evolved considerably, and it is very unlikely he would articulate this kind of distinction today.
9   Thunberg, *Our House Is on Fire*, 131. See also https://www.theguardian.com/environment/2020/jun/20/tipping-point-greta-thunberg-hails-black-lives-matter-protests.
10 W. Carson Byrd, Rachelle J. Brunn-Bevel, and Sarah M. Ovink, *Intersectionality and Higher Education* (2019).
11 Todd LeVasseur, "Activism, Religious Studies, and Embodied Teaching in an Era of Rapid Climate Changes," *Worldviews: Global Religions, Culture, and Ecology* 25, no. 1 (2021): 6.
12 Thunberg, *No One Is Too Small*, 10–11.
13 Patricia O'Connell Killen, and John De Beer, *The Art of Theological Reflection* (New York: Crossroad Publishing Company, 1994), x.
14 Patricia O'Connell Killen, "Midrange Reflection: The Underlying Practice of Wabash Center Workshops, Colloquies, and Consultations," *Teaching Theology & Religion* 10, no. 3 (2007): 144.
15 Killen, and Beer, *Art of Theological Reflection*, 2–3.
16 Killen, "Gaps and Gifts," 7, 8.
17 Thunberg, *No One Is Too Small*, 92–3.
18 Killen, "Midrange Reflection," 144.
19 Particularly useful texts include Stephanie Kaza, and Kenneth Kraft, *Dharma Rain: Sources of Buddhist Environmentalism* (Boston, MA: Shambhala Publications, 2000); Ibrahim Abdul-Matin, *Green Deen: What Islam Teaches about Protecting the Planet* (San Francisco, CA: Berrett-Koehler Publishers, 2010); Pope Francis, *Laudato Si': On Care for Our Common Home* (Vatican City: Encyclical Letter, 2015); Melanie L. Harris, *Ecowomanism: African American Women and Earth-Honoring Faiths* (Maryknoll: Orbis Books, 2017).
20 For example, I have found discussions of John Brown and Frederick Douglass resonant and helpful in my environmental ethics courses.
21 Killen, "Midrange Reflection," 147.

Bibliography

Abdul-Matin, Ibrahim. *Green Deen: What Islam Teaches about Protecting the Planet*. San Francisco, CA: Berrett-Koehler Publishers, 2010.

Byrd, W. Carson, Rachelle J. Brunn-Bevel, and Sarah M. Ovink. *Intersectionality and Higher Education*. 2019.

Harris, Melanie L. *Ecowomanism: African American Women and Earth-Honoring Faiths*. Maryknoll: Orbis Books, 2017.

Kaza, Stephanie, and Kenneth Kraft. *Dharma Rain: Sources of Buddhist Environmentalism*. Boston, MA: Shambhala Publications, 2000.

Killen, Patricia O'Connell. "Gaps and Gifts." *Prism: A Publication of the Division of Humanities at Pacific Lutheran University* 12 (1999): 6–8.

Killen, Patricia O'Connell. "Midrange Reflection: The Underlying Practice of Wabash Center Workshops, Colloquies, and Consultations." *Teaching Theology and Religion* 10, no. 3 (2007): 143–9.

Killen, Patricia O'Connell, and John De Beer. *The Art of Theological Reflection*. New York: Crossroad Publishing Company, 1994.

Killen, Patricia O'Connell, and Eugene V. Gallagher. "Sketching the Contours of the Scholarship of Teaching and Learning in Theology and Religion." *Teaching Theology & Religion* 16, no. 2 (2013): 107–24.

LeVasseur, Todd. "Activism, Religious Studies, and Embodied Teaching in an Era of Rapid Climate Changes." *Worldviews: Global Religions, Culture, and Ecology* 25, no. 1 (2021): 1–16.

Lipka, Sara. "'I Didn't Know How to Ask for Help': Stories of Students with Anxiety." February 4, 2018. Available online: https://www.chronicle.com/article/i-didnt-know-how-to-ask-for-help-stories-of-students-with-anxiety/, accessed August 11, 2021.

Llewellyn Ihssen, Brenda. "Learning with Lessened Limitations: Choose Your Own Adventure." *The Wabash Center Journal on Teaching* 21, no. 1 (2021): 49–54.

McKibben, Bill. *The Comforting Whirlwind: God, Job, and the Scale of Creation*. Grand Rapids, MI: W.B. Eerdmans Pub. Co., 1994.

O'Brien, Kevin J. "Approaching Crisis in a Subjunctive Mode." *Worldviews: Global Religions, Culture, and Ecology* 25, no. 1 (2021): 33–47.

Pope Francis. *Laudato Si': On Care for Our Common Home*. Vatican City: Encyclical Letter, 2015.

Thunberg, Greta. *No One Is Too Small to Make a Difference*. 2019.

Thunberg, Greta, Svante Thunberg, Beata Ernman, and Malena Ernman. *Our House Is on Fire*. New York: Penguin Books, 2020.

2

Paschal Pedagogy

Mara Brecht
Loyola University Chicago

Ten years ago, I was fortunate enough to attend a Wabash Center teaching workshop led by Patricia Killen. She taught me to be a student of teaching. I learned the value of reading about the practice of teaching, studying the behaviors and comportment of teachers I admire, and reflecting regularly on my own teaching.

Over the past decade, Patricia and I have grown as conversation partners. We think together with questions about pedagogies at faith-based institutions. She and I share roots in the Roman Catholic tradition, and both of us share the position of lay women educators in the Church. In fact, I credit Patricia with helping me *realize* my identity as a lay woman Catholic educator interested in the intersection of spirituality and pedagogy.

Patricia has helped me not only see and develop my teaching practices, but also integrate my faith commitments into my teaching and grow in my faith through teaching. She has profoundly "imprinted" on me and continues to be one of my most significant mentors. I am honored to offer an essay that celebrates her and her manifold contributions to our guild and, as I propose at the conclusion of this essay, to the Catholic community more broadly. My essay will explore the place where Patricia most deeply and lastingly affected me—where faith and teaching meet.

Easter and the Empty Tomb

I begin biblically and theologically, with the Easter mystery.[1] Christians, it bears reminding, preserve two sets of memories as to how the first followers came to proclaim "He Is Risen!": the *appearance traditions* and the *empty tomb traditions*.

In the appearance traditions, Jesus walks among the disciples, speaks with them, and breaks bread at their table. He comes to his followers and even invites those who doubt to touch his wounds, as in the case of Thomas. He touches Jesus and cries out, "My Lord and my God!" (John 20:28). The doubting disciple is blessed with the knowledge of Jesus through his *presence*.

In the empty tomb traditions, by contrast, there is no Jesus to see, hear, break bread with, or touch. There is instead only an empty space. The evangelist Luke begins the story of Easter Sunday this way: "But on the first day of the week, at early dawn, they came to the tomb, taking the spices that they had prepared. They found the stone rolled away from the tomb, but when they went in, they did not find the body" (Luke 24:1-3).

It's easy to imagine the scene: The women come to the tomb, expecting to find a dead body. They find nothing. Their expectations are completely upended. They stand quietly, peering into the blackness of the tomb. They wait for their eyes to adjust to the dark, and their minds to settle on what it all must mean. And then, Luke reports, two "dazzling figures" appear to the women and pose a piercing question, *Why do you look for the living among the dead?*

In the Gospel-writer Matthew's account, the angels are more direct about the meaning of the emptiness: "He is not here; for he has been raised, as he said" (Matthew 28:6). And how do the women who have witnessed the empty tomb—who have been invited to make meaning from it—respond? With fear and joy, and with an urgent message for the other disciples. They share the message of Easter, and the message of the paschal mystery itself: He who died is raised, that which was broken is made whole. There was nothing to see at the tomb, which was, indeed, exactly what they needed to see.

Patricia teaches and trains teachers in a style that can be likened to the way of the empty tomb. She models the wisdom of moving out of the way, allowing darkness to loom and quiet to rest around those who gather. Another way of thinking about Patricia's form of teaching is as design-focused teaching. It operates from the premise that, like the empty tomb, empty spaces are disclosive and dwelling in them is meaningful. This kind of teaching cuts against the grain of dominant models of teaching, which place teacher at the center and grant exclusive primacy to the materials of learning.

I first learned this alternative way of teaching, design-focused teaching, at my Wabash Center workshop. In an essay on Wabash teaching workshops, Patricia describes their methodology: The facilitator sets up "sequences of questions, activities, and processes that deliberately direct participants' attention to particular teaching events and issues in specific ways that lead to new observations, that spark discovery, and that provide a framework to organize the discovery, internalize it, and translate it appropriately to potential new contexts."[2] In short, participants undergo the experience of learning that Patricia teaches them to design for their own classrooms. This allows participants to "learn twice" the way of design-focused teaching.

As a facilitator, Patricia is highly skilled at "rendering visible" the processes and practices of teaching.[3] I am a direct beneficiary of her skill. Being able to "see" teaching allows teachers to develop their practice, in particular how they set up and plot out learning experiences. The following sections address this area of teaching: design.

A Highly Composed Classroom

I was recently a part of another teaching workshop Patricia led. Before the workshop, she gave our group an assignment, asking us to describe "teaching at its best." Don't give it too much thought, she instructed, but write descriptively about a classroom moment when we knew—deep in our guts—that teaching and learning was happening in the best way it could. We didn't even have to be sure of exactly why the experience constituted teaching at its best, just that we *knew* somehow it did. Maybe it would even be better if we didn't know why the moment worked, so we could unpack and analyze our experiences, make our way toward explanations together.

Here's the moment I shared with the group: I was teaching a majors and minors theology course on the development of Christian doctrine of God. My students were working in small groups to puzzle through a short section of Irenaeus' *Against Heresies*, a second-century text. The ideas were difficult. I'd given students a series of questions to help them along, and my hope was that students would work together to "arrive" at some answers and hypotheses about the reading. After working in small groups, the class came together to talk through our ideas and interpretations. One of my students—a math major and theology minor—had an insight, the kind of lightbulb-on-over-the-head-a-ha! moment that seems to only happen in cartoons.

The student wanted to share his idea with the whole class, and so he asked to use the board. Students were scattered in small groups across the room, and the student scrambled through them to the front of the class. I handed him the chalk. On the board, he sketched a diagram, and, as he did, he gave the class a basic two-minute introduction to binary code. Once we had a grasp of the concept, he connected the logic of binary to the Ireneaus's logic in his attack on Marcion. Lightbulbs switched on across the classroom. More a-ha! moments.

As my student stepped up to the board, I didn't know what was going to happen, I had no idea what he would say. But he made an exciting connection, and I could see the fire in his eyes. I trusted the moment. It worked. And not only did the students understand better the debate between Ireneaus and Marcion, they also saw a fellow classmate model intellectual creativity.

For me, the event was thrilling. I knew it to be *teaching at its best* because it felt like that moment on the rollercoaster ride when your car just peeks out over the crest of the track and begins barreling forward. All the tension of the long uphill climb is released. You catch some air in your seat. Your hands are up and everyone around you is screaming, sharing in the same abandon and yet knowing you're following a defined path to a definite end. *That's* what *teaching at its best* feels like.

Back at the teaching workshop discussion, I attributed the success of the situation to my student more than to myself, though I explained that the moment expressed my larger pedagogical values: learning is a social event, the classroom is a laboratory, students take ownership for their learning, and so on. My colleagues in the group pushed me in my self-analysis. "Didn't *your* actions play an important role too?" they challenged. "You decentered the authority in the class so they could step in."

I wasn't so sure about all that, but I conceded that my pedagogy did aim to make room for students to be active leaders and learners. Patricia intervened in our discussion and, as she has so frequently done for me, shifted my way of seeing the situation. In one way, my moment of *teaching at its best* represented decentered authority, yes. But she called attention to the highly structured set of events that led to the moment of the student going to the board.

My moment of *teaching at its best* happened not because I stepped aside and let the students run amok, nor because the class declared mutiny against structure. Instead, my teaching was very carefully planned out, and in that planning, I created space for students to take over and initiate their own learning. Mine was the highly composed classroom, and I learned to create it by giving attention to design.

The Design of Learning

Learning design, I learned from Patricia, hinges on three questions: What is the context? What is the purpose? What is the path? *What is the context?* The first question looks at students and asks, what's their institutional location, the wider social situation, and cultural factors that are significant for their learning.

What is the purpose? The second question gets at where we want our students to end up. Teaching and learning are teleological. We should always point students in a direction, even if they're not aware of where they're headed. We might invite students into a learning activity that looks like leisurely fooling around in a text, but even that seeming aimlessness ought to have a purpose. Everything we do in our teaching—every interaction we set up, every activity we construct, every piece of writing we read, every question we ask—ought to be oriented toward the end we've defined.

What is the path? is late-stage work. It's tempting to think first about books we want our students to read, films we'd like them to see, and assignments we imagine giving them. But content materials and assignments—however compelling in the abstract—are only meaningful for learning when arranged to serve a purpose, which also must be appropriate to the context. You can't just pull a book you love off the shelf, hand it to a student, and expect learning to happen.

By understanding *context*, we see the specific needs and capacities of our students. By identifying *purpose*, we become explicitly clear about the ends we imagine for them. To forge a *path* we use readings and lessons aligned with the ends of the course, which are shaped relative to their needs and capacities. The path is therefore dependent on context and purpose.

This is the work of backward teaching design, wherein teachers choose material and create assignments only after determining the basic shape of the class. When I work through the question of *path*, I imagine myself as an author telling a story or, better yet, as a board game designer arranging sequences of events. What incremental "moves" will lead students toward an idea? What plot line will each class meeting follow? *Context, purpose, path* becomes a mantra—and with years of recitation, have become axiomatic—as I design a course.

Another axiom of Patricia's teaching wisdom is the arc. To work effectively, classes need a clear beginning, middle, and end–like a book with a narrative arc. We begin somewhere. We move in a particular way. We arrive at our destination. This needs to be true for a particular class. And for a particular unit. And for the entire semester. There's no "Let's pick up where we left off." No, Patricia taught me that every class begins where it begins and then ends where it ends, according to a plan.

Knowing context helps locate the beginning point of learning. Having a goal or purpose lets us know what the end will be. Planning a path is how we chart the middle and what we use as our milestones along the way. Whether an individual class session or a semester course, Patricia has taught generations of teachers how to design arcs of learning that move students from one place to another in a clear progression. The arced path that Patricia places students on, I suggest and develop in the next section, is expressive of a deep, Christian impulse—the paschal mystery.

Pedagogy and the Paschal Mystery

"He Is Risen!" These three simple words capture the essence of Christian faith. When Christians speak these words, they tell an abbreviated version of a much longer story, namely that Jesus Christ died and rose from the dead. The words also speak volumes theologically. To draw out just a few theological points, the phrase reminds us that "He" is the incarnation, God made flesh. His resurrection represents God's victory over death. The exclamation point is telling too, because it's a joyful sentence to speak. When we slow down to think about it, "He Is Risen!" always points us back to the paschal mystery, the mystery of Jesus' death and resurrection.

All Christians profess faith in the paschal mystery, although it figures variously into their theological imaginations and lives of practice. Catholics are fairly explicit about the centrality of the paschal mystery, particularly following the Second Vatican Council.[4]

Catholic weekly practice speaks to this. The culminating point of the Mass occurs in the Liturgy of the Eucharist. In this ritual, the priest and the people speak in a dialogue of prayer in an exchange that does the sacramental work of thanksgiving and sanctification. By offering this prayer together, the priest and the people fulfill their shared apostolic command to keep alive the paschal memory of Christ, "his blessed Passion, glorious Resurrection, and Ascension into heaven."[5]

One of the many things Vatican II did for the Catholic Church was emphasize the importance of the people as full participants in Mass. Through this key liturgical rite (the Mass) the people of God explicitly participate in the paschal mystery.[6] But our experience with the paschal mystery extends far beyond the Mass itself, and is fundamental to everyday life. The great Jesuit theologian Karl Rahner refers to the daily experience of the paschal mystery—of Christ's dying and rising—"the liturgy of the world."[7] The paschal mystery is always present to us, for the experience of life includes myriad deaths and resurrections.

The world is broken and fragmented and, at the very same time, a jewel to behold, a dawning light, a ripened peach ready to be picked, a still and placid lake. In and through the thick of living—with its griefs and joys—ordinary people connect to the death and resurrection of Christ. The arc of our day-to-days fit into the larger arc of our lives, which themselves fit into the arc of God's own story, a redemptive story.[8] In the end, Christians profess, all is made whole. This is what the women discovered at the empty tomb.

Patricia's spiritual sensibilities, like my own and like those of Catholics around the world, have been shaped by regularly participating in the liturgical rituals that call forth the paschal mystery, as well as by a theological outlook that connects the events of our day-to-days to this deepest truth of our faith tradition. The paschal mystery is foremost in our shared spirituality, even if it is not explicitly articulated or expressed. It bears on all we do, including teaching.

This is why the late scholar of Catholic education, Mario O. D'Souza, CSB argues for a necessary link between the paschal mystery and Catholic education. He writes,

> Catholic educators, undoubtedly, engage with this mystery implicitly at different levels ... Such an education is more than religious education or instruction, of course, but everything that Catholic education stands for ... is, or should be, founded upon and situated within the paschal mystery, both implicitly and explicitly understood.[9]

When I reflect on Patricia's teaching, her skill at schooling teachers in the way of design-focused teaching, I find there the dynamic of the paschal mystery.

Learning as a "Paschal" Dynamic

Learning entails discomfort, disruption, and disorientation. We ask our students to examine their assumptions, view their commitments in a stark new light, acknowledge how narrow their slice of the world is. This can be especially painful in classes examining faith, God, and religious traditions. Students frequently experience discomfort in our classes, at the beginning of their learning.

But we do not leave our students in the place of disorientation and disruption, instead we invite them to new possibilities by following us along a carefully-plotted path. With our pedagogical guidance, students learn to see another way, to arrive at different thoughts, to collect and assemble into new patterns what they've heard and understood. A basic duty of teaching is to help something new arise for our students.

Even in the space of an individual class meeting, students find their ideas broken apart and then made whole again. Consider a lesson where students begin by identifying the main idea of an assigned reading. They jot it out in their notebooks or share it on the board. Then, through guided questioning, the instructor helps students pull apart the reading, analyze its parts, and revisit and refine their initial ideas. It's hard work, both to so carefully attend to a reading and to reassess what they first thought. By the end of class, students have a deepened grasp of the material, a stronger sense of its meaning, maybe even a new insight into the world. In learning, our knowledge—and even our very selves—are remade. It's a kind of resurrection.

Patricia teaches that well-designed learning experiences, both small and large, should always move along in such a way, with a beginning, middle, and end. The cycles of learning each class, each week, each unit also unfold in the space of the larger course. Each beginning, middle, and end merges into another beginning, middle, and end. Each dying and rising opens to another dying and rising.

At the same time, the cycles are also oriented toward learning goals, the specific ends we've designated for student learning. The cycles of learning in the well-designed class, it seems to me, are liturgical in their rhythm and ultimately expressive of the paschal mystery. Just as Catholics are called to connect the daily dyings-and-risings of life to the death and resurrection of Christ celebrated and enacted in Mass, the daily dyings-and-risings of learning do bigger work.

The ultimate end to which Patricia leads her students—and I speak here as a student of her teaching practice—exceeds the precise learning ends of the courses or workshops. They draw us into the darkness, and toward the loving mystery at the heart of the universe.

It Was *Women* at the Tomb: A Final Note on "So What?"

Feminists draw inspiration from the empty tomb traditions, both for what it means for women in the Christian tradition, for the nature of faith itself, and—I will add—for the future of the Catholic Church.

Amy Jill Levine calls attention to the fact that, women are "the first witnesses to the resurrection and the first missionaries of the church" even if they are not among the twelve disciples. Women, Levine reminds us, play a "substantiative role" in the Easter story.[10] This is a role that Christianity's collective memory hangs onto, even as centuries of androcentric forces work against it. Carolyn Osiek emphasizes the fact that the empty tomb tradition is an epiphany story.[11]

That is, the women are led into a new truth—and indeed the central truth of Christian faith—*because of* an absence. The empty tomb creates a space for the women to step into and to discover a totally new idea, He Is Risen!

I take it as significant that Patricia is—like the women at the tomb—a woman. The women were "entrusted with the first Easter encounter and the first mandate to proclaim it."[12] They play a substantive role in the story. They "encountered" resurrection in the empty dark, and then made good on the promise to spread the message, even when their credibility was questioned, as in Luke, "However, this story of theirs seemed to be nonsense, and the apostles did not believe them" (Luke 24:11).

In her decades of teaching and training teachers, Patricia invites others to encounter. She radiates credibility and emanates authority without also placing herself at the center. In a faith tradition that has long-denied the authority of women, Patricia assumes it with an easy grace. She, like the women at the tomb, shows the prodigious capacity of women to be in touch with the paschal mystery and to invite others to the same even while that capacity is questioned.

In the conclusion to a volume on the future of the American Catholic Church, Patricia echoes the unifying message of the volume's contributors. If the American Church is to endure, she writes, it must "embrace the virtues of elasticity in thought and practice" and be generous to difference.[13] Many in the Church work to stretch the tradition's elasticity so as to include greater lay leadership as well as increased roles for women, to herald these forms of difference in the Church's structure.

As a woman in the tradition, I draw inspiration and strength from the lay leadership of Patricia and I maintain hope that Catholic educators, particularly laywomen educators, will be among the most significant sowers of the "seeds of renewal" so needed by the Church. Patricia's gift to me, to countless teachers, and to the Church is to inspire, give strength, and kindle the hope of resurrection that is found at the empty tomb.

Notes

1 All biblical references use the New Revised Standard Version, Anglicized Catholic Edition.
2 Patricia O'Connell Killen, "Midrange Reflection: The Underlying Practice of Wabash Center Workshops, Colloquies, and Consultations," *Teaching Theology & Religion* 10, no. 3 (2007): 147.

3   Patricia O'Connell Killen, "Editor's Note," *Teaching Theology & Religion* 13, no. 2 (2010): 93. Patricia begins this note with a concern about some of the pitfalls that render teaching invisible to its practitioners.
4   D'Souza notes the theological attention given to the paschal mystery at the Council, how the term *paschale mysterium* came to occupy a place of primacy in the conciliar documents. Mario D'Souza, "Paschal Mystery and Catholic Education," *Heythrop Journal* 54 (2013): 848.
5   *General Instruction of the Roman Missal*, 3rd edn. (Washington, DC: United States Catholic Conference of Bishops, 2011), 78–9.
6   Ormond Rush, *The Vision of Vatican II: Its Fundamental Principles* (Collegeville, MN: Liturgical Press, 2017), 42.
7   Michael Skelley, *The Liturgy of the World: Karl Rahner's Theology of Worship* (Collegeville, MN: Liturgical Press, 1991), 99–101.
8   Ibid., 100.
9   D'Souza, "Paschal Mystery and Catholic Education," 847.
10 Amy-Jill Levine, "Matthew," *Women's Bible Commentary*, rev. edn., ed. Carol A. Newsom, Sharon H. Ringe, and Jacqueline E. Lapsley (Louisville, KY: Westminster John Knox Press, 2012), 477.
11 Carloyn Osiek, "The Women at the Tomb: What Are They Doing There?" *Feminist Companion to Matthew*, ed. Amy Jill Levine, (New York: Bloomsbury, 2001), 220.
12 Ibid.
13 Patricia O'Connell Killen, "Conclusion: The Shape of the American Catholic Future," *The Future of the American Catholic Church*, ed. Patricia O'Connell Killen and Mark Silk (New York: Columbia University Press, 2019), 344.

Bibliography

D'Souza, Mario. "Paschal Mystery and Catholic Education." *Heythrop Journal* 54 (2013): 846–58.

Killen, Patricia O'Connell. "Midrange Reflection: The Underlying Practice of Wabash Center Workshops, Colloquies, and Consultations." *Teaching Theology & Religion* 10, no. 3 (2007): 143–9.

Killen, Patricia O'Connell. "Editor's Note." *Teaching Theology & Religion* 13, no. 2 (2010): 93–4.

Killen, Patricia O'Connell. "Conclusion: The Shape of the American Catholic Future." In *The Future of the American Catholic Church*, edited by Patricia O'Connell Killen and Mark Silk, 331–48. New York: Columbia University Press, 2019.

Levine, Amy-Jill. "Matthew." In *Women's Bible Commentary*, rev. edn., edited by Carol A. Newsom, Sharon H. Ringe, and Jacqueline E. Lapsley, 465–77. Louisville, KY: Westminster John Knox Press, 2012.

Osiek, Carloyn. "The Women at the Tomb: What Are They Doing There?" In *Feminist Companion to Matthew*, edited by Amy Jill Levine, 205–20. New York: Bloomsbury, 2001.

Rush, Ormond. *The Vision of Vatican II: Its Fundamental Principles*. Collegeville, MN: Liturgical Press, 2017.

Skelley, Michael. *The Liturgy of the World: Karl Rahner's Theology of Worship*. Collegeville, MN: Liturgical Press, 1991.

United States Conference of Catholic Bishops. *General Instruction of the Roman Missal*, 3rd edn. Washington, DC: United States Catholic Conference of Bishops, 2011.

3

Art and the Unexpected

Alicia J. Batten
Conrad Grebel University College

Introduction

The Coronavirus pandemic forced the majority of college and university instructors throughout the world to adapt their teaching in some manner. This essay attempts to honor Patricia and Gene by reflecting upon a teaching "practice" that I began to use more systematically because of the pandemic, a practice that more successfully contributed to the students' achievement of the learning goals of the course than I had anticipated. The practice features the use of art when teaching a biblical studies class, specifically an exegesis course on the Gospel of Mark. Images have been part of the Christian tradition from its early days,[1] and art continues to be an important resource for many instructors. Beyond the study of religion, some scholars employ art not only to teach but also to engage in research and to write about their subject. For example, in his book, *Vermeer's Hat*, historian Timothy Brook includes several full-page color plates of Dutch paintings as doors that one enters to discover how and why particular objects became coveted items of trade in the seventeenth century. Throughout the book, Brook engages the details of the paintings, and the particular material objects that appear there such that the reader repeatedly examines the plates, and notices elements of them that they may not have paid particular attention to otherwise. Brook refers to an observation by art critic James Elkins, who argues that "paintings are puzzles that we feel compelled to solve in order to ease our perplexities about the world in which we find ourselves, as well as our uncertainties as to just how we got here."[2] I think that such an observation is relevant for understanding why students in the Gospel of Mark class made connections to some of the learning goals in a more explicit manner than students had done in previous years. My hunch is that the works of art prompted some students to reflect more deeply about elements of the Gospel narrative and the complexity of interpretation.

The Place and the Practice

The course on the Gospel of Mark was for the MTS (Master of Theological Studies) program at Conrad Grebel University College, a Mennonite college affiliated with the University of Waterloo in Ontario, Canada. The college and the university confer the MTS degree jointly. Students are from a range of backgrounds with regard to education, age, ethnicity, and nationality. Theologically, they are also very diverse, including some from mainline Protestant church affiliations, Roman Catholic, Anabaptist, evangelical, non-denominational, and some who are agnostic or may not identify as Christian but are curious about the Christian tradition. Not surprisingly, they represent a diverse array of political and social perspectives. Some people enroll because they want to engage in Christian ministry professionally, others wish to continue on to do a PhD, while still others pursue the program out of interest and the desire for personal enrichment. It is a privilege to teach such students as they are highly motivated, they consistently come to class prepared, and most of them are very eager to engage with one another.

The MTS program has a list of learning goals that it hopes all students enrolled will achieve. These are as follows: (1) demonstrate skills in effective communication; (2) gain knowledge of Christianity from a variety of disciplinary, theological, contextual, and experiential perspectives; (3) engage scholarship through research and critical analysis of primary sources and contemporary scholarly debates; (4) interpret Christian texts and traditions in light of present contexts; (5) interact with issues of justice and peace; (6) attend to voices of the marginalized, and increase the capacity for intercultural competence; (7) nurture personal formation through practices such as self-reflection, openness to others, leadership training, faith development, and participation in a diverse learning community; (8) enhance the capacity for life-long learning. There are some additional objectives for students enrolled in the Applied Studies option of the program, as well for those pursuing the Thesis option.[3]

Not every course can address all of these aims, and some classes engage with certain objectives more intensively than others do. There is an emphasis on the first goal in most courses, given the importance of writing and seminar discussion across the curriculum. The class on Mark also stresses the fourth goal ("interpret Christian texts and traditions"), as well as the third ("engage scholarship"). Through required readings, class discussion, and assignments, we also attend to the importance of perspective, especially the significance of ancient and modern contexts (objective #2) as well as questions of what difference it makes to interpret a text from a marginalized position (objective #6). My hope is that the goals of personal formation (objective #7) and life-long learning (objective #8) are addressed throughout the course through content, discussion, and assignments.

Everyone at the college and university switched to fully remote teaching in fall 2020. As mandated by the university, the amount of synchronous time that we could spend with classes was 90 minutes as opposed to 180 minutes per week. Therefore, I needed to "flip" my "classroom" such that I could provide the content ahead of our ninety-minute class meetings. I created recorded lectures that included Power Point slides with images and text. Our initial few weeks centered upon student reactions to reading the entire Gospel in one sitting, as well as attention to methodological questions, especially the difference that method makes. We then explored the question of the genre of Mark and aspects of its composition and rhetoric before we turned to working through a close examination of the chapters of the Gospel, week by week, in consecutive order. Assignments throughout the semester included an initial "response paper" that describes how each student experienced reading through the Gospel of Mark in one sitting, including noting what surprised or confused them.[4] A written review and discussion leadership of an academic article had to be completed once throughout the semester as well as multiple posts on the discussion board of the learning platform. At the close of the course, students submitted a book review, and a final research exegesis paper on a small portion of the Gospel.

Puzzlement

My experience of teaching the New Testament and Christian origins over the years has been that for students who have never engaged with critical scholarship and with all of the unknowns and ambiguities about the origins and meanings of these texts, a close and critical examination of the literature can be rather challenging. Often, students begin a class with very particular understandings of what this body of literature meant and means, and these understandings are precious to them. Therefore, as many who teach in my field will likely agree, a course in academic biblical study can be disorienting, and threatening to the theological orientation of some students. One has to think carefully about how to design the class in order to create a setting in which what Eugene Gallagher describes as "intellectual hospitality" can thrive.[5] Moreover, the strongly held convictions of some of the students are not generally a problem, but a "resource" or "point of energy," as Patricia O'Connell Killen has put it,[6] that students can identify, explore together, and draw from as we move through the material.

In my experience, resistance to and anger about an academic approach to the literature of ancient Christ groups are more characteristic of a survey class, where one has less time to get into the minutiae of each text. However, in a course focused on one single document—in this case, the Gospel of Mark—we have the advantage of entering into a much closer examination. In addition, the Gospel of Mark is itself quite enigmatic and invites a great deal of puzzlement. Why does Jesus continually tell people to be quiet about what he has done and who he is? Why are the disciples such buffoons, and why does Jesus seemingly snub his own family (Mark 3:31-35)? The identity and significance of the young man who flees naked when Jesus is arrested (Mark 14:51-52) almost became a running joke in the class, as people were so baffled by this figure, and they often searched for details and clues throughout the narrative that would help solve the mystery of the "naked man." There is plenty in Mark to be confounded by and therefore studying the specifics of a particular passage, or perhaps the question of why the Gospel ends as it does,[7] students have more opportunity to engage in puzzlement together. This sort of engagement with the mysteries of the narrative contributes to a certain "slowing down," as they participate in a more immersive practice of study.[8]

Although I had used artistic images in many of my classes before, in the Power Point lectures posted on the learning platform I integrated images (mostly paintings but also some mosaics, sculptures, manuscript illuminations, and icons) that connected to the section of the Gospel that we were discussing that week. The choice of artwork was based on whether it was an image that I had a legal "right" to post on the board as well as a host of more subjective judgments. For example, did it reflect what I deemed to be an interesting portrayal of the particular story in the Gospel? Did it offer a different interpretation of the passage, pushing the viewer to consider questions of diversity and marginality? It was very important that I find artistic interpretations that included images of non-white people, for example, given the dominance of a white Jesus and white biblical characters in Western art. In addition, I chose artwork that I found to be aesthetically interesting and that I found to be vivid and arresting in some way. Using artwork from the early church was also important, as it enabled students to appreciate how some of the early Christians portrayed these stories (e.g., Jesus is usually without a beard in early frescoes; or he sometimes appears as a magician). I also searched for artworks that I hoped would challenge the viewer in some way.[9]

Students were required to "watch" my lectures prior to our ninety-minute synchronous session online. Each week I began the class by asking them to provide questions or comments they had in response to the lecture, and it became evident that the artwork was engaging some of them. They also posed questions and made observations to each other on the discussion board, where they were required to participate throughout the semester. The images did not dominate any of their conversations, but it was interesting that they brought up the images when I had not explicitly asked them to, and in some cases, made connections to both the primary and secondary readings. For example, during the week that we focused on Mark 9, with particular attention to the Transfiguration (Mark 9:2-8), I had included a slide of a wooden sculpture depicting Jesus between the priests of two different Yoruba gods. My lecture commented that the artist wanted to illustrate that Jesus did not judge or condemn the Yoruba tradition. One of the students responded very enthusiastically; he thought that the sculpture had turned Jesus into a Black African, effectively decolonizing the story. The student continued on to highlight the importance of art for offering a different perspective, and that he had really appreciated seeing images and thinking through the text alongside the images. Other students responded positively to his post, voicing their agreement, and indicating how the visual component was causing them to think about how diverse interpretation could be. They said that the artwork was prompting them to reflect upon particular stories in new ways, or at least, to consider possible additional dimensions of well-known passages. During another week, I included a painting depicting the widow and the Temple treasury pericope (Mark 12:41-44) in which the widow is a young Black woman. Students commented appreciatively about the fact that she was Black, which made them imagine the story differently as they considered the element of race as part of her overall oppression even though that feature is not evident in the account itself. One student was initially confused by the fact that the woman in the painting was young, indicating that she had always assumed that the widow was elderly. However, this perplexity was productive because the student then observed that in reality, it was probable that the widow was a young woman given the much shorter life spans of people in Mediterranean antiquity. Additionally, an assigned reading for that week had analyzed the story of the widow through the lens of intersectionality, and it was interesting to read a student post stating that the painting had brought this theme of intersectionality to life, that the image reinforced ideas in the reading. I did not make these connections in the pre-recorded lectures; the students noticed these particular elements of the painting and their connection to the reading. Their observations were somewhat unexpected.

Art and Teaching Biblical Studies

Lynn Huber and Dan Clanton's insightful essay on the use of art for teaching biblical studies describes several benefits that such a practice can provide. They point out how our students often need to be taught how to "see" even obvious elements in ancient texts, and the fact that in Western cultures we are regularly bombarded with images and texts in rapid fire such that we are often hampered in our ability to notice smaller details. Thus, using images, slowly and with attention to their particularities,[10] can assist in highlighting the details in texts.[11] Indeed, we could spend more time on the specifics of the narrative in a class focused on one text, but I conjecture that the use of art occasionally led students to re-examine some of their assumptions about aspects of the story, and to discover elements that they had not paid attention to before. For example, the story of the Syrophoenician Woman (Mark 7:24-30) features a witty, Gentile woman who talks back to Jesus (after he has insulted her, calling her a "dog"), causing him to change his mind. Students are often shocked by various elements in this story, but I wanted to demonstrate to them how significant a female figure she was and thus deliberately included a modern icon of the figure who looks squarely at the viewer, exuding strength. Jesus is obviously absent in the icon. Students did not post about the image on the discussion board; however, they did comment in class that although the story was initially disturbing to them, they had come to appreciate this female figure (as well as other female characters such as the bleeding woman in Mark 5). My distinct impression was that students had understood that although Jesus is at the center of Mark's account, these minor characters were important and essential to the story. Student recognition of this aspect of Mark had not been as discernible in the past.

Huber and Clanton also observe that students, especially those from more "conservative" backgrounds, often need to be "prodded to see the possibility of multiple interpretations in text, especially texts that many hold as sacred."[12] The illustration of the Transfiguration story, described above, is an example of how at least some of the students understood that a text could be interpreted in multiple ways. One student had posted on the discussion board that art has the ability to show us a different perspective and that, in the student's view, this ability is largely overlooked in theological studies. This focus on perspective is consistent with the learning objectives of the course, as it contributes to thinking about what it means to read and think from, for example, a marginal position. Although at first some students may have been bothered or puzzled by some of the images, these visual interpretations eventually drew them in, and caused them to think about how another person or community might take a different approach to the story.

Art is also useful as a means of illuminating biblical texts.[13] For example, Simon of Cyrene (Cyrene is the equivalent of ancient Libya) would not have been a white person, despite the fact that he is portrayed most often as a white. Thus, I included a sculpture of a Black Simon of Cyrene, and the students were thankful, indicating that they had not consciously paid attention or thought about this aspect of Simon before. This recognition is connected to one of the overall aims of the course, which is to appreciate the ancient context. Likewise, the image of the young Black widow at the Temple forced the students to think more about the role of ethnicity and race when it comes to biblical interpretation, but they also had to reckon with the fact that the widow could be *young*. Her age was an element that they had not considered previously as most of them had grown up in a country where people tend to live to a greater age than in the ancient world. In addition, while lecturing on the crucifixion of Jesus, I included Marc Chagall's *White Crucifixion* (1938), now found in the Art Institute of Chicago.[14] Chagall makes it obvious what Jesus' ethnic identity is by portraying him on the cross partially covered by a *Tallit* or prayer shawl instead of the usual linen cloth. Students are not accustomed to seeing Jesus with a *Tallit*. The image forces them to think. Although they understood that Jesus was a Judean, it was important to emphasize this feature consistently throughout this course (and others). The vitriol against the Pharisees and scribes is so strong in the gospel literature that it becomes tempting to separate Jesus from his Judean identity because he is so often in conflict with these groups, which are anachronistically lumped together in Mark's Gospel.

Conclusion

Teaching courses in New Testament and Christian Origins can be a fraught experience given the impact that raising difficult questions about historicity and meaning can have on students who uphold strong convictions about the Bible and the Christian tradition. However, the puzzlement and even disorientation that some students may experience in the class can also be a source of energy. Infused into such a teaching situation, art can assist as instructors attempt to illustrate and sensitize students to the complexity of interpretation. Artistic interpretations of biblical texts provide a visual construal of a story that can point to elements in the text that are not stated or obvious, thus underlining the significance of context. Like the text itself, art can function as a source of puzzlement for it possesses the power to arrest or confuse the viewer. An artwork may trigger the observer to think about aspects of a story's meaning in a new way. Additionally, it may cause a person to consider that other people might understand a biblical story quite differently, and that these variations in interpretation connect with the context and identity of the interpreter. Moreover, an artistic depiction of a beloved story can sensitize the viewer, at least in some ways, to what it might mean to read a particular text from a marginalized position.

James Elkins has written that art is among the experiences he relies on to alter who he is. He writes, "I do not *want* to see things from a single point of view ... I want to continue to change—I do not wish to remain the same jaded eye that I was a moment ago."[15] Such a desire is fundamental to notions of ongoing formation and life-long learning. Art, then, can assist us in cultivating dispositions in students that contribute to their ultimate flourishing.

Notes

1. Margaret R. Miles, "Image," in *Critical Terms for Religious Studies*, ed. Mark C. Taylor (Chicago: University of Chicago Press, 1998), 165.
2. Timothy Brook, *Vermeer's Hat: The Seventeenth Century and the Dawn of the Global World* (Toronto: Viking Canada, 2008), 9.
3. See Conrad Grebel University College Master of Theological Studies Learning Objectives. https://uwaterloo.ca/theological-studies/about (accessed August 24, 2021).
4. The assignment is based solely on the student experience of reading the Gospel from start to finish, to which they then return at the end of the course to see if their perspective has changed. This exercise encourages metacognition in that the students can reflect upon their learning and how and why their thinking may have changed.
5. Eugene V. Gallagher, "Welcoming the Stranger," *Teaching Theology & Religion* 10 (2007): 137–42.

6   Patricia O'Connell Killen, "Students' Inner Conflicts: A Pedagogical Resource," *Teaching and Learning Forum*, Pacific Lutheran University (Spring 2000): 2.
7   Most scholars think that the Gospel of Mark originally ends in Mark 16:8, where the women flee the empty tomb in terror, saying nothing to anyone.
8   On the importance of slowing down the learning process, see Jennifer L. Roberts, "The Power of Patience," *Harvard Magazine* (November–December 2013); available online: https://www.harvardmagazine.com/2013/11/the-power-of-patience (accessed July 20, 2021).
9   My choice of images was comparable to my choice of secondary readings for the course. Apart from the copyright issue, I look for recent work that is academically solid, interesting, provocative, diverse, and that represents a perspective that I "think" students may not have encountered before.
10 See Roberts, "The Power of Patience."
11 Lynn R. Huber and Dan W. Clanton Jr., "Introduction: Teaching the Bible with Art," in *Teaching the Bible through Popular Culture and Art*, ed. Mark Roncace and Patrick Gray; SBL Resources for Biblical Study 53 (Atlanta: Society of Biblical Literature, 2007), 175.
12 Ibid., 176.
13 Ibid., 177.
14 Marc Chagall, *White Crucifixion*, available online: https://jstor.org/stable/community.15022168 (accessed July 29, 2021).
15 James Elkins, *The Object Stares Back* (New York: Simon and Schuster, 1996), 41.

Bibliography

Brook, Timothy. *Vermeer's Hat: The Seventeenth Century and the Dawn of the Global World*. Toronto: Viking Canada, 2008.

Chagall, Marc. *White Crucifixion*. Available online: https://jstor.org/stable/community.15022168, accessed July 29, 2021.

Conrad Grebel University College Master of Theological Studies Learning Objectives. Available online: https://uwaterloo.ca/theological-studies/about, accessed August 24, 2021.

Elkins, James. *The Object Stares Back*. New York: Simon and Schuster, 1996.

Gallagher, Eugene V. "Welcoming the Stranger." *Teaching Theology & Religion* 10 (2007): 137–42.

Huber, Lynn R. and Dan W. Clanton, Jr. "Introduction: Teaching the Bible with Art." In *Teaching the Bible through Popular Cultures and the Arts*, edited by Mark Roncace and Patrick Gray, 175–86. SBL Resources for Biblical Study 53. Atlanta: Society of Biblical Literature, 2007.

Killen, Patricia O'Connell. "Students' Inner Conflicts: A Pedagogical Resource." *Teaching and Learning Forum*, Pacific Lutheran University (Spring 2000): 1–2.

Miles, Margaret R. "Image." In *Critical Terms in Religious Studies*, edited by Mark C. Taylor, 160–72. Chicago: University of Chicago Press, 1998.

Roberts, Jennifer L. "The Power of Patience." *Harvard Magazine*. November–December, 2013. Available online: https://www.harvardmagazine.com/2013/11/the-power-of-patience, accessed July 20, 2021.

4

Laughter in the Temple: Hermeneutics and Humor in Teaching Religion

Anita Houck
Saint Mary's College

"We need to watch this clip from Colbert."

"Colbert? I don't think we've got time for that."

That was true, as far as it went: our syllabus in Heaven and Hell gave us plenty of dense texts to discuss. But I was also nervous. I didn't know *The Colbert Report* well; what if my students and I had different senses of humor, and I ended up looking like some old curmudgeon? I recalled an observation of Reinhold Niebuhr: "[t]here is laughter in the vestibule of the temple, the echo of laughter in the temple itself, but only faith and prayer, and no laughter, in the holy of holies."[1]

My students continued: "No, really, it's really good theology. We need to watch it." The students, of course, were right. Colbert was interviewing Stanford psychologist Philip Zimbardo about his book *The Lucifer Effect*. Zimbardo made a series of statements about hell and damnation, and Colbert came back with measured, sound responses from Catholic theology. Finally, Zimbardo, flustered, rejoined, "Obviously, you learned well in Sunday school." Colbert replied with a line probably never before spoken in English: "I *teach* Sunday school, professor"—except that, instead of saying "professor," he used an epithet from George Carlin's list of "Seven Words You Can Never Say on Television."[2]

The interview drew media attention because Colbert stepped out of his pundit persona, and, yes, because of that closing line.[3] But the students were interested in the eschatology, not the scatology. They had recognized in their everyday world a connection to their work in theology, evaluated its content astutely, and shared their insight with others. Colbert's humor drew them toward the kind of learning teaching aims for.

"Religious worlds," Stephanie N. Brehm writes, "are not solely serious." Instead, humor is "an arena for the expressions of religious identities and relationships."[4]

As a result, humor can be an ally in teaching religion and theology. It can be a helpful pedagogical technique; it's a compelling aspect of lived religion; and, above all, it's a fundamental component of human relationships within and beyond the classroom, whether the classroom is physical or virtual. Yet, particularly in a culture where humor is often politicized and polarized,[5] humor can entrench views rather than motivate us to examine them. To move past that potential impasse, it's helpful to use hermeneutic processes that integrate affect and cognition. In teaching, those processes work best when they become familiar enough to help us encounter the unfamiliar.

Laughter in Theory: Dissecting the Frog

E.B. White and Katharine S. White famously cautioned against the study of humor, contending that "Humor can be dissected, as a frog can, but the thing dies in the process and the innards are discouraging to any but the purely scientific mind."[6] But anyone invested in critical thinking has good reason to study humor. Humor suffuses the cultural worlds of students and teachers alike. As Caty Borum Chattoo and Lauren Feldman note, "In the still-evolving digital era, the opportunity to consume and share comedy has never been as available."[7] We and our students are citizens of a world in which the Proud Boys claim that they're not Nazis, just "funny dudes."[8] Humor also inhabits the religious worlds learners are called to engage. In many courses, students exploring the complexities of religion will, and should, encounter the laughter of Sarah and Abraham in Genesis, festival plays about the butter-thief Krishna, the warm humor about "bad hijab days" in the video "Hijabi World,"[9] or the issues surrounding the cartoons published in *Charlie Hebdo*.

What makes humor so important, wherever it's found, is that it expresses and shapes relationships,[10] evoking what philosopher Ted Cohen calls "the intimacy of joking."[11] That intimacy requires shared background knowledge. Background knowledge allowed the students to appreciate Colbert; it lies behind esoteric lightbulb jokes ("How many surrealists does it take to screw in a lightbulb?"[12]); and it's what out-of-touch professors seek when they scramble to urbandictionary.com to decode a link sent by a student (a meme showing Jesus emerging from the tomb, surrounded by the caption "YOLO JK LOL"). Humor also requires an affective connection, namely a shared taste for what's funny and a shared sense of what's appropriate in particular contexts. These similarities are difficult to gauge, much less ensure, especially amid the power dynamics of a classroom—hence my nervousness when Colbert showed up in class. Discovering similarities in our knowledge and taste creates intimacy; uncovering differences can divide.

The relational networks humor creates are often more complex than we realize. Humor's intimacy links a source (e.g., the joke-teller) and an audience to each other. But humor also links them to the object or target of their joke, present or absent, as well as to the surrounding culture or cultures that define what deserves mockery or approval, and when. Equally important, laughter and humor come in many tones, from affiliative (laughing with) to derisive (laughing at), and that tone is often difficult to interpret and quick to change.[13] Religion has sometimes resisted laughter because it assumed that laughter is always derisive, and assumed that, when laughter showed up in religion, its target is always the sacred—Niebuhr's "holy of holies." In fact, much religious humor is quite reverent toward the sacred. When it derides, its derision is usually directed toward the religious foibles of the pious, as in the Emo Philips creation voted "the funniest religious joke of all time."[14]

The concepts of intimacy, relational networks, and ambiguous tone provide a good basic toolkit for thinking critically about humor. Two other points complicate matters. First, there's no agreed-upon definition of humor; in fact, the word often refers to a broad semantic field that includes (among others) laughter, smiling, comedy, jokes, and play. In particular, pedagogical research on humor often conflates humor and laughter (as I confess I often do here), an understandable but sometimes misleading connection. In fact, psychologist Robert R. Provine found that, in ordinary conversation in the United States, only about 10–20 percent of laughter actually responds to something funny. The rest is relational, made up of unremarkable affirmations, greetings, and questions.[15] Second, there's no scholarly consensus about what causes something to be humorous. Charles R. Gruner has compiled a list of 88 theories,[16] others 100.[17] Incongruity is currently the most popular theory,[18] including in pedagogical research.[19] But other approaches, especially Plato's and Hobbes's theory that laughter expresses superiority, and Freud's explanation of laughter as psychological release,[20] often shed more light on how humor works and on the values that underlie our different senses of humor. If teachers think of humor primarily as joking based on incongruity, we'll miss important aspects of humor and laughter that can contribute to teaching and learning.

Laughter in Research: Humor in Teaching and Learning

The state of research into humor and pedagogy is, well, pretty sad. In 1995, James Teslow offered a glum evaluation of the field, and matters haven't improved much since: "much of the basic research is two [now four or five] decades old, little replication has taken place, most studies involve young children, findings have been equivocal …. Is this any way to treat a basal cultural phenomenon?"[21]

Despite the limitations, the research overall suggests that humor can enhance teaching and learning, especially when it's relevant to course content and avoids appearing aggressive or offensive.[22] Humor, especially in the form of laughter, can enhance wellbeing, particularly by reducing stress.[23] It can improve classroom climate,[24] students' view of instructors' credibility,[25] teaching evaluations,[26] and student-teacher rapport within and outside the classroom.[27] The evidence is more mixed on academic learning: humor works well to gain students' attention,[28] but it's less clear that it promotes understanding and retention, especially in the long term.[29] Some evidence suggests that humorous illustrations can effectively reinforce material that's also presented straightforwardly;[30] other evidence suggests that even unintentional humor can improve student learning.[31]

As in the semantic field noted above, humor in these studies can refer to a wide range of behaviors, from jokes, wordplay, and physical comedy to more Provinian actions that Melanie Booth-Butterfield and Melissa Bekelja Wanzer classify as "other orientation" ("communication that shows awareness and adaptation to the audience members and their response to humor") or "expressiveness/general humor" ("being friendly, enthusiastic, positive, and happy").[32] Teachers' self-deprecatory humor sometimes enhances relationships but can also hinder them;[33] either way, as Hannah Gadsby's *Nanette* suggests, it can entrench damaging expectations of members of marginalized groups.[34] Excessive humor distracts from learning; some research settled on a recommendation of three to four jokes per class.[35] Humor on quizzes and tests may be effective when tied closely to humor used in instruction, but may be unhelpful overall, and even detrimental for students who experience anxiety.[36] Several researchers caution that humor works only if students think it's funny,[37] a dauntingly high bar. As John Banas and colleagues observe, "Not everyone is funny, and Ziv (1988) commented that there are few things worse than an unfunny person trying to be humorous." The less-funny among us, they recommend, might use videos and cartoons to "inject humor but make the burden of spontaneous humor less cumbersome."[38]

If humor does promote learning, the mechanisms by which it does so aren't clear.[39] But San Bolkan and Alan Goodboy suggest that any potential cognitive benefits derive from humor's well-established relational benefits, "creating a positive affective experience that fulfills students' needs to feel connected and enjoy a sense of belonging."[40]

Many studies of pedagogical humor are based on observations of particular courses and teachers, and it's not clear how much can be generalized from one academic field to another. In 2013–14, in connection with the Wabash Center's mid-career workshop on religious commitments in the classroom, I conducted a small study researching the question "In what ways might humor be an effective tool in religious studies and theology classes, particularly for engaging religious commitments?" Study participants represented nine US colleges and universities, all (because of other research questions) Catholic-sponsored.[41] Nine faculty and eighty-six of their students completed online surveys,[42] and eight of the faculty participated in a follow-up discussion.[43]

Overall, the findings agreed with the research literature: students reported feeling more comfortable and learning better when their instructors used humor. However, this was less often true for students who found the course to be more challenging than their other courses. Students and faculty agreed that several kinds of humor can be helpful, provided the humor used is "not intended to demean or attack others." "Humor to illustrate course content (for instance, humorous examples)" was seen as helpful by the largest percentage of students (76.7 percent), followed by "humor on general topics, like pop culture or college life" (67.4 percent) and "humor to lighten the mood when the class is dealing with serious topics" (66.3 percent). Differences between faculty and students arose on "jokes to keep the class attentive" (considered helpful by 66.3 percent of students, 33.3 percent of faculty) and "teachers making fun of themselves" (51.2 percent of students, 100 percent of faculty). Considerable minorities rated "good-natured joking about students in the class" as helpful (46.5 percent of students, 44.4 percent of faculty), despite the challenges such humor entails. No students evaluated "humor on tests or quizzes" as helpful, compared to 20.9 percent of faculty. Finally, continuing an embarrassing trend in the literature, 66.6 percent of the teachers reported using humor "in most or almost every class," but only 44.2 percent of students agreed.

The survey also asked participants to describe an example of humor in their religion or theology class and explain why the humor was or was not helpful. Coding revealed that improving classroom atmosphere was important for both students and faculty. But almost all student examples were content-related, often translations of course concepts into familiar experiences—for instance, telling a story about scraping ice off a windshield to illustrate Buddhist detachment, or turning a misspoken reference to "cheap grapes" (rather than cheap grace) into jokes about the cost of produce. Students' examples also singled out physical humor and creative activities like story-telling and drawing.[44]

Students and faculty agreed with the statement "It's healthy for people to have a sense of humor about their own religious commitments," but students' responses were somewhat less positive than faculty's (73.2 percent of students and 100 percent of faculty agreed or strongly agreed). Moreover, students who placed more importance on their own religious commitments, and students who had more clarity regarding their own religious commitments, were less likely to agree. A total of 75.5 percent of students said that "teachers' use of humor helps me learn about others' religious commitments" either "sometimes" (30.2 percent) or "often" (45.3 percent), as compared to only 22.2 percent of teachers. While the study is small and limited, this last finding suggests that humor might contribute to a fundamental goal in religion and theology: understanding people different from ourselves.

Laughter in the Circle: Humor in Hermeneutics

The study of religion invites learners to encounter deeply different ways of looking at and being in the world. Like humor, it's often a matter of feeling at least as much as a matter of intellect. While religious studies and theology, as Patricia O'Connell Killen observes, share critical-thinking goals with other disciplines in the humanities, "the subject matter of religion adds a particularly emotionally charged dimension to the process. In religion courses, students learn that religion does not insulate humans from life, that it is part of making sense of living, loving, hoping, creating, suffering, and joy."[45]

Learning about such personal topics, and learning in the presence of affect, doesn't come naturally to most of us. In many courses, then, we may have to teach how to do it. The approach I now teach started when I noticed a class was going well and tried to identify what was happening. Now called "the hermeneutic circle," this approach, which I tweak most semesters, is part of the first week's curriculum in every course I teach, and it's practiced throughout the course.[46] The purpose of the circle is to slow down: to give learners space to notice their reactions to what they're encountering, to integrate cognitive and affective aspects of learning, and ultimately to bridge what we're learning in class with the world we inhabit the other 165 hours a week. The circle aims, to borrow Killen's words, both to "evoke affective connection to material and create

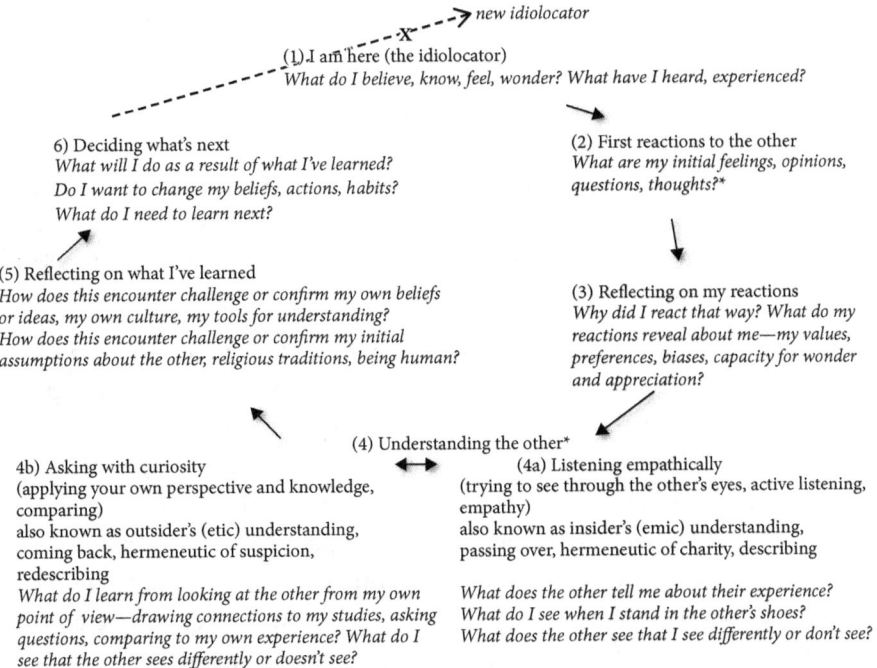

Figure 4.1 The Hermeneutic Circle (with thanks to Fall 2000's RLST 213 class)

cognitive distance from it."[47] Teaching it also provides an opportunity to signal that humor has a place in the class.

The circle begins with each person's starting point regarding whatever we're about to engage—our "furnished and familiar mental homes," as Killen puts it.[48] This point is called an idiolocator, repurposing (with a touch of silliness) the technical term for the "You are here" mark on a map. It includes everything a learner brings to an encounter, consciously or unconsciously: feelings, assumptions, stereotypes, experiences, questions, knowledge, and things heard that may or may not be true. Valuing each person's idiolocator affirms, as bell hooks puts it, "that everyone influences the classroom dynamic, that everyone contributes. These contributions are resources. Used constructively they enhance the capacity of any class to create an open learning community."[49] Yet idiolocators include not only information and insights, but also misinformation and blind spots. So the circle fosters not only affirmation, but also examination of our idiolocators. As Eugene V. Gallagher observes of introductory classes,

> the students who populate our courses may well be ill- or uninformed about religion, ... but that does not mean that they have had no experience with religion. That is, whether they are deeply or shallowly involved in the practice of a religion, hazily conscious of some of the roles religions play in American civic life or simply vaguely aware that religion is something that some other people do, they are unaccustomed to thinking critically about religion.[50]

Explicitly articulating this starting point can be useful, especially in approaching topics that are often associated with strong feelings or misinformation. Usually, though, our idiolocators become clearer once we encounter something specific—a text, an artifact, an event—and notice how we react. This response is Step 2 in the circle, the first reactions to (what I imperfectly call) the other. Three guidelines define a good Step 2. The main criterion is honesty: we all have reactions we're not proud of, and being aware of them allows us to notice how they shape our learning and, if we choose, to change the idiolocators they come from. Second, first reactions are where we begin an encounter, not where we end it. Finally, first reactions generally reveal more about ourselves—our preferences, values, prejudices—than about what we're encountering. So the next step in the circle is dedicated to reflecting on these reactions (Step 3). To illustrate these steps, I've sought stories that use humor, tap into the course's content, and echo students' own experience. For instance, a passage from *The Book of Joy* by the Dalai Lama and Desmond Tutu tells the story of the Archbishop being cut off in traffic, responding with "exasperation and a head-shaking chuckle," then expressing compassion.[51] A short self-deprecating story relates my efforts to change my intransigent habit of assuming authority figures are male; students often (alas) confess they, too, initially imagine all doctors, researchers, and judges as men.[52]

Step 4 shifts the focus from ourselves to the other. Like many models, such as the hermeneutic of charity and the hermeneutic of suspicion, the circle defines understanding as a process in two movements. Step 4a requires listening, echoing the first stages of Bloom's taxonomy (recalling and explaining):[53] grasping key concepts, summarizing claims and evidence in a text, accurately observing a ritual. Step 4b applies that knowledge to more dialogic tasks like comparing and interrogating: pondering whether Rama's treatment of Sita fits certain views of dharma, or analyzing how a comedian relates to their audience and object. Understanding then moves back and forth between the steps, as questions require more knowledge and knowledge inspires more connections. Step 5 reflects on the process, comparing first responses to stances that are now better informed and more self-aware. Step 6 articulates decisions that follow from this reflection, often decisions to pursue further learning. A new idiolocator is the result.

In the course, the circle becomes a familiar practice for encountering the unfamiliar, structuring our encounters with the most personally challenging material. It allows feelings and assumptions to become not failures of learning, but important first steps in learning. The circle also provides shared, fairly neutral language for talking to each other. I used to flail when a student's first reactions expressed something I heard as a prejudice; my own feelings were engaged (my step 2), and it was difficult to resist the impulse to demand more open-mindedness—as if I could teach open-mindedness by immediately dismissing someone else's view (my step 3). With the circle as shared language, I can instead commend the student for articulating an honest first response, then point toward the self-reflection of step 3. The circle also transfers out of the class; students have said they use it not only in other courses, but also in relations with roommates.

Laughter in the Temple: Humor in Interfaith Encounter

Most of us are more used to consuming humor than to analyzing it. The circle can help us apply critical thinking to humor—without, in my experience, dissecting away the funniness. When a class on Spirituality and Comedy watched TED talks by Maysoon Zayid[54] and Negin Farsad,[55] two Muslim comics, students liked both videos, but most preferred Zayid's (step 2), finding the video easier to relate to (step 3). When we applied our study of Islam and humor (step 4), we noticed that, while Zayid mentions Islam and Ramadan, she foregrounds her experience of cerebral palsy rather than her religion, and she ends with an encouraging universal message. These aspects of her humor can allow easier affiliation with her non-Muslim audience (including all of my students). In contrast, Farsad, a self-identified "social justice comedian," foregrounds Islam and includes derisive humor about Islamophobia and, well, Florida. Acknowledging and analyzing our reactions illuminated our humor preferences and interfaith attitudes. At the same time, watching female Muslim comics who, against many students' expectations, do not cover their hair, may have helped correct stereotypes.

Even unbidden, humor is likely to show up in our classes, whether we accidentally refer to cheap grapes, students bring in a comic video, or the guide at the Hindu Temple jokes that he sometimes feels lazy about coming to the daily aarti service. Interfaith encounters, which by definition engage what's unfamiliar, can make humor especially difficult to negotiate. When the Rabbi of a nearby congregation started visiting my classes, her light joking met with silence. The reason, students later told me, was that they didn't want to offend. They were afraid it was inappropriate to laugh at a guest, an authority figure, or a religion, and most of all afraid of misunderstanding the humor of (for many of them) the first Jewish person they'd ever met. In the face of that fear, humor couldn't perform the relationship-building functions Provine and Cohen describe.

Fear of offending in interfaith situations isn't something we can easily dispel, even, perhaps, in ourselves. But acknowledging that fear provides another opportunity for self-reflection and learning. In this case, as often, fear was rooted in respect for our guest and a tacit but wise awareness of the limits of our intercultural competence, in particular, of how humor works in unfamiliar situations. My job as teacher, I realized, had to include educating them on humor, a topic not covered in *How to Be a Perfect Stranger*, the classic guide to interfaith etiquette.[56] The next semester, when I was preparing the class for the Rabbi's visit, I gave the needed information: I told the students that the Rabbi is known for her dry sense of humor (true) and it's okay to laugh. That time, when she joked, they laughed. Weeks later, when they attended Shabbat service, the Rabbi made a couple jokes for the benefit of her guests, the students laughed again, and the congregation smiled with them. Both situations show how effectively humor can express and shape relationships.

Students have sometimes reflected on similar experiences in the observation logs, based on the hermeneutic circle, that they complete after site visits. Some students chose to attend a three-hour Shabbat service, followed by lunch. "At the end of the service," a first-year student wrote, "a man came up to us, and he was amazed that we stayed the whole time. He said, 'You all stayed for the whole service! Your [sic] all Jew-ed up now!'. The girls and I just laughed at this statement." When the log asked the student to reflect on her response, she insightfully analyzed the relational context of the humor:

> I believe I responded the way I did because the energy shifted towards the end of service. Children began re-uniting with their families, so the energy shift allowed me to focus on their community and the dynamic the community has as a whole.

> Humor in many scenarios is a risk, but I was able to see the man's intent over his comment because the transition from the service to lunch was occurring.

She was completely right that context shapes humor, and that humor entails risk. She also noticed rightly that humor, when accepted, could help defuse the risks that inhere in meeting across interfaith differences.

Being able to negotiate such comic terrain is a worthy goal of education.[57] After all, if evolutionary psychologist Robin Dunbar is right, from the earliest days of human society, laughter has been essential in helping people get along.[58] Jonathan P. Rossing has argued compellingly for considering humor as a civic virtue that helps us both understand and act in our communities: "By playing with knowledge constructions and destabilizing conventional truths," he writes, "humor helps audiences recognize not only the social practices and truths of our shared world but also the processes by which people collectively create, recreate, maintain, and accept that reality." He concludes, "we would do well to recognize the ways of thinking and acting that humor cultivates for addressing an array of problems in everyday life, private and public, and to apply these sensibilities across multiple contexts."[59]

Rossing's comments tie into goals many instructors share as they seek to enable students to think critically about their worlds. But they also point toward a different kind of learning students often show when they enter unfamiliar territory: gaining the ability not only to observe and understand, but also to practice generosity in the company of others. It may not be clear that humor helps students acquire and retain knowledge, but perhaps it helps in other ways that might be of even more lasting value. Though little known today, *eutrapelia*, literally "well turning," the virtue of appropriate humor, was advocated by Aristotle[60] and, following him, Aquinas.[61] Both reasoned that neither the overly dour nor the overly flippant could participate well in community. It's the person with an appropriate sense of humor, good-spirited and agile in responding to others, who contributes to the common good. Perhaps, by welcoming humor into our courses, we can help students along the way to that virtue, and thus to more insightful human encounters across unfamiliar terrain. It's clearly a goal that students can meet with skill and grace.

When I attended a Wabash workshop for pre-tenure faculty led by Patricia O'Connell Killen, the project I brought to work on was the first iteration of the hermeneutic circle. Killen immediately noted that I had it wrong. In that early version, students reflected on themselves first and then encountered and responded to the other. Killen pointed out that those steps needed to be reversed: we learn about ourselves *by* engaging the other, not before. In my version, my students and I could enter the world of religion thoroughly prepared, armed with solid self-knowledge. Learning, it turns out, is riskier than that. It's often offered before we're fully ready and comes bearing surprises not only about our world but about ourselves. But the risks are worthwhile if we have the tools to learn from what we encounter, above all from the people we meet.

Notes

1. Reinhold Niebuhr, "Humour and Faith," in Reinhold Niebuhr and Robert McAfee Brown, *The Essential Reinhold Niebuhr: Selected Essays and Addresses* (New Haven: Yale University Press, 1987), 60.
2. The word begins with m; the list is published in "Seven Dirty Words," Wikipedia, last modified November 12, 2020, https://en.wikipedia.org/wiki/Seven_dirty_words#cite_note-umkc-1.
3. Philip Zimbardo, interview by Stephen Colbert, *The Colbert Report*, Comedy Central, February 11, 2008, http://www.cc.com/video-clips/8sjpoa/the-colbert-report-philip-zimbardo. Among commentators who have weighed in on the interview are Jesse Carey, "6 Times Stephen Colbert Got Serious About Faith," *Relevant*, April 14, 2014, https://www.relevantmagazine.com/culture/6-times-stephen-colbert-got-serious-about-faith/; James Poniewozik, "Stephen Colbert's Night Vision," *Time*, August 27, 2015, https://time.com/4012855/stephen-colberts-night-vision/; and Stephanie N. Brehm, *America's Most Famous Catholic (According to Himself): Stephen Colbert and American Religion in the Twenty-first Century* (New York: Fordham University Press, 2019), 97.
4. Brehm, *America's Most Famous Catholic*, 3.
5. See, for instance, Dannagal Goldthwaite Young, *Irony and Outrage: The Polarized Landscape of Rage, Fear, and Laughter in the United States* (New York: Oxford University Press, 2020); and Paul Lewis, *Cracking Up: American Humor in a Time of Conflict* (Chicago: University of Chicago Press, 2006).
6. E. B. White and Katharine S. White, preface to *A Subtreasury of American Humor* (New York: Coward-McCann, 1941), xvii, quoted in Steve Wilkens, *What's So Funny about God?: A Theological Look at Humor* (Downers Grove, IL: IVP Academic/InterVarsity Press, 2019), 7.
7. Caty Borum Chattoo and Lauren Feldman, *A Comedian and an Activist Walk into a Bar: The Serious Role of Comedy in Social Justice*, Communication for Social Justice Activism (Oakland, CA: University of California Press, 2020), 5.
8. Driesbach, Tom, "How Extremists Weaponize Irony to Spread Hate," *All Things Considered*, NPR, 26 April 2021, https://www.npr.org/2021/04/26/990274685/how-extremists-weaponize-irony-to-spread-hate.

9   Dina Sayedahmed and Hamna Saleem, "Hijabi World," Newest Americans, 2015, https://newestamericans.com/hijabi-world/.
10 For more on the relational nature of humor, see Anita Houck, "Holiness and Humour," *HTS Theological Studies* 72, no. 4 (2016), doi: 10.4102/hts.v72i4.3464.
11 Ted Cohen, *Jokes: Philosophical Thoughts on Joking Matters* (Chicago: University of Chicago Press, 1999), 40.
12 Fish.
13 For more on these distinctions in pedagogical humor, see the excellent review article by John Banas et al., "A Review of Humor in Educational Settings: Four Decades of Research," *Communication Education* 60, no. 1 (January 2011), 122.
14 Emo Philips, "The Best God Joke Ever—and It's Mine!," *The Guardian*, September 29, 2005, https://www.theguardian.com/stage/2005/sep/29/comedy.religion.
15 Robert R. Provine, *Laughter: A Scientific Investigation* (New York: Viking, 2000), 40–1.
16 Charles R. Gruner, *The Game of Humor: A Comprehensive Theory of Why We Laugh* (New Brunswick, NJ, and London: Transaction Publishers, 1997), 10–12.
17 H. Foot and M. McCreaddie, "Humour and Laughter," in *The Handbook of Communications Skills*, ed. O. Hargie (New York: Routledge, 2006), quoted in Melanie Booth-Butterfield and Melissa Bekelja Wanzer, "Humor and Communication in Instructional Contexts: Goal-Oriented Communication," in *The SAGE Handbook of Communication and Instruction*, ed. Deanna L. Fassett and John T. Warren (Los Angeles: SAGE, 2010), 223.
18 Scholars who promote incongruity theory also debate how incongruity should be defined. See, for example, Elliott Oring, "Appropriate Incongruity Redux," in *Engaging Humor* (Urbana and Chicago: University of Illinois Press, 2003), 1–12.
19 Incongruity is the basis for IHTP, Instructional Humor Processing Theory, perhaps the most prominent theory explaining how humor improves instruction; see Melissa B. Wanzer, Ann B. Frymier, and Jeffrey Irwin, "An Explanation of the Relationship between Instructor Humor and Student Learning: Instructional Humor Processing Theory," *Communication Education* 59, no. 1 (2010): 1–18. Bolkan and Goodboy's study challenges IHTP but, like many studies, nonetheless relies on incongruity to define humor ("intentional messages that lead to laughter and amusement through incongruous meanings," 45). San Bolkan and Alan K. Goodboy, "Exploratory Theoretical Tests of the Instructor Humor-Student Learning Link," *Communication Education* 64, no. 1 (2015), with discussion of IHTP on 46–8. For additional discussion, see Banas et al., "A Review of Humor in Educational Settings," 117, 119.
20 For a helpful introduction to humor theory, see John Morreall, "Philosophy of Humor," *Stanford Encyclopedia of Philosophy*, last modified August 20, 2020, https://plato.stanford.edu/entries/humor/.
21 James L. Teslow, "Humor Me: A Call for Research," *Educational Technology Research and Development* 43, no. 3 (1995): 7.

22 Banas et al. explain, "The use of positive, nonaggressive humor has been associated with a more interesting and relaxed learning environment, higher instructor evaluations, greater perceived motivation to learn, and enjoyment of the course. Conversely, the use of negative or aggressive humor aimed at students has been associated with many of the opposite outcomes, including a more anxious and uncomfortable learning environment, lower evaluations of instructors, increased student distraction and less enjoyment of class." Banas et al., "A Review of Humor in Educational Settings," 137. For studies of appropriate and inappropriate humor, see Booth-Butterfield and Wanzer, "Humor and Communication in Instructional Contexts"; and Ann Bainbridge Frymier, Melissa Bekelja Wanzer, and Ann M. Wojtaszczyk, "Assessing Student Perceptions of Inappropriate and Appropriate Teacher Humor," paper presented at the annual convention of the National Communication Association, November 2007, Chicago, Illinois.

23 For a review of studies, see Marney A. White, "Academic Course Evaluations in Health Sciences Can Be a Joke: A Cross-Sectional Examination of Whether Students Appreciate a Professor's Sense of Humor," *American Journal of Health Education* 50, no. 6 (2019): 398; Amy Wortley, and Elizabeth Dotson, "Stand Up Comics: Instructional Humor and Student Engagement," *Journal of Instructional Research* 5 (January 2016): 15–16; and Victoria D. Smith and Amy Wortley, "'Everyone's a Comedian.' No Really, They Are: Using Humor in the Online and Traditional Classroom," *Journal of Instructional Research* 6 (January 2017): 18–23. Though it focuses primarily on students' humor, also relevant is Melanie Booth-Butterfield, Steven Booth-Butterfield, and Melissa Wanzer, "Funny Students Cope Better: Patterns of Humor Enactment and Coping Effectiveness," *Communication Quarterly* 55, no. 3 (2007): 299–315, doi:10.1080/01463370701490232.

24 Crystal McCabe, Katie Sprute, and Kimber Underdown, "Laughter to Learning: How Humor Can Build Relationships and Increase Learning in the Online Classroom," *Journal of Instructional Research* 6 (January 2017): 4–7; Booth-Butterfield and Wanzer, "Humor and Communication in Instructional Contexts," 224–6; Banas et al., "A Review of Humor in Educational Settings," 130–1.

25 Booth-Butterfield and Wanzer, "Humor and Communication in Instructional Contexts," 232; see also Banas et. al., "A Review of Humor in Educational Settings," 130–1.

26 For a review of research, see Banas et al., "A Review of Humor in Educational Settings," 129; for a delightful and potentially suggestive (if limited) study, see White, "Academic Course Evaluations in Health Sciences Can Be a Joke."

27 Banas et al., "A Review of Humor in Educational Settings," 127. Rapport is one of the benefits noted by Drew C. Appleby in his succinct review of research on humor in college teaching, which also includes a report on his own research in his classes in introductory psychology. Drew C. Appleby, "Using Humor in the College Classroom: The Pros and the Cons," *Psychology Teacher Network*, American

Psychological Association, February 2018, http://www.apa.org/ed/precollege/ptn/2018/02/humor-college-classroom.

28 San Bolkan and Darrin J. Griffin, "Catch and Hold: Instructional Interventions and Their Differential Impact on Student Interest, Attention, and Autonomous Motivation," *Communication Education* 67, no. 3 (2018): 269–86; Erik Rosegard and Jackson Wilson, "Capturing Students' Attention: An Empirical Study," *Journal of the Scholarship of Teaching and Learning* 13, no. 5 (December 2013): 1–20.

29 Booth-Butterfield and Wanzer, "Humor and Communication in Instructional Contexts," 226. Banas et al. reviews the mixed results (131–2) and concludes that some studies, when carefully controlled, do show some benefits, demonstrated not only by self-report but by retention on final exams: "Laboratory experiments (e.g., Schmidt, 2002) have repeatedly demonstrated that, when context is held constant, humorous information is recalled more easily than nonhumorous information. Additionally, naturalistic experiments revealed that humor-treatments increased test scores compared to no-humor controls (Ziv, 1988)." Banas et al., "A Review of Humor in Educational Settings," 137.

30 Banas et al., "A Review of Humor in Educational Settings," 135.

31 "Humor has been found to affect memory in both intentional and incidental humorous memory situations (Carlson, 2011), meaning students' retention of material is positively affected by classroom humor whether or not it was intentional on the part of the instructor." Wortley and Dotson, "Stand Up Comics," 16.

32 Booth-Butterfield and Wanzer, "Humor and Communication in Instructional Contexts," 227.

33 Wortley and Dotson, "Stand Up Comics," 15. Booth-Butterfield and Wanzer's subjects identified self-disparaging humor as both appropriate and inappropriate in "Humor and Communication in Instructional Contexts," 230.

34 Gadsby's groundbreaking performance called into question the familiar self-deprecatory tropes expected of comics, especially when comics are part of marginalized groups: "I built a career out of self-deprecating humor. That's what I built my career on. And I don't want to do that anymore. Because do you understand what self-deprecation means when it comes from somebody who already exists in the margins? It's not humility. It's humiliation. I put myself down in order to speak, in order to seek permission to speak." Hannah Gadsby, *Nanette*, filmed at the Sidney Opera House, Netflix, 2018.

35 Banas et al., "A Review of Humor in Educational Settings," 134.

36 Ibid., 134–5.

37 White's study finds that the students who gave her the strongest course evaluations were also the students who shared her appreciation of a joke that was, "per this professor/author's subjective interpretation, objectively hilarious" (402): "In the glorious 1980s, your professor was the singer for a punk-rock band called The Prevention. They were better than The Cure" (399). White readily admits the

study's limits (402) but sees it confirming other research. White, "Academic Course Evaluations in Health Sciences Can Be a Joke." For other cautions, see Booth-Butterfield and Wanzer, "Humor and Communication in Instructional Contexts," 231. Appleby wryly connects repeated failures at pedagogical humor with research showing that incompetence often correlates with overconfidence.

38 Banas et al., "A Review of Humor in Educational Settings," 135. See also Wortley and Dotson, "Stand Up Comics," 14.

39 Banas et al., "A Review of Humor in Educational Settings," 119–20. Bolkan and Goodboy propose an alternative to IHTP in "Exploratory Theoretical Tests of the Instructor Humor-Student Learning Link," 58–9.

40 Bolkan and Goodboy, "Exploratory Theoretical Tests of the Instructor Humor-Student Learning Link," 58.

41 The study included a research question designed to guide a decision at my own Catholic institution: "Does the name of a department—Theology, Religious Studies, or Theology and Religious Studies—shape students' expectations of how a course will engage their and their teachers' religious commitments?"

42 Each faculty member chose a class to study, and all student participants from that institution were from that class. The aim was to include at least ten students from each class, though some classes were not that fully represented. The students' religious self-identifications were as follows: 48 (55.8 percent) Catholic, 14 no affiliation, 1 agnostic, 1 Hindu, 2 Muslim, 1 pluralist, 1 Orthodox, and 18 non-denominational or denominational Protestant. There were no significant differences in responses based on gender or religious identity.

43 The nine faculty participants included three assistant professors; six associate professors, including three department chairs and one holding an endowed chair; two members of underrepresented racial or ethnic groups; and representatives of the three kinds of departments being studied (Religious Studies, Theology, and Theology and Religious Studies). Faculty participants were selected in part based on their reputations as excellent teachers.

44 Students who provided examples (fifty-seven of the eighty-six) were not altogether representative of the sample as a whole: they had lower self-reported GPAs, were more likely to be White and in their first year of college, and reported their religious commitments as less important and less clear.

45 Patricia O'Connell Killen, "'Keeping the Power of Wisdom Accessible': Religion Departments in Church-Related Colleges in Our Time," *Perspectives in Religious Studies* 46, no. 4 (Winter 2019): 409.

46 A more detailed explanation of the circle can be found in Anita Houck, "You Are Here: Engagement, Spirituality, and Slow Teaching," in *Becoming Beholders: Cultivating Sacramental Imagination and Actions in College Classrooms*, ed. Karen E. Eiffler and Thomas M. Landy (Collegeville: Michael Glazier/Liturgical Press, 2014), 70–85. The handout provided to students includes this text: "Other sources that

have contributed to this circle are Thomas Groome's work on catechetical praxis, for instance in *Sharing Faith: A Comprehensive Approach to Religious Education and Pastoral Ministry: The Way of Shared Praxis* (HarperSanFrancisco, 1991); Gary L. Comstock's discussion of empathic and critical approaches in *Religious Autobiographies*, 2nd edn. (Wadsworth, 2004); Patricia O'Connell Killen's insightful suggestions—particularly on ordering steps 2 and 3—in a 2003 workshop of the Wabash Center for Teaching and Learning in Theology and Religion; and a helpful conversation with Rodger Narloch in January 2015."

47 Patricia O'Connell Killen, "Editor's Note," *Teaching Theology & Religion* 10, no. 4 (2007): 213–14, doi: 10.1111/j.1467-9647.2007.00373.x.

48 Patricia O'Connell Killen, "Gracious Play: Discipline, Insight, and the Common Good," *Teaching Theology & Religion* 4, no. 1 (2001): 4.

49 bell hooks, *Teaching to Transgress: Education as the Practice of Freedom* (New York: Routledge, 1994), 8.

50 Eugene V. Teaching Gallagher, "Teaching for Religious Literacy," *Teaching Theology & Religion* 12, no. 3 (July 2009): 210.

51 Bstan-'dzin-rgya-mtsho [the Dalai Lama] and Desmond Tutu, with Douglas Abrams, *The Book of Joy: Lasting Happiness in a Changing World* (New York: Avery/Penguin Random House, 2016), 101–2.

52 Students also volunteer their experience wrestling with the famous riddle about the surgeon; see Douglas R. Hofstadter, "Changes in Default Words and Images Engendered by Rising Consciousness," *Metamagical Themas: Questing for the Essence of Mind and Pattern* (New York: Basic Books/HarperCollins, 1985), 142, https://leeclarke.com/courses/intro/readings/Hofstadter_Changes_in_Default-_Words_and_Images.pdf.

53 Patricia Armstrong, "Bloom's Taxonomy," Vanderbilt University Center for Teaching, last modified 2020, https://cft.vanderbilt.edu/guides-sub-pages/blooms-taxonomy/.

54 Maysoon Zayid, "I Got Ninety-Nine Problems … Palsy Is Just One," TEDWomen, December 2013, https://www.ted.com/talks/maysoon_zayid_i_got_99_problems_palsy_is_just_one.

55 Negin Farsad, "A Highly Scientific Taxonomy of Haters," TED, February 2016, https://www.ted.com/talks/negin_farsad_a_highly_scientific_taxonomy_of_haters.

56 Stuart M. Matlins, and Arthur J. Magida, eds. *How to Be a Perfect Stranger: The Essential Religious Etiquette Handbook*, 6th edn. "Perfect Stranger" Series (Woodstock, Vermont: SkyLight Paths Publishing, 2015).

57 Booth-Butterfield, Booth-Butterfield, and Wanzer go so far as to "propose that it would be useful to incorporate information regarding competently communicated humor into freshman orientation sessions, staff training sessions, first-year experience programs, and counseling center workshops. This is being initiated at some colleges and universities." "Funny Students Cope Better," 310.

58 Dunbar and colleagues hypothesize that laughter may have allowed early human communities to overcome social tensions and thus reach sizes large enough to enhance survival. P. Ghosh, "Study Reveals Laughter Really Is the Best Medicine," *BBC News*, September 13, 2011, http://www.bbc.com/news/science-environment-14889165. More detailed review of the hypothesis can be found in R. I. M. Dunbar et al., "Social Laughter is Correlated with an Elevated Pain Threshold," *Proceedings of the Royal Society B* 279 (2012): 1161–7, doi:10.1098/rspb.2011.1373.

59 Jonathan P. Rossing, "A Sense of Humor for Civic Life: Toward a Strong Defense of Humor," *Studies in American Humor* 2, no. 1 (2016): 14–15, 17, doi:10.5325/studamerhumor.2.1.0001.

60 Aristotle, *Nicomachean Ethics*, trans. Martin Ostwald, The Library of Liberal Arts, New York: Macmillan 1962, IV.8, 107–9.

61 Thomas Aquinas, "Question 168. Article 2. Whether there can be a virtue about games?" *The Summa Theologiae of St. Thomas Aquinas*, trans. by Fathers of the English Dominican Province, 2nd and rev. edn. (1920), online edition 2017, New Advent, II.II.168.2, https://www.newadvent.org/summa/3168.htm#article2.

Bibliography

Appleby, Drew. C. "Using Humor in the College Classroom: The Pros and the Cons." *Psychology Teacher Network*. American Psychological Association. February 2018. Available online: http://www.apa.org/ed/precollege/ptn/2018/02/humor-college-classroom.

Aquinas, Thomas. "Question 168. Article 2. Whether There Can Be a Virtue about Games?" *The Summa Theologiae of St. Thomas Aquinas*. Translated by Fathers of the English Dominican Province. 2nd and rev. ed. (1920), online edition 2017. New Advent. Available online: https://www.newadvent.org/summa/3168.htm#article2.

Aristotle. *Nicomachean Ethics* IV.8. Aristotle, *Nicomachean Ethics*, trans. Martin Ostwald, 107–9. The Library of Liberal Arts, New York: Macmillan 1962.

Armstrong, Patricia. "Bloom's Taxonomy." Vanderbilt University Center for Teaching, last modified 2020. Available online: https://cft.vanderbilt.edu/guides-sub-pages/blooms-taxonomy/.

Banas, John, Norah Dunbar, Dariela Rodriguez, and Shr-Jie Liu. "A Review of Humor in Educational Settings: Four Decades of Research." *Communication Education* 60, no. 1 (January 2011): 115–44.

Bolkan, San and Alan K. Goodboy. "Exploratory Theoretical Tests of the Instructor Humor-Student Learning Link." *Communication Education* 64, no. 1 (January 2015): 45–64.

Bolkan, San and Darrin J. Griffin. "Catch and Hold: Instructional Interventions and Their Differential Impact on Student Interest, Attention, and Autonomous Motivation." *Communication Education* 67, no. 3 (2018): 269–86.

Booth-Butterfield, Melanie, Steven Booth-Butterfield, and Melissa Wanzer. "Funny Students Cope Better: Patterns of Humor Enactment and Coping Effectiveness." *Communication Quarterly* 55, no. 3 (2007): 299–315. doi:10.1080/01463370701490232.

Booth-Butterfield, Melanie and Melissa Bekelja Wanzer. "Humor and Communication in Instructional Contexts: Goal-Oriented Communication." In *The SAGE Handbook of Communication and Instruction*, edited by Deanna L. Fassett and John T. Warren (Los Angeles: SAGE, 2010), 221–39.

Borum Chattoo, Caty, and Lauren Feldman. *A Comedian and an Activist Walk into a Bar: The Serious Role of Comedy in Social Justice*. Communication for Social Justice Activism, 1. Oakland, California: University of California Press, 2020.

Brehm, Stephanie N. *America's Most Famous Catholic (According to Himself): Stephen Colbert and American Religion in the Twenty-first Century*. New York: Fordham University Press, 2019.

Bstan-'dzin-rgya-mtsho [the Dalai Lama] and Desmond Tutu, with Douglas Abrams. *The Book of Joy: Lasting Happiness in a Changing World*. New York: Avery/Penguin Random House, 2016.

Cohen, Ted. *Jokes: Philosophical Thoughts on Joking Matters*. Chicago: University of Chicago Press, 1999.

Dunbar, R. I. M., Rebecca Baron, Anna Frangou, Eiluned Pearce, Edwin J. C. van Leeuwen, Julie Stow, Giselle Partridge, Ian MacDonald, Vincent Barra, and Mark van Vugt. "Social Laughter Is Correlated with an Elevated Pain Threshold." *Proceedings of the Royal Society B* 279 (2012): 1161–7, doi:10.1098/rspb.2011.1373.

Farsad, Negin. "A Highly Scientific Taxonomy of Haters." TED 2016, February 2016. Available online: https://www.ted.com/talks/negin_farsad_a_highly_scientific_taxonomy_of_haters.

Frymier, Ann Bainbridge, Melissa Bekelja Wanzer, and Ann M. Wojtaszczyk. "Assessing Student Perceptions of Inappropriate and Appropriate Teacher Humor." Paper presented at the annual convention of the National Communication Association, November 2007, Chicago, Illinois.

Gadsby, Hannah. *Nanette*. Filmed at the Sidney Opera House, Netflix, 2018.

Gallagher, Eugene V. "Teaching for Religious Literacy." *Teaching Theology & Religion* 12, no. 3 (July 2009): 208–21.

Ghosh, P. "Study Reveals Laughter Really Is the Best Medicine." *BBC News*, September 13, 2011. Available online: http://www.bbc.com/news/science-environment-14889165.

Gruner, Charles R. *The Game of Humor: A Comprehensive Theory of Why We Laugh*. New Brunswick, NJ, and London: Transaction Publishers, 1997.

Hofstadter Douglas R. "Changes in Default Words and Images Engendered by Rising Consciousness." *Metamagical Themas: Questing for the Essence of Mind and Pattern*, 142–8. New York: Basic Books/HarperCollins Publishers, 1985. Available online: https://leeclarke.com/courses/intro/readings/Hofstadter_Changes_in_Default-_Words_and_Images.pdf.

hooks, bell. *Teaching to Transgress: Education as the Practice of Freedom*. New York: Routledge, 1994.

Houck, Anita. "You Are Here: Engagement, Spirituality, and Slow Teaching." In *Becoming Beholders: Cultivating Sacramental Imagination And Actions in College Classrooms*, edited by Karen E. Eifler and Thomas M. Landy, 70–85. Collegeville: Michael Glazier/Liturgical Press, 2014.

Houck, Anita. "Holiness and Humour." *HTS Theological Studies* 72, no. 4 (2016): 1–8. doi:10.4102/hts.v72i4.3464.

Killen, Patricia O'Connell. "Gracious Play: Discipline, Insight, and the Common Good." *Teaching Theology & Religion* 4, no. 1 (2001): 2–8.

Killen, Patricia O'Connell. "Editor's Note." *Teaching Theology & Religion* 10, no. 4 (2007): 213–14. doi:10.1111/j.1467-9647.2007.00373.x.

Killen, Patricia O'Connell. "'Keeping the Power of Wisdom Accessible': Religion Departments in Church-Related Colleges in Our Time." *Perspectives in Religious Studies* 46, no. 4 (Winter 2019): 403–15.

Matlins, Stuart M., and Arthur J. Magida, eds. *How to Be a Perfect Stranger: The Essential Religious Etiquette Handbook*. 6th edn. "Perfect Stranger" Series. Woodstock, Vermont: SkyLight Paths Publishing, 2015.

McCabe, Crystal, Katie Sprute, and Kimber Underdown. "Laughter to Learning: How Humor Can Build Relationships and Increase Learning in the Online Classroom." *Journal of Instructional Research* 6 (January 2017): 4–7.

Morreall, John. "Philosophy of Humor." *Stanford Encyclopedia of Philosophy*, last modified August 20, 2020. Available online: https://plato.stanford.edu/entries/humor/.

Niebuhr, Reinhold. "Humour and Faith." In *The Essential Reinhold Niebuhr: Selected Essays and Addresses*, edited by Reinhold Niebuhr and Robert McAfee Brown, 49–60. New Haven: Yale University Press, 1987.

Oring, Elliott. "Appropriate Incongruity Redux." In *Engaging Humor*, 1–12. Urbana and Chicago: University of Illinois Press, 2003.

Philips, Emo. "The Best God Joke Ever—And It's Mine!" *The Guardian*, September 29, 2005. Available online: https://www.theguardian.com/stage/2005/sep/29/comedy.religion.

Provine, Robert R. *Laughter: A Scientific Investigation*. New York: Viking, 2000.

Rosegard, Erik and Jackson Wilson. "Capturing Students' Attention: An Empirical Study." *Journal of the Scholarship of Teaching and Learning* 13, no. 5 (December 2013): 1–20.

Rossing, Jonathan P. "A Sense of Humor for Civic Life: Toward a Strong Defense of Humor." *Studies in American Humor* 2, no. 1 (2016): 1–21. doi:10.5325/studamerhumor.2.1.0001.

Sayedahmed, Dina and Hamna Saleem. "Hijabi World." *Newest Americans*, 2015. Available online: https://newestamericans.com/hijabi-world/.

"Seven Dirty Words." Wikipedia, last modified November 12, 2020. Available online: https://en.wikipedia.org/wiki/Seven_dirty_words.

Smith, Victoria D., and Amy Wortley. "'Everyone's a Comedian.' No Really, They Are: Using Humor in the Online and Traditional Classroom." *Journal of Instructional Research* 6 (January 2017): 18–23.

Teslow, James L. "Humor Me: A Call for Research." *Educational Technology Research and Development* 43, no. 3 (1995): 6–28.

Wanzer, Melissa B., Ann B. Frymier, and Jeffrey Irwin. "An Explanation of the Relationship between Instructor Humor and Student Learning: Instructional Humor Processing Theory." *Communication Education* 59, no. 1 (2010): 1–18.

White, Marney A. "Academic Course Evaluations in Health Sciences Can Be a Joke: A Cross-Sectional Examination of Whether Students Appreciate a Professor's Sense of Humor." *American Journal of Health Education* 50, no. 6 (2019): 398–404.

Wilkens, Steve. *What's So Funny about God?: A Theological Look at Humor*. Downers Grove, IL: IVP Academic/InterVarsity Press, 2019.

Wortley, Amy, and Elizabeth Dotson. "Stand Up Comics: Instructional Humor and Student Engagement." *Journal of Instructional Research* 5 (January 2016): 13–18.

Young, Dannagal Goldthwaite. *Irony and Outrage: The Polarized Landscape of Rage, Fear, and Laughter in the United States*. New York: Oxford University Press, 2020.

Zayid, Maysoon. "I Got Ninety-Nine Problems … Palsy Is Just One." TEDWomen 2013, December 2013. Available online: https://www.ted.com/talks/maysoon_zayid_i_got_99_problems_palsy_is_just_one.

Zimbardo, Philip. Interview by Stephen Colbert, *The Colbert Report*, Comedy Central, February 11, 2008. Available online: http://www.cc.com/video-clips/8sjpoa/the-colbert-report-philip-zimbardo.

5

Planning for Playfulness

Richard S. Ascough
Queen's University

Introduction

In his *Ars Poetica*, the late first century BCE Roman poet Horace wrestles with the nature of poetry in a way that I think proves helpful for thinking about pedagogy. Horace opines that although poets might have some innate abilities, they must also work on their skills as writers of poetry, applying discipline and practice to their development while being open to criticism from self and others. A poem does not just "happen." The well-crafted poem requires all of the design skill at the disposal of the poet. But when designed well, it brings both teaching and enjoyment. The poet, he says, "who has managed to blend profit with delight wins everyone's admiration, for he gives his reader pleasure at the same time as he instructs him" (*Ars Poetica* 342).

Horace is onto something in helping us think about pedagogy, which is one of the two core facets of his conception of poetry. Poems instruct but do so in a way that also brings pleasure; the aim is "to give profit or delight or to mix the giving of pleasure with useful precepts for life" (*Ars Poetica* 333–334). For Horace, learning is not separated from enjoyment; his is a far cry from the view of Menander: "The one who is not flogged is not educated" (*Sententia* 422). The notion of "delight" can, of course, be unpacked in many ways. In this essay, I want to point to a way in which our honorees have both, together and separately, embodied the conception of "profit with delight" through their use of pedagogical play alongside emphasis on solid design principles.

Pedagogy of Play

Some two decades ago, Patricia Killen published an article on the theme of play in the study of religion and theology in which she argued that "university teaching involves creating spaces of gracious play that are potentially transformative for students and faculty."[1] For Patricia, "gracious play" is the nexus of discipline, insight, and the common good.[2] It involves companions, rules, and innovation, with the graciousness stemming from being "caught up in play" and thus experiencing "self-transcendence," resulting in "delight in being."[3] Patricia makes the call for creating space in higher education for such gracious play in which students are supported in their learning even while being "caught up" in its graciousness. It does not just happen, however, as she well recognizes. It must be anticipated, planned, and designed.

The Wabash workshops in which I have participated in some capacity with Patricia and/or Gene in leadership had the three key hallmarks of playful learning: choice, wonder, and delight.[4] Although there was always a particular flow to the workshops, the overall design was built around broad themes identified by the leadership team, enacted in detail as the subthemes that arose from the applications of the participants themselves. Although subtle, arriving at a workshop that forefronts themes that are important to participants provided them with a sense of ownership, motivation, and empowerment. As the workshop progressed, an increasing amount of the design and delivery of content was negotiated among the participants themselves. Such collective decision-making processes enhanced the sense of empowerment and ownership among learners.[5] The workshops were also filled with experiences of wonder—"improvising or exploring, creating or inventing, pretending or imagining, and taking risks or learning from trial and error"[6]—through the various interactive sessions that asked participants to illustrate, role-play, compose, create, and so on. Finally, the delight at the workshop was palpable, not just in the gracious hospitality that Patricia and Gene so affirmed,[7] but also in sessions and especially in the "off-hours" gatherings, when participants could "smile, laugh, joke, or perhaps be silly."[8] Such antics are not, however, by-products of the time together but are reflectively structured and encouraged within the overall workshop design.

Mardell and his colleagues in the "pedagogy of play" project blandly but boldly state that "unfortunately, a sense of delight is often missing in schools."[9] Although they are speaking about primary and secondary education, my own sense is that there is a distinct lack of choice, wonder, and delight in higher education. Or, as Farné suggests, it is the false juxtaposition of "play" and "learning" that has relegated play, and thus pleasure, to the margins in favor of learning as "mandatory duty" and "work."[10]

University is unnerving for students, as Patricia noted two decades ago. Students find the disciplinary focus and the rigor of methodology alien and threatening, and they fear the development of a critical consciousness that asks them to deconstruct much of their own worldview.[11] This is certainly something that my colleagues and I have noticed at our own institution, where students seem overburdened with anxiety to the extent that it cripples their ability to engage fully in the educational experience. They seem conditioned to think of the university experience, at least the formal courses within the curriculum, as overly serious; it is a path to a career, and they must prove themselves each step along the way. And while certainly it is, in part, that very thing, the pressures our students face make them seem incapable of figuring things out on their own. This is poignantly illustrated by the oft-heard cry of instructors that the answer to the question is "on the syllabus" if students would only actually sit down and read it! This is, of course, a widespread problem that involves many complex factors and manifests itself in a lot of mental health issues on our campuses.

Perhaps the issue is that students are entering university with experiences of the "new culture of learning" from K-12, and higher education has not fully caught up with it in all of its aspects. This new culture of learning recognizes not just the important shift from teaching-centered to learning-centered pedagogy but also the role of games within the learning environment.[12] Thomas and Seely Brown see this manifesting in the growth not just of a network of digital resources but in the way these can be used in what they call the "petri dish" of a "bounded environment of experimentation" to create a "new culture of learning" based on "information and experimentation" in which "play is the central tool for inverting the traditional hierarchy of learning and knowing."[13]

Gene engages with the idea of a *new* culture of learning with characteristically humorous aplomb: "Thomas and Seely Brown have come late to the party, but they have brought their smart phones."[14] He rightly argues that the shift from instruction to learning as a pedagogical paradigm has long been underway in higher education and that the new digital media are new ways of deploying active learning strategies rather than the impetus for them. In his article, Gene asks whether teachers can even make the case for students coming to class, whether physically or online; what is the value added of the classroom experience? Naturally, Gene answers his own question affirmatively, pointing to the classroom as the location of multi-dialogical, "disciplined pursuit of knowledge" among the professor, student, and material.[15] He does admit, however, the disconnect that can take place between what students want to learn and what instructors teach; "teachers need to figure out ways to bring into dynamic and productive relationship certain bodies of material, the 'stuff' of courses, and the 'things that really interest' their students."[16] And it is here where he concedes that gaming is important, but limited, rightly noting that "cooperation, imagination, and creative play mark many other communities of discourse beyond that of online gamers."[17]

A new(er) culture of learning, or at least a pedagogical reflection on the culture of learning can and should recognize the importance of playfulness as a key element of student learning.[18] We need, however, to think of it as going beyond "children"; using it with young adults such as those in our colleges and universities might mitigate some of the issues noted above, reducing the stress and anxiety that our students experience.[19] As Farné shows, "adult identity is not built on the negation of loss of childhood, but it is achieved starting from its development and exploitation."[20] While other developmental aspects are distinctive to particular stages (e.g., "student," "worker," "pensioner"), play is something that begins with childhood and continues on;[21] witness the cultural impact in North America of such things as participating in sports, online gaming, or adult games like Cards Against Humanity. This continuation suggests that learners in higher education can and will be positively oriented to participating in play as part of their education, not just at the primary school level.

This is not an original suggestion by any means. Play has a long history in educational theory, being initiated with Locke in 1693 and brought into the mainstream with the work of Rousseau in 1762 and carried into the modern period in the thinking of pedagogues such as Montessori, among others.[22] "Play characterizes the two fundamental guidelines which are at the basis of education; the spontaneous and natural direction on the one side, and the intentional one on the other side."[23] Yet it seems to me that it has not fully been recognized for the impact it can have in our classrooms. And while designing for playfulness is not a panacea for all the stress impacting our students, it is one small way that instructors might contribute not only to the lessening of our students' anxiety but, in fact, to the enhancement of their overall learning.

Playfulness in the Classroom

A few years ago, I introduced into my second-year undergraduate course on the New Testament a game I call "Discipleship Survivor." Riffing off a well-known TV series and its spin-offs, on the first day of class I suggest that perhaps Peter is not all that Jesus thought him to be when he promised him the keys to the kingdom (Matt 16:15-19), since later Peter will deny Jesus three times. I reveal a toy boat that has Jesus and his twelve disciples in it, and I challenge the students either to defend Peter or find someone more worthy of key possession by nominating a disciple to be removed each week of the twelve-week semester. The "survivor" will then be granted the keys. I give students very little direction other than to "look up" what the disciples did. During the ensuing weeks, students develop their research skills, abilities to distinguish reliable and non-reliable sources (both primary and secondary), and proficiency in offering arguments and counter arguments. The exercise ends up taking at least thirty minutes of each three-hour class period and has proven to be more effective pedagogically than I first imagined.[24]

This activity has all the principles of good gaming (challenge, community, narrative, competition, and multimedia) and play (choice, wonder, and delight).[25] It is, as Lester asserts for games, engaging and provides "a venue in which concepts are introduced to the learner or reinforced in a fun, low-fear environment,"[26] or, as Schell puts it, "a problem-solving activity, approached with a playful attitude."[27] The students are first and foremost engaged in the competitive nature of the task, sometimes forming ad hoc coalitions in order to save or eliminate a particular disciple. It is only on later reflection that they realize and recognize the nature of the learning that has been going on through the game.

Contributors to Whitton and Moseley's volume on games in education[28] identify five characteristics of games that make them effective for use within more traditional teaching practices: challenges toward reaching a goal, developing communities of practice and/or engagement, narrative structures and complex plot lines, healthy competition within oneself or with others, and the use of multimedia that engage more than one or two senses and different ways of knowing. "Gaming can be an individual or shared experience," they write, "but always involves construction, synthesis, and application of knowledge" and thus lends itself well to a constructivist approach to teaching and learning.[29] Constructivism is "the idea that knowledge, like reality, is not an objective data to be mechanically transmitted and acquired, but it is the outcome of a relationship in which the subject and the object are involved in a process of *construction of meaning*."[30]

Through games, students create their own learning about a given subject through active engagement that builds upon past knowledge and experiences.[31] Games can be a fun way of engaging the students' attention, but, as Whitton and

Moseley rightly caution, "the use of games in education must be driven by the pedagogic goals and needs of the learners."[32] This is where the principles of backward design are critical. These principles are foundational to Patricia's approach to the "design of intellectual experiences." Drawing on Wiggins and McTighe,[33] among others, Patricia advocates first identifying student learning outcomes and using them as the basis for the course assessments and assignments, which in turn leads to determining the course content and activities. And it is within this broader framework of backward design that we must look for opportunities for playfulness, through games or other activities, that can be used in order to provoke or enhance students' initial forays into the material, facilitate their integration of new material with what they know, or provide them with opportunities to demonstrate how they have done the integration and thus learned.[34]

Equally important to the pedagogy of play is designing for spontaneity. This is, I admit, a bit of an oxymoron as it tries to capture both the importance of clear and careful design for interactive learning while recognizing that there is a place for extemporaneity in the classroom. One cannot "design" spontaneity in detail, but one can design the intellectual experience of students in a way that leaves room—both in terms of time and content—to involve students' own interests and passions while still staying the course with the material at hand. For example, an unexpected breakthrough occurred during the mid-point break in my class on Greek and Roman Religions which allowed me to harness a piece of contemporary popular culture for my own teaching ends. Students at one of the tables were watching the trailer for the new Gilmore Girls show that was shortly to appear on Netflix (December 2016). They were laughing about being "fangirls" of the early 2000s series, calling it a "cult." They jokingly asked me to let them show the trailer to the entire class, which, to their great surprise, I allowed. I then started asking them why they, and the rest of the class, thought it was a "cult" and what made it the same and/or different from the Dionysos mystery "cult" we were discussing that day. I segued that into a mini-lecture/discussion on Jonathan Z. Smith and the comparative method in Religious Studies.[35] In their post-class comments, a quarter of the students noted how positive and helpful this connection had been. My impromptu decision to utilize what students were "fooling around" with at the break resulted in significant unplanned learning—for example, one student noted, "Gilmore Girls explanation was useful, made more sense of the course as a whole!"

To be sure, seizing the moment in order to spark student interest can be daunting, not to say risky. But as Nikki Pugh declares, "there's huge scope for more playfulness in education and by playfulness I basically mean not-being-afraid-to-be-wrong-ness."[36] And I would add to that, a large element of not-afraid-to-fail-ness. Engaging students where they are at with the material they care about can connect learning to the meaning and value they find in their own lives. Thus, playfully and spontaneously reacting to issues raised is one way—certainly not the only way—of engaging our students. And in having fun ourselves, even when taking risks, students are more likely to adopt the same playful yet risk-taking approach in their own learning. Although they may not necessarily like taking playful risks—as one of my students said of a role-playing activity: "I kinda hate skits, … but I think it works"—they recognize the potential rewards.[37]

Conclusion

What Farné claims for children can be extended to the young adults in our college and university classrooms where, through playfulness, they experience familiarity "with a changeable dimension of reality, where risks and unexpected events can take place at any time, where it is necessary to face them, and where it is not possible to be completely sure of relationships, which can turn out to be ambivalent and conflicting (just as often happens in real life)."[38] This kind of processing goes beyond formal games and even impromptu, informal games such as hide-and-seek or "cops-and-robbers" that younger children initiate. By introducing playfulness into the classroom (or workshop), we are creating conditions where students must fashion their own (bounded) path through the subject matter, learning together to navigate and negotiate the dataset that is "course content" and forge for themselves new ways of understanding and applying the material at hand.

The above examples from my own teaching illustrate how playfulness can be integrated into a course. These activities have worked well in my own courses but would never have been possible—in fact, I doubt I ever would have attempted them—without the mentorship of Patricia and Gene. Patricia trained me in the theory and practice of pedagogical design while allowing me to engage in playfulness, both inside and outside of the formal leadership times in various Wabash workshops. For his part, Gene both embodied and encouraged thoughtful playfulness in ways that did not allow me to take myself too seriously while at the same time driving home just what is at stake in teaching. For both Patricia and Gene, each and every moment with students and workshop participants is an opportunity for profit with delight when our design of intellectual experiences includes thoughtful engagement with playfulness.

Notes

1. Patricia O'Connell Killen, "Gracious Play: Discipline, Insight, and the Common Good," *Teaching Theology & Religion* 4 (2001): 2.
2. Ibid., 3.
3. Ibid., 6.
4. Ben Mardell, Daniel Wilson, Jen Ryan, Katie Ertel, Mara Krechevsky, and Megina Baker, "Towards a Pedagogy of Play. A Project Zero Working Paper," 2016. Available online: http://www.pz.harvard.edu/sites/default/files/Towards%20a%20Pedagogy%20of%20Play.pdf, accessed October 14, 2020, 7–8. See further the "PoP Playbook" at https://pz.harvard.edu/sites/default/files/PoP%20Playbook.pdf. The Pedagogy of Play project is a research collaboration between Project Zero at the Harvard Graduate School of Education and the LEGO Foundation (see http://www.pz.harvard.edu/projects/pedagogy-of-play). The project explores the role of play in education in order to establish and develop a working set of playful learning principles, practices, and tools and ultimately a pedagogy of play framework. As a "pedagogy," it is "a systematic approach to the practice of playful learning and teaching" (Mardell et al., "Towards a Pedagogy of Play," 2).
5. Mardell et al., "Towards a Pedagogy of Play," 7.
6. Ibid., 8.
7. Cf. Patricia O'Connell Killen, "Midrange Reflection: The Underlying Practice of Wabash Center Workshops, Colloquies, and Consultations," *Teaching Theology & Religion* 10 (2007): 143–9; Eugene V. Gallagher, "Welcoming the Stranger," *Teaching Theology & Religion* 10 (2007): 137–42.
8. Mardell et al., "Towards a Pedagogy of Play," 8.
9. Ibid., 9.
10. Roberto Farné, "Pedagogy of Play," *Topoi* 24 (2005): 169.
11. Killen, "Gracious Play," 6.
12. See Douglas Thomas and John Seely Brown, *A New Culture of Learning: Cultivating the Imagination for a World of Constant Change* (Lexington, KY: Authors, 2011), 96–9; cf. Mary E. Hess, "A New Culture of Learning: What are the Implications for Theological Educators?" *Teaching Theology & Religion* 17 (2014): 228.
13. Thomas and Seely Brown, *New Culture of Learning*, 116–17.
14. Eugene V. Gallagher, "Is the 'New Culture of Learning' All That New?" *Teaching Theology & Religion* 17 (2014): 232.
15. Ibid., 234.
16. Ibid., 236.
17. Ibid., 238.
18. Note: "These terms—play, playful, and even learning—are complex and complicated constructs with ambiguous relationships between and among them. For instance,

not all play is playful (e.g., professional football). Nor does all that might be considered *playful* (e.g., a conversation) resemble what would ordinarily be called play" (Mardell et al., "Towards a Pedagogy of Play," 2). Mark Carnes goes so far as to identify as "bad play" some co-curricular activities such as sports events, early literary societies, fraternity initiations, and even online role-playing games, since they interfere with full student engagement ("From Plato to Erikson: How the War on 'bad play' has Impoverished Higher Education," *Arts and Humanities in Higher Education* 14 [2015]: 383–7; idem, *Minds on Fire: How Role-Immersion Games Transform College* [Cambridge, MA: Harvard University Press, 2014], 37–62).

19   In their comprehensive literature review of studies of the game-based learning platform Kahoot!, Alf Inge Wang and Rabail Tahir found that ten of fourteen studies showed that it "reduced student anxiety related to asking questions" and could "reduce stress and tension," encourage participation without concern about being judged, add humor, and enable "shy students to get involved" ("The Effect of Using Kahoot! For Learning—A Literature Review," *Computers & Education* 149 [2020]: 13; https://doi.org/10.1016/j.compedu.2020.103818).

20   Farné, "Pedagogy of Play," 170. Farné demonstrates how the "discovery" of childhood as a category in the seventeenth century is inextricably linked to the development of childhood toys and games and that play was and is the ongoing symbol of childhood culture (Ibid., 170–1).

21   Ibid., 179.

22   Ibid., 170–5.

23   Ibid., 169.

24   For a full description of this activity and a comprehensive qualitative analysis of its effectiveness, see Richard S. Ascough and Christina D'Amico, "Active Learning in Lecture Based Courses: 'Discipleship Survivor' as a Case Study," *Wabash Journal on Teaching* 2, no. 1 (2021): 33–48.

25   See further below. On gaming in higher education see Carnes, *Minds on Fire* and the essays in Nicola Whitton and Alex Moseley, eds., *Using Games to Enhance Learning and Teaching: A Beginner's Guide* (New York, NY: Routledge, 2012). For application to Religious Studies and Theology, see the special issue of *Teaching Theology & Religion* 21/4 (2018) on "Games & Learning." For use of an online gaming platform such as Kahoot!, see Wang and Tahir (2020) and more practically Carolyn M. Plump and Julia LaRosa, "Using Kahoot! in the Classroom to Create Engagement and Active Learning: A Game-Based Technology Solution for eLearning Novices," *Management Teaching Review* 2, no. 2 (2017): 151–8.

26   G. Brooke Lester, "What IF? Building Interactive Fiction for Teaching and Learning Religious Studies," *Teaching Theology & Religion* 21 (2018): 265.

27   Jesse Schell, *The Art of Game Design: A Book of Lenses*, 2nd edn. (Boca Raton, FL: CRC Press, 2015), 47.

28 Whitton and Moseley, *Using Games*.
29 Ibid., 5; Benjamin E. Zeller, "'Make Your Own Religion': The Fictive Religion Assignment As Educational Game," *Teaching Theology & Religion* 21 (2018): 334.
30 Farné, "Pedagogy of Play," 172, his emphasis.
31 Nicola Whitton, "Good Game Design Is Good Learning Design," in *Using Games to Enhance Learning and Teaching: A Beginner's Guide*, ed. Nicola Whitton and Alex Moseley (New York, NY: Routledge, 2012), 11.
32 Whitton and Moseley, *Using Games*, 5.
33 Grant Wiggins and Jay McTighe, *Understanding by Design*, 2nd edn. (Alexandria, VA: Association for Supervision and Curriculum Development, 1998).
34 Whitton suggests that "playfulness" is one of six aspects of games that "support and enhance the processes around learning," the other five being practice, engagement, scaffolding, feedback, and digital literacy ("Good Game Design," 14). While I do not think she is incorrect, I think this is a limited way of thinking about "playfulness." Play is so much more than gaming, although it can include gaming.
35 On comparison in religious studies, see Eugene V. Gallagher and Joanne Maguire, *The Religious Studies Skills Book: Close Reading, Critical Thinking, and Comparison* (London: Bloomsbury, 2019), 119–39.
36 Quoted in Whitton and Moseley, *Using Games*, 15.
37 On role-playing, see Melanie A. Howard, who notes that "Because the world of the [role-playing] game lets students explore different perspectives without necessarily claiming those viewpoints as their own, it offers students a safe space to explore difficult questions without posing a direct threat to the religious views that they already hold" ("A Game of Faith: Role-Playing Games as an Active Learning Strategy for Value Formation and Faith Integration in the Theological Classroom," *Teaching Theology & Religion* 21 [2018]: 286).
38 Farné, "Pedagogy of Play," 177.

Bibliography

Ascough, Richard S. and Christina D'Amico. "Active Learning in Lecture Based Courses: 'Discipleship Survivor' as a Case Study." *Wabash Journal on Teaching* 2, no. 1 (2021): 33–48.

Carnes, Mark C. *Minds on Fire: How Role-Immersion Games Transform College*. Cambridge, MA: Harvard University Press, 2014.

Carnes, Mark C. "From Plato to Erikson: How the War on 'bad play' has Impoverished Higher Education." *Arts and Humanities in Higher Education* 14 (2015): 383–7.

Farné, Roberto. "Pedagogy of Play." *Topoi* 24 (2005): 169–81.

Gallagher, Eugene V. "Welcoming the Stranger." *Teaching Theology & Religion* 10 (2007): 137–42.

Gallagher, Eugene V. "Is the 'New Culture of Learning' All That New?" *Teaching Theology & Religion* 17 (2014): 232–8.

Gallagher, Eugene V., and Joanne Maguire, *The Religious Studies Skills Book: Close Reading, Critical Thinking, and Comparison*. London: Bloomsbury, 2019.

Hess, Mary E. "A New Culture of Learning: What Are the Implications for Theological Educators?" *Teaching Theology & Religion* 17 (2014): 227–38.

Howard, Melanie A. "A Game of Faith: Role-Playing Games as an Active Learning Strategy for Value Formation and Faith Integration in the Theological Classroom." *Teaching Theology & Religion* 21 (2018): 274–87.

Killen, Patricia O'Connell. "Gracious Play: Discipline, Insight, and the Common Good." *Teaching Theology & Religion* 4 (2001): 2–8.

Killen, Patricia O'Connell. "Midrange Reflection: The Underlying Practice of Wabash Center Workshops, Colloquies, and Consultations." *Teaching Theology & Religion* 10 (2007): 143–9.

Lester, G. Brooke. "What IF? Building Interactive Fiction for Teaching and Learning Religious Studies." *Teaching Theology & Religion* 21 (2018): 260–73.

Mardell, Ben, Daniel Wilson, Jen Ryan, Katie Ertel, Mara Krechevsky, and Megina Baker. "Towards a Pedagogy of Play. A Project Zero Working Paper." 2016. Available online: http://www.pz.harvard.edu/sites/default/files/Towards%20a%20Pedagogy%20of%20Play.pdf, accessed October 14, 2020.

Plump, Carolyn M., and Julia LaRosa. "Using Kahoot! in the Classroom to Create Engagement and Active Learning: A Game-Based Technology Solution for eLearning Novices." *Management Teaching Review* 2, no. 2 (2017): 151–8.

Schell, Jesse. *The Art of Game Design: A Book of Lenses*. 2nd edn. Boca Raton, FL: CRC Press, 2015.

Thomas, Douglas, and John Seely Brown. *A New Culture of Learning: Cultivating the Imagination for a World of Constant Change*. Lexington, KY: Authors, 2011.

Wang, Alf Inge, and Rabail Tahir. "The Effect of Using Kahoot! For Learning—A Literature Review." *Computers & Education* 149 (2020): 1–22. https://doi.org/10.1016/j.compedu.2020.103818.

Whitton, Nicola. "Good Game Design Is Good Learning Design." In *Using Games to Enhance Learning and Teaching: A Beginner's Guide*, edited by Nicola Whitton and Alex Moseley, 9–18. New York, NY: Routledge, 2012.

Whitton, Nicola, and Alex Moseley, eds. *Using Games to Enhance Learning and Teaching: A Beginner's Guide*. New York, NY: Routledge, 2012.

Wiggins, Grant, and Jay McTighe. *Understanding by Design*. 2nd edn. Alexandria, VA: Association for Supervision and Curriculum Development, 1998.

Zeller, Benjamin E. "'Make Your Own Religion': The Fictive Religion Assignment as Educational Game." *Teaching Theology & Religion* 21 (2018): 321–35.

6

The Tao of the Post-It: Empowering Student Engagement in Gene Gallagher's Classroom

Lydia Willsky-Ciollo
Fairfield University

The color-wheel standard for nostalgia is "rosy," right? For me, when thinking about Gene Gallagher—at various, often overlapping, times my teacher, advisor, and mentor—all I see is neon yellow. The Day-glo yellow-green of a Post-It note, more accurately. When we co-taught a course at my alma mater, Connecticut College—me, an adjunct on the brink of my dissertation defense and Gene, the seasoned classroom vet—Gene would write his plan for the day on a single Post-It. In six bullet points or less—each bullet often comprised of only one word each—written in red pen and in his distinctive block lettering, Gene's Post-Its contained universes.

At the outset of my teaching career, I found such pithiness equal parts intimidating and baffling: how could one fill a seventy-five-minute bloc of time without a detailed plan and a contingency plan if that failed? Now, more seasoned but still pedagogically green in my own mind, I understand better the purpose, function, and brilliance of the Post-It. The Post-It note centers the student in the design of an entire course, specific assignments, a particular class, and a single discussion. This student is never hypothetical or imagined, but present and real. The simplicity of the Post-It enables flexibility and expects that students will come to class with different levels of knowledge, interest, and expectation. As a symbol and a physical artifact of student-centered learning, Gene Gallagher's Post-Its propose that students are more engaged when their input is invited, valued, and synthesized in the content and outcomes of the course, while leaving room for challenging held assumptions in a way that sparks dialogue rather than silencing or disenfranchising. In this essay, I will elaborate on the

Gene Gallagher's "Tao of the Post-It," which is reflective of his teaching career and a theory of pedagogy that de-centers the professor, moves beyond content-delivery, and invests in the idea that students learn best when actively engaged.

Leaning into the Silence

"Lecturing is easier," Gene once told me. On the side of preparation, perhaps not. The work that goes into writing and synthesizing material into a cogent lecture takes time and skill. Nonetheless, the primary work of a lecture, from this standpoint, occurs outside rather than inside the classroom. A good lecture, in theory, could proceed apace without the lecturer even present. Lecture, in the classic sense reflects the "instruction paradigm" theorized by Robert B. Barr and John Tagg.[1] Lecture imparts content and students are recipients of this content. Lectures fill the space with ideas, stories, facts, and statistics; lectures are designed to fill the silence.

Post-It note plans lean into the silence. The first time I asked my students a question and the only sound, to my ears at least, was my quickening pulse, I sprung into action and answered my own question. Later, Gene asked me how long I thought the pause between question and answer had been, my estimate far exceeded the mere seconds of silence that passed in reality. His reply (though I paraphrase it here) was "Next time, count to ten, slowly, in your head. If there is still no response, rephrase the question. Count to ten again. If they are still silent, give an example, poll the room with a yes-or-no question, or move on if you think it's a dead-end." Sometimes they will need more guidance, but delivering "the answer" perpetuates passive learning. Even more significant, answers, particularly in humanities courses, are various, multi-faceted, and often contingent upon *who* delivers them—but there is a high likelihood that students will record *your* answer as "gospel." As Gene wrote once regarding his assessment of why teachers matter and why they do not, "Apprenticing yourself to someone from whom you can learn a lot can be an exhilarating intellectual experience. Staying in such an uneven relationship can be stultifying. Pretty quickly, simply replicating your mentor's insights does neither you nor your mentor any good."[2]

The Post-It plan presumes that the gaps in a lesson plan are as generative as the moments of content delivery; that the content you choose is important, but equally important is the space to absorb, challenge, discuss, or meditate on a question. Nearly a decade into my teaching career, I have found the moments of silence a more comfortable space in which to dwell. Sometimes students simply need a moment to collect their thoughts; sometimes they do not wish to appear too eager, so they hold back for a time; sometimes they are unsure that they know what they actually know.

Silence also means, sometimes, that you asked a bad question. Witnessing Gene have a question fall flat, which he followed with a wry laugh, a "Well that went over well," and a pivot to the next thing, was a paradigm-shifting moment for a neophyte. Adaptation in the moment is both a skill (requiring knowledge of content and pedagogical tools) and a learned behavior (requiring resilience, an acceptance of failure, and a willingness to laugh at oneself). The Post-It plan expects that the instructor will have thought through the run of a particular class and its "thesis," while also allowing space to try different things; see what works and what does not; and to lean into, not run from, silence.

Teach the Students that You Have

Every instructor who has ever taught two sections of the same class simultaneously or back to back semesters of the same course can report how disjointed it can feel to teach the same material to different sets of students. One might have a loquacious bunch one hour and a reserved group the next; a group made of those taking the course solely for credit and then a group with a handful of invested Majors or Minors in the next; on one group your jokes fall flat and with the other you develop a consistent, informal kind of banter for the duration of the course. The bottom line is that rarely does the same teaching style work for each set of students, requiring one to heed Gene's advice: to "teach the students you have, not the ones you wish you had."[3] A detailed lesson plan may accomplish little if the class does not have the interest, prerequisite experience or knowledge, or level of engagement that the instructor assumes. Thus, essential to the planning of an entire course and individual classes with your students in mind is, first, to know who is sitting in front of you.

Knowing who your students are is a cumulative process and one that usually spans the course. Nonetheless, this does not mean that the process cannot begin immediately. What Gene has called "discussion starter papers" and I have adapted in my courses in various forms are assignments often performed simply for credit and based entirely on students' own knowledge, presuppositions, and experiences.[4] During our semester of co-teaching a course on Religion in the United States, Gene suggested that we have our students write about their own religious histories, thereby prompting them to think about the ways that they may fit into the American religious landscape. I continue to use the "My Religious History" in my solo version of that course, which serves as a useful touchstone for students when discussing the course's major "thesis": that there are multiple stories and modes of telling the story of American religion, often depending upon who is asked.

In my course on Afro-Caribbean and Afro-American religions, which is a class about race as much as it is a class about religion, students begin by reading the short story "Recitatif" by Toni Morrison. Through these papers I get to know my students' comfort level with discussions of race, implicit bias, and white privilege, as well as their "meta-awareness" of the purpose of the assignment. Based upon these papers and the accompanying discussions they spawn between students and with me, I am able to adapt the frame of each class, even if the essential content does not change. For example, if I have a set of students who felt upset or even angry at being compelled to address any implicit assumptions about race, I often choose to reveal my own biases and struggles with them as an attempt to forge a bridge; for another set of students, who feel ready to talk about race and white privilege and their own self-assessment, to bring the focus to myself in such a way would be the wrong move and might shut down discourse that is already happening. An added benefit of these starter assignments is that they can often double as self-assessment tools: the last class of the semester, students re-read their papers and consider whether after having completed the course they would answer in the same way and why. My students re-read their "Recitatif" papers at the end of the course, which I accompany with the question "what would you want to teach your 'beginning-of-the-course' self, now that you stand at the end of the course?" Besides being a means for me to see students put into their own words what has been most salient in their learning (and whether it matches with my "objectives" for the course), it is a moment for students to take on the role of teacher themselves, a role that prompts ownership of their acquired skills and knowledge.

What Do You *Really* Want Students to Learn?

By constitution and choice of discipline, scholars of Religious Studies are committed to the idea that knowledge about religion is essential to human society and daily life. Teachers of Religious Studies, many of whom teach in departments whose function is to "serve" CORE or General Education requirements, cannot presume that their students will feel similarly. Many students will tick the appropriate box and never darken the door of a Religious Studies course again. For this reason, Religious Studies courses, particularly introductory courses, must be designed "with the knowledge that it may well be the only course in the study of religion that the students enrolled will take."[5] Hence the question: what do you *really* want students to learn? What is important as takeaway?

Given that students are often shy on details about what they learned the previous week, often specific content, facts, and details is not what will stick. "Backward course design" has emerged as a way to reverse-engineer courses, beginning with questions, goals, and outcomes for courses, rather than the specific topics and material to be covered.[6] Designing courses this way does not rule out one's expertise as a starting point, but for students in Religious Studies courses, the aim for teachers is usually not to make experts in our field. So with each text chosen, each theme explored, the question should always be: why am I giving this to my students and what do I hope they will glean from it?

In Religious Studies classes, the answer to this question may relate to "skills"—strengthening analytical reading and writing abilities, developing a critical or theoretical toolbox handy in many fields, or building public speaking skills—but it often relates to questions of "religious literacy," and what that means for our students who will be contributors to society in the future. The concept of religious literacy presumes that knowledge of religion is essential to functioning and living in the United States (and the world). What precisely this knowledge should be is the purview of the instructor, thus the development of precise metrics for assessing religious literacy is difficult. (This fact compounds the ever-increasing pressure upon Religious Studies, as a Humanities discipline, to defend its existence as a viable and necessary area of study for the undergraduates as consumers. But I digress ....) Learning objectives or "goals" have become a way of gesturing toward what students will learn in the course and Gene, whose learning objectives he designed to be non-content specific, allow for varying degrees of preparedness among students, and to incorporate content as "needed."

As noted in the previous section, the student cohort for a given class may help to dictate what content requires focus, what questions require probing, and what modes of assessment would work best to measure students' response. While teaching my course on New Religious movements at my current institution, Gene served as a guest co-teacher for a class where the topic was the "anticult movement." Prior to the class, I handed Gene a stack of "Weekly Posts": short reflections written by my students on the reading for that day and a practice that I "stole freely" (to employ the verbiage of the Wabash Center) from Gene.

The students were nearly unanimous in their censure of the tactics of the anticult movement. My lesson plan took a predominantly critical tack as well, thus I was feeling quite chuffed that my students were already on the same page. Gene, after reading the posts, determined that he would focus his portion of the class on swinging the pendulum back, focusing on the reasons behind anticult activism and the real people whose fear for family and children had led them to seek help. Gene's portion of the class enabled a balanced lesson that equipped my students with a more humanized understanding of anticult activism. However, even when that specific knowledge faded, hopefully what remained was the memory of testing different interpretations, examining multiple perspectives, and reading critically those with personal or professional biases or agendas—even those of their instructors. Teaching religious literacy, from my perspective and as modeled by Gene, is asking students to recognize that religious ideas, peoples, and institutions are complex, that rarely is there a soundbite that perfectly summarizes any of them, and that it is best to proceed from a perspective of curiosity-seeking-balance that avoids passively accepted "tropes," cultural myths, or "accepted wisdom."[7] Whereas religious systems may be exclusive in belief or worldview, religiously literate citizens are open to understanding the religions of others, acknowledging their own lacunae, and testing their assumptions. In this way, religious literacy implies a learning process, moreso than a learning outcome.

This same openness is required of instructors as well, particularly when it comes to the ways that their own learning has progressed. Across semesters, the answer to the question, "what do I hope students will get from the course" will likely shift. In their undergraduate (and possibly graduate) careers, every student will take a class from a professor who has not changed the syllabus or lecture notes in a decade. To remain frozen in time, in a pedagogical sense, it presumes that students are interchangeable; it also presumes that the instructor has not changed or gained new understanding and knowledge that would be relevant to the question. Thus, the question becomes how to protect one's time, as an instructor, while remaining active and engaged in guiding students to content and questions that bear relevance for them at their particular moment. Gene's rule of thumb was to revise the syllabus each go-around by changing around two weeks of content and, on a class-by-class basis, by leaving space to bring in current events.

As a caveat to all of this: centering students in the learning process and building space for adaptation—crucial components of the Post-It model of pedagogy—does not preclude the instructor from delivering content that s/he/they think that students simply need to know. Consensus is sometimes as important as entertaining multiple perspectives. As Gene once said, "[eventually] the engineers better decide in common how to build the bridge, so they need consensus at that point."[8] As I tell my students, there are some days where my aim is to "build their knowledge base." For example, it would be nearly impossible to examine the controversy (and misunderstandings) of "the Principle" (plural marriage) in my course on Mormonism, if I did not spend the previous class detailing the ins-and-outs of Mormon cosmology. Having laid out the required knowledge, I can then decide based on who my students are and what they have chosen to write about in their posts whether to focus our discussion on the support of the Principle by both women and men, the feminist response to its practice, or the cultural assumptions and obsession with the practice, among other possible angles.

Beyond the Post-It

If you visited my classroom today, would you see me teaching from a Post-It? No. To paraphrase what Gene so sagely said, students who seek to replicate their mentor do both a disservice. For me, writing out lesson plans is how I think them through—to have written something out in full, cements it in my psyche. The better question is: do I subscribe to the Tao of the Post-It, to centering my students in my planning and running of each class? Yes. For example, at the outset of each class, I write "Framing Questions" on the board, the intention of which is to focus students on the major ideas we should be thinking about each day (as well as linking them to the greater themes of a given course). These give me a certain flexibility to pick and choose what information I will bring up or what examples and case studies I will use to illustrate my points. Working within the "frame" of the Framing question is my version of the Post-It.

On a more personal level, meditating on Gene and the Post-It has reminded me how important it is to trust what you know and what you can do. I do not know that I could have said I trusted either at the outset of my career ("imposter syndrome" is real). It takes a great deal of self-belief and trust to bring your students into the plan in a way that cedes to them some authority and occasionally passes them the reigns entirely. As a student in Gene's classroom, an undergraduate "teaching assistant" and later co-teacher of Gene's, and a mentee, Gene passed the reigns at my own pace and without my knowing it. He taught the student that he had.

Notes

1. Robert B. Barr and John Tagg, "From Teaching to Learning—A New Paradigm for Undergraduate Instruction," *Change* 27, no. 6 (1995): 12–25.
2. Eugene V. Gallagher, "Autobiography of Malcolm X Imparts Important Lessons about Teaching and Learning," *Diverse: Issues in Higher Education* 23, no. 1 (2006): 47.
3. Eugene V. Gallagher, "Teaching for Religious Literacy," *Teaching Theology and Religion* 12, no. 3 (2009): 212.
4. Eugene V. Gallagher, "'Discussion Starter' Papers," *Teaching Theology and Religion* 13, no. 3 (July 2010): 241–2.
5. Gallagher, "Teaching for Religious Literacy," 210.
6. Grant Wiggins and Jay McTighe, "Backward Design," in *Understanding By Design*, 2nd edn. (Alexandria, VA: Association for Supervision & Curriculum Development, 2005).
7. Gallagher, "Teaching for Religious Literacy," 215.
8. Jill DeTemple, Eugene V. Gallagher, Kwok Pui-lan, and Thomas Pearson, "Reflective Structured Dialogue: A Conversation with 2018 American Academy of Religion Excellent in Teaching Award Winner Jill DeTemple," *Teaching Theology and Religion* 22 (2019): 230.

Bibliography

Barr, Robert B. and John Tagg. "From Teaching to Learning—A New Paradigm for Undergraduate Instruction." *Change* 27, no. 6 (1995): 12–25.

DeTemple, Jill, Eugene V. Gallagher, Kwok Pui Lan, and Thomas Pearson. "Reflective Structured Dialogue: A Conversation with 2018 American Academy of Religion Excellent in Teaching Award Winner Jill DeTemple." *Teaching Theology and Religion* 22 (2019): 230.

Gallagher, Eugene V. "Autobiography of Malcolm X Imparts Important Lessons about Teaching and Learning." *Diverse: Issues in Higher Education* 23, no. 1 (2006): 47.

Gallagher, Eugene V. "Teaching for Religious Literacy." *Teaching Theology and Religion* 12, no. 3 (2009): 212.

Gallagher, Eugene V. "'Discussion Starter' Papers." *Teaching Theology and Religion* 13, no. 3 (July 2010): 241–2.

Wiggins, Grant and Jay McTighe. "Backward Design." In *Understanding by Design*, Second Edition. Alexandria, VA: Association for Supervision & Curriculum Development, 2005.

Taking the General Education Student Seriously

Bruce David Forbes
Morningside University

In my initial semester of full-time college teaching, the first course assigned to me was one with which many of us have become very familiar: Introduction to Religion (or some kind of rough equivalent). Over time, personal reflection on my early years of teaching, fresh out of graduate school, plus anecdotal conversations with a variety of colleagues about teaching introductory courses as part of a liberal arts undergraduate core curriculum, found me growing increasingly uneasy. I began to suspect that, in those introductory level courses, too many of us over-emphasized transmitting the terminology and theories of Religious Studies, recruiting students into our department, and preparing students for graduate school. This might not be a problem if all of the students were declared or exploring Religious Studies majors. However, in many cases, the vast majority of students taking the introductory course do so to fulfill core curricular or general education liberal arts requirements. This may be the one and only college level religion class they will ever take, in their entire lives. Do we take those students and their needs seriously enough, not just in style, but in the very design of the course? The focus of the following discussion is on introductory Religious Studies courses that include many non-majors.

I am not inclined to advocate any singular model for such an introductory course. What I have developed for myself, however, is a series of four questions I try to reflect upon, at least briefly, every time I prepare an introductory course syllabus for a new semester, questions that serve the purpose of reminding me about the general education students who usually constitute the majority of students in those courses. Perhaps other faculty will find the questions helpful as well.

1) What factors minimize my awareness of, and attention to, general education students in my class? (It helps me to name the factors.)
2) What are the backgrounds, interests, attitudes, and assumptions that general education students bring with them into the classroom?
3) What is the rationale for including Religious Studies in a liberal arts curriculum?
4) In light of the answers to the above three questions, what are appropriate goals and outcomes for general education students in my introductory courses?

I am convinced that this reflection should influence not simply teaching techniques, or the selection of readings, but also the overall intentions, the basic design, of any course with large numbers of non-majors.

One book that helped throw the issue into bold relief for me is *Teaching Nonmajors: Advice for Liberal Arts Professors*, by P. Sven Arvidson. Arvidson identifies himself as a professor who primarily teaches "core" philosophy courses to students who are not philosophy majors, and he has written a brief volume for busy teachers in similar situations. He envisions his readers as "a history professor teaching sociology majors, an English professor teaching electrical engineering majors," and so on, and his book offers specific, practical teaching tips for liberal arts professors who want to "engage these students who are not majors in your discipline and are in your classroom because it is required, not directly because they have chosen this course."[1] The chapters consider strategies for better lectures, class discussions, assignments, and policies, all of which would seem to apply to courses across the board, whether for majors or non-majors. Arvidson grants as much, acknowledging it as advice for better teaching in general.

What is most striking is that Arvidson never raises, not even in a single sentence, the basic question of whether a course for non-majors might have different goals or objectives than a course for majors. That, it seems to me, is a fundamental issue. If Arvidson taught two sections of an Introduction to Philosophy course, one entirely filled with students who intended to major in the department, and one filled with non-majors who were fulfilling general education requirements and were unlikely to take another philosophy course, would the objectives and content be identical in both sections?

Of course, the contrast may not be that sharp. For many of us in similar situations, the actual student composition of our classes is mixed. Clearly, circumstances vary by institution, curriculum, and course. In my setting in a small midwestern church-related university, a typical Introduction to Religion class of thirty students might include one or two students who enter the course intending to major or minor in Religious Studies. Another four or five may become interested in a major or minor in Religious Studies as a result of taking the course. In my earliest years of teaching, I designed the Introduction to Religion course with those five or six students in mind, hoping to offer something so fascinating and exciting that I would recruit a growing number of majors into the department and facilitate their discovery of skills and background knowledge to prepare them for other Religious Studies courses. Over time it dawned on me, too slowly, that if that was my primary intention, the overwhelming majority of the students in the class then became "failures" in a sense, because they were not successfully recruited into the academic fold of our department. The students themselves would not be failures, but the failure would be mine if the measure was attracting majors. When the cold reality is that most of the students are taking the one and only Religious Studies class they will ever take in college, what is my responsibility to them? I believe it is unethical to design the course with little reflection on the background, needs, and interests of that majority.

(As an aside, this same reality applies to many courses in addition to introductory religion classes, depending on the institution and curriculum. In settings where students can make "cafeteria choices" of courses even at upper levels to fulfill certain general education requirements, those classes also may enroll a large number of non-majors. In my case, that included 300 level courses in the History of Christianity and Religion in America and topical courses like Religion and Popular Culture. Again, how should the preponderance of non-major students in a class influence the basic design of the course, if at all? Applying this question to upper division courses raises an array of additional issues. For the purposes of this discussion, I focus only on introductory courses.)

If one searches the literature about teaching introductory Religious Studies courses, a common assumption is that such courses should provide "an introduction to the field." In an older collection of essays published by Scholars Press in 1991 (*Teaching the Introductory Course in Religious Studies: A Sourcebook*), Ninian Smart writes that "an introductory course should have four kinds of balance: dimensional balance, ancient-modern balance, East-West balance, and large-small balance." In addition, "we may want to mix in a treatment of various theories of religion – such as those of Durkheim, Freud, and Levi-Strauss. It might be useful if theories could illustrate some of the diverse disciplines in religious studies."[2] Smart recognizes the potential problem of "overloading the syllabus" and understands the need to be selective, but the over-riding assumption is that the course will introduce the academic field and encourage students to pursue Religious Studies further. Many other authors in the same volume seem to share the assumption.

Obviously, an introductory Religious Studies course will be about religion, but with what goals and what emphases, especially when the majority are general education students? For them it will not be the basic building block for other religion courses they will take, because that is not their path. To wrestle with this, I have gravitated to the following four questions I ask myself, about the role of general education students, non-majors, in my introductory level courses.

1) What factors minimize my awareness of, and attention to, general education students in my class? I suppose this is a sort of neo-Freudian attempt to raise subconscious assumptions to the level of consciousness, so that I might wrestle with them more forthrightly. What has distracted me from fully recognizing the number of general education students in my classes and their legitimate educational needs?

A primary factor, as I have suggested already, is the temptation to view introductory courses as recruiting grounds for the major. Indeed, students who previously have never considered the topic of religion from critical perspectives may find themselves fascinated and want to learn more, which certainly contributes to the health of the department. Yet this disregards the student who is committed to another career path and has room for only this one general education religion course in his or her four-year academic plan.

A second problem arises when the introductory course is made a prerequisite for other classes in the department. The class is then viewed as the first step on a journey toward upper division courses, graduate school, and prominence in professions that will make the department proud. As a result, akin to science and math courses where the introductory classes deliver vital content that all other departmental courses are built upon, we feel obligated to begin the process of introducing terminology (jargon?), theories, and methodologies so that such basic notions do not have to be retaught at the upper level. Thus, some introductory courses are built around books like Daniel Pals' *Eight Theories of Religion* or Mircea Eliade's *The Sacred and the Profane*, because they provide foundational conceptualizations in the field.[3] I believe that such books will be very helpful to Religious Studies majors somewhere along the way, but I doubt that they are most crucial for a student who will never take another religious studies course.

A third distraction is when we see most "service courses" as a burden rather than an opportunity, standing in the way of teaching in our specialties. Students sometimes talk about general education courses as ones they need to "get out of the way," and faculty can echo the same language. The attitude changes when I get excited about what I can offer to future nurses, history teachers, engineers, business leaders, lawyers, and artists that might genuinely make a difference in their lives and careers. It also is exciting to think about what they might offer to this class that an entire room of religious studies majors could not.

2) What are the backgrounds, interests, attitudes, and assumptions that general education students bring with them into the classroom? Just as any good speaker or writer must know his or her audience in order to connect with them, the same certainly is true of teachers. Yet my formal educational background, and most of my early academic research and writing, focused almost totally on *what* I teach but included virtually no attention to *who* I teach and how I teach. Now, belatedly, I have become more aware of academic literature in developmental psychology, characterizations of generational trends, and studies of faith formation in adolescents and young adults, literature that I previously was content to leave to psychologists, sociologists, and ministers while I followed my own teaching path in religious studies. Yet if I am concerned to relate not just to Religious Studies majors (students with special intellectual curiosity about religion and/or with religion-related career intentions), but also to other students across a wide spectrum of interests and careers, some attempt to understand their inclinations and development would seem appropriate.

Because I work mostly with traditional age college students, that might involve reviewing the classic developmental theories of Erickson and Piaget or exploring understandings of moral development and personal formation in the work of Kohlberg, Kegan, Gilligan, and Fowler. Focusing more specifically on religion or spirituality among young adults, one book I have found helpful is Sharon Daloz Parks' *Big Questions, Worthy Dreams: Mentoring Young Adults in Their Search for Meaning, Purpose, and Faith,* prompting reflection upon the dynamics of post-adolescent meaning-making.[4] In terms of trends, tendencies, and differences among generations, *Generation Z: A Century in the Making* (Seemiller and Grace) is both data-based and wide-ranging, including sections on both religion and higher education.[5]

It would also be helpful to understand what students want to get out of a class like this, even if I am not in a position to address some of those interests. Barbara Walvoord is very helpful in that regard, as reported in her *Teaching and*

*Learning in College Introductory Religion Courses.*⁶ Her main (and not especially surprising) conclusion is a "great divide" between students and faculty in their goals for learning in the introductory course. The generalization is that faculty choose the goal of critical thinking more frequently than students do, and students include their own religious and spiritual development as a goal more often than faculty do. Examination of the data reveals, however, that faculty and students are very similar in endorsing some goals, such as factual knowledge and understanding other religions, and the contrast regarding critical thinking is not total (approximately 85 percent of faculty identify analysis and evaluation as a goal, but more than 60 percent of the students do so as well). The greatest divide is about the goal of developing students' own religious beliefs and/or spiritual practices, chosen by approximately 65 percent of students and approximately 30 percent of faculty. Numbers vary between church-related and public institutions, but the overall patterns are similar in each. Such survey findings touch off protests by many faculty, including me, that spiritual development is not the primary task of college level academic study of religion. Some of us may attempt to find spaces in our courses where students can have structured occasions to integrate the analysis and critical thinking encouraged in class with their own spiritual reflection, while others of us may find it important to maintain careful distinctions between course considerations and the personal religious search. Whatever the choice about what will happen in the class, it would be important for faculty to at least be cognizant of the intense attention to meaning-making that preoccupies most young adults who are enrolled in our classes.

Also in the interest of "knowing your audience," I have become increasingly curious about any demographics our university can provide about the incoming class. In addition, I ask questions about students' personal backgrounds during organizational sessions of a course at the beginning of the term, orally in class or on anonymous distributed forms. How many students have friendships with persons from a religion other than their own? How many have traveled outside the United States? How many know a language other than English? To what extent was any study of world religions included in their high-school classes? How many students discuss religion-related topics with their friends? How many students are turned off by traditional, institutional religions? What are their vocational goals? And so on. I have asked some similar questions in upper division classes as well, but in introductory classes both the questions and the answers help remind me of the variety of general education students who are enrolled.

3) *What is the rationale for including religious studies in a liberal arts curriculum?*

The simple purpose of this question is to remind myself why any college's curriculum committee, and the general faculty, would see fit to include religious studies courses among the general education requirements as part of a liberal arts education. It is doubtful that the principal intention is to provide religious studies faculty a sporting chance to recruit students into their department. For insight on religious studies in the liberal arts, we find suggestions in national conversations and perhaps in our own particular institutions' mission statements.

One possible answer is that Religious Studies is not the point. Rather, at the introductory level, religious studies simply participates with other liberal arts courses, especially in the humanities, to help students develop their abilities in reading, writing, and speaking, offering and analyzing arguments. Religion is simply one of many options of subject matter through which one might work on those skills. One of the most noted, provocative voices for this view is the distinguished scholar of the history of religions, Jonathan Z. Smith, who spent much of his career teaching introductory courses in his college at the University of Chicago. His starting point, which he would apply to introductory courses in many fields, is that "an introductory course serves the primary function of introducing the student to college level work, to work in the liberal arts." He sees liberal education as "training in argument about interpretations," and in such training "particular subject matter serves merely as the excuse, the occasion ...." Overall, he writes, "our task, in the long run, is not to introduce or teach our field for its own sake, but to use our field in the service of the broader and more fundamental enterprise of liberal learning."[7]

Another possible answer is the need for greater religious literacy in American society, which Stephen Prothero highlighted in *Religious Literacy: What Every American Needs to Know—and Doesn't*. He argues for teaching about religion both in public high schools and in higher education, not advocating particular religious beliefs and practices but learning about them. He maintains that basic religious literacy is needed for citizens "to participate meaningfully – on both the left and the right – in religiously inflected public debates. High school and college graduates who have not taken a single course about religion cannot be said to be truly educated."[8] This argument applies to introductory courses because it seeks to better equip the American public in general, not only those who are especially interested in religion.

A third answer about the relationship of religious studies to general education, in public and private schools of all kinds, pertains to the particular institution's mission, vision, or value statements. The variety here is so great that it is impossible to generalize, but many of the words and phrases are familiar: critical thinking, community service, global citizen, holistic, ethical leadership, social justice, and more. Many of us have learned that when a prioritization review arises at a school, the relationship of a department or particular courses to the institution's mission statement is regularly cited as one of the criteria for evaluation, even if it may not be the central one. Curriculum committees sometimes refer to mission statements in their decisions as well. If those statements are to be more than mere rationalizations, when a course I am teaching qualifies to satisfy one of my school's education requirements, and thus attracts general education students, it certainly is appropriate to reflect upon how this class helps develop in my students those capacities designated by the mission statement.

4) In light of the answers to the above three questions, what are appropriate goals and outcomes for general education students in my introductory course? This final question is my occasion to integrate the preceding discussions and reflections into some practical decisions about how I design my course. I fully respect that my colleagues may reach conclusions very different from mine, but I believe that if we at least ask these questions, we can keep the needs and interests of general education students in mind while also serving those students who may pursue additional study of religion.

For the record, here are my personal conclusions in shaping an Introduction to Religion course. First, I do not believe that a primary purpose of the course should be to introduce students to the language, theories, and methodologies of the "field" of Religious Studies. Some elements arise along the way, of course. For example, we discuss how religion scholars define "myth" differently from the popular understanding of the word, and students encounter Freudian and Marxist critiques of religion. Yet a full systematic consideration of basic religious studies theories and the breadth of the field is not the main focus. That can come later in courses for those pursuing a major.

I have two major intentions in teaching the course. One is to introduce students to religious variety, in essence to widen their world a bit and contribute to basics of religious literacy. Most of my students have had little exposure to world religions and are at the same time very uninformed about the religions of their own background. The first half of the semester is devoted to this consideration of variety. The course begins with Hesse's *Siddhartha*, to raise the theme of religion as a personal search, followed by a thumbnail overview of the world's major religions.[9] A disproportionate amount of time is devoted to Islam, because of the special needs for understanding in the world's current context. A brief consideration of differences among Christians concludes this section, because of great student confusion about variations even within a religion that they assume they know best. At the end of this section, we explicitly discuss the variety of perspectives people have in evaluating "other" religions (exclusive, inclusive, and pluralist views), and students write a discussion paper in which they offer their personal responses to the three options, with supporting arguments drawn from information gleaned in the first half of the semester. In light of the discussions above, this first half of the course seeks to improve basic religious literacy which is important for all citizens, relevant to domestic issues and world events. It also addresses what Walvoord identified as one of the goals upon which faculty and students of all kinds agree, the importance of some basic factual knowledge about a variety of religions.

My second major intention is to encourage critical analysis and reflection about religion. As one student said, "oh, this is more than just Sunday School with extra reading." Rather than organize this section with an Eliade template of symbol, myth, and ritual, or with a consideration of basic religious studies theories (Durkheim, Weber, Freud, etc.), I have described my approach as "looking at religion from different angles" and those angles are other academic fields, specifically psychology, sociology, and the natural sciences. It becomes a series of dialogues between academic fields that many general education students may have chosen as majors: psychology and religion (Freud, Maslow, and Frankl), sociology and religion (Marx, Bonhoeffer, communal religious groups), and natural sciences and religion (the creationism-evolution controversies, typologies of several possible relationships between science and religion). I believe that this approach fully integrates most students into the discussions, whatever their intended majors and careers, and it fits well with intentions for general education.

My particular choices are not especially important. What is important is that we take non-majors, general education students in our classes, seriously. They are not disposable supplemental enrollees while we teach the students we prefer, those who are inclined to join our guild. The variety of their backgrounds and interests can actually enhance our reflection on religion. Introductory courses filled with non-majors offer an exciting opportunity for dialogue and reflection with students who will enter all sorts of professions, critically informed and engaged in aspects of life beyond their specialties.

Notes

1. P. Sven Arvidson, *Teaching Nonmajors: Advice for Liberal Arts Professors* (Albany: State University of New York Press, 2008), xii.
2. Ninian Smart, "Teaching Religion and Religions: The 'World Religions' Course," in *Teaching the Introductory Course in Religious Studies: A Sourcebook*, ed. Mark Juergensmeyer (Atlanta: Scholars Press, 1991), 203.
3. Daniel Pals, *Eight Theories of Religion* (New York: Oxford University Press, 2006). Mircea Eliade and Willard R. Trask, *The Sacred and the Profane: The Nature of Religion* (New York: Harcourt, Inc., 1987).
4. Sharon Daloz Parks, *Big Questions, Worthy Dreams: Mentoring Young Adults in Their Search for Meaning, Purpose, and Faith* (San Francisco: Jossey-Bass, 2000).
5. Corey Seemiller and Meghan Grace, *Generation Z: A Century in the Making* (New York: Routledge, 2019).
6. Barbara E. Walvoord, *Teaching and Learning in College Introductory Religion Courses* (Malden, MA: Wiley-Blackwell, 2007), Chapter 1.
7. Jonathan Z. Smith, "The Introductory Course: Less Is Better," in *Teaching the Introductory Course in Religious Studies: A Sourcebook*, ed. Mark Juergensmeyer (Atlanta: Scholars Press, 1991), 186, 188, 192.
8. Stephen Prothero, *Religious Literacy: What Every American Needs to Know—and Doesn't* (New York: Oxford University Press, 2009), 17.
9. Hermann Hesse, *Siddhartha*, many editions.

Bibliography

Arvidson, P. Sven. *Teaching Nonmajors: Advice for Liberal Arts Professors*. Albany: State University of New York Press, 2008.

Daloz Parks, Sharon. *Big Questions, Worthy Dreams: Mentoring Young Adults in Their Search for Meaning, Purpose, and Faith*. San Francisco: Jossey-Bass, 2000.

Eliade, Mircea and Willard R. Trask. *The Sacred and the Profane: The Nature of Religion*. New York: Harcourt Inc., 1987.

Hesse, Hermann. *Siddhartha*. New York: Bantam, 1982.

Pals, Daniel. *Eight Theories of Religion*. New York: Oxford University Press, 2006.

Prothero, Stephen. *Religious Literacy: What Every American Needs to Know—and Doesn't*. New York: Oxford University Press, 2009.

Seemiller, Corey and Meghan Grace. *Generation Z: A Century in the Making*. New York: Routledge, 2019.

Smart, Ninian. "Teaching Religion and Religions: The 'World Religions' Course." In *Teaching the Introductory Course in Religious Studies: A Sourcebook*, edited by Mark Juergensmeyer. Atlanta: Scholars Press, 1991.

Smith, Jonathan. "The Introductory Course: Less Is Better." In *Teaching the Introductory Course in Religious Studies: A Sourcebook*, edited by Mark Juergensmeyer. Atlanta: Scholars Press, 1991.

Walvoord, Barbara. *Teaching and Learning in College Introductory Religion Courses*. Massachusetts: Wiley-Blackwell, 2007.

8

The Challenges of Teaching as Racial and Ethnic Minority Scholars

Kwok Pui-lan
Candler School of Theology

In the summer of 2020, protests swept across the United States and other parts of the world in support of Black Lives Matter. After the killing of George Floyd, Breonna Taylor, and other Black people by the police, there was a national reckoning around issues of systemic racism and police brutality. In August, athletes across the American sports world held an unprecedented strike in protest by refusing to play their regularly scheduled games. Following their example, many professors took part in #ScholarStrike in September to show their solidarity against police violence and racial injustice. Over the course of two days, they were asked to pause their classes, lead teach-ins about racial violence, and highlight specific issues, such as intellectual gatekeeping and over-policing of college campuses, on their own campuses.[1]

As an Asian American teaching theology in a predominantly white theological school, the #ScholarStrike movement provided an occasion for self-examination. Three years ago, I moved to live in the American South for the first time when I began to teach at Candler School of Theology. I have never had so many Black students in my classes before. In a course on Christology and Cultural Imagination, more than a quarter of the students were Black, hailing from different parts of the United States. To understand where my Black students were coming from, I went to worship in about a dozen Black churches. These included independent churches and those belonging to the United Methodist Church, the African Methodist Episcopal Church, the Baptist Church, and the Pentecostal tradition. These visits exposed me to the diversity of Black churches and their worshipping styles and highlighted the gulf between the theology and cultural ethos in these Black churches and those found in predominantly white, mainline theological schools.

After these visits, I began to ponder these existential questions: Am I teaching theology in a way that is preparing students to lead Black churches? Have I perpetuated white hegemony in my course contents and pedagogies? How can I help students broker the differences between the academy and Black churches?

These questions are pertinent not only for me but also for many teaching in seminaries and divinity schools. According to The Association of Theological Schools in the United States and Canada (ATS), about 45 percent of the students of ATS schools belong to racial and ethnic minority (REM) communities. Because of the decline of membership of white mainline denominations, theological schools must attract diverse students by reaching out to REM students and nontraditional students. With demographic changes in the student body, I wonder if theological schools have adapted to their new situations by reexamining their curriculum and teaching? Black Lives Matter and the summer protests should be a wake-up call and a moment of reckoning for theological schools.

During this season of critical reflection, I want to explore the challenges of teaching as REM scholars. My colleagues Patricia O'Connell Killen and Eugene Gallagher have helped many professors reflect on their roles as teachers and their teaching practices through their writings and teaching workshops. In their classic essay sketching the contours of scholarship of teaching and learning in theology and religion, Killen and Gallagher point out that scholars have not only examined the usual topics, such as classroom practices, the person of the professor, the purposes of teaching, and pedagogies and theories, but they have also challenged the conceptualization of the fields and well-established ways of teaching, and brought new resources to bear on their teaching.[2] Indeed, in order to address systemic racism, professors have to challenge Eurocentric conceptualization of the fields of theology and religion and the privileging of Euro-American voices and experiences in the classroom. In the following, I want to discuss embodied scholarship, transformative pedagogy, and conscientious assessment.

Embodied Scholarship

During the first class of my courses, I teach students to write my name in Chinese characters (郭 佩 蘭). Such an exercise is not meant to be ego-boosting, but to underscore the fact that their teacher has come from and grown up in another culture. I know that for many students, this is their first-time learning theology from an Asian female professor. I also know that even before I utter my first word, my embodiment as a female, racialized person in the classroom will elicit curiosity, and might invite stereotypical projections.

For many theology professors, the gender, race, class, and sexuality of the professors do not matter. They are to impart theological knowledge that they have acquired through rigorous learning to their students. Their job is to help students understand the Christian theological tradition and to be able to critically reflect upon it. These professors are usually white, middle-class, cisgender males who are often oblivious to the privileges they have.

They teach theology almost in the same way as they were taught as students. A review of some of the syllabi of courses in theology or systematic theology posted on the Wabash Center website shows that the majority of required texts are written by European and Euro-American male theologians. There is not much acknowledgment of the work of REM scholars in the United States and of the global nature of theology. Only one required text, and often none, is by a theologian outside North America, usually Gustavo Gutiérrez's work on liberation theology.[3]

Some may argue that a syllabus on theology focusing on European males is justified because they have made the most significant contributions to the field. This argument is biased and ahistorical, as William A. Dyrness points out: a Eurocentric and Western orientation has had the "unfortunate consequence of marginalizing not only what we call the Eastern tradition but the still vibrant Syriac, North African, and Asian strands of the larger Christian tradition, to say nothing of the newer traditions in Africa and Latin America."[4] Since Syrian Christianity arrived in China as early as the seventh century, this oversight is particularly glaring.

A theology class that privileges white male voices may prompt someone like me, who is neither white nor male, to ask: "why am I not learning something about theology from my culture?" As we wonder, we can learn from Nobel Laureate Toni Morrison who noted a parallel erasure of African American presence in American literature. Her strategy is not to ask, "why am I, an Afro-American, absent from it?" Rather, she teaches us to ask, "what intellectual feats had to be performed by the author or his critic to erase me from a society seething with my presence, and what effect has that performance had on the work? What are the strategies of escape from knowledge? Of willful oblivion?"[5]

One of the main "strategies of escape from knowledge" in the discipline of theology is to treat theology as "universal" and "objective," and everywhere the same. The other strategy is to assume that white male theologies are superior to theologies done by other peoples. What is hidden from view is the question of "race" in the conceptualization of the theological tradition. Race and racism are the "unspeakable things unspoken,"[6] as Toni Morrison puts so well.

To demystify the white washing of theology, the strategies that Toni Morrison suggests to her colleagues in American literature can be adapted to good use in theology. First, we must build our own intellectual neighborhood. This work includes the recovering of past scholarship and archives; the building of academic networks; the development of research, scholarship, and publication; and the encouragement of students and younger scholars to labor in the field. In addition, we have to develop a critical assessment of theology that accommodates REM theological scholarship, "one that is based on its culture, its history, and the artistic strategies the works employ to negotiate the world it inhabits,"[7] as Morrison says.

The second strategy is the examination of the theological canon, the founding texts, for the ways that race has shaped "the choices, the language, the structure … in other words, for the ghost in the machine."[8] Willie James Jennings's award-winning text *The Christian Imagination* serves as a model for this task. Jennings examines the construction of race and differences in the Christian tradition dated back to the Medieval period in various locales.[9] I have also pointed out how the construction of an asexual Jesus in the nineteenth century emerged at the same time when the colonized natives were depicted as lustful, promiscuous, and sexually deviant.[10]

The third strategy is to examine the presence of race, including REM narratives, persons, and idiom, in contemporary and/or noncanonical theology. This includes the works of both white and REM scholars.[11] I remember some thirty years ago, there was a debate about whether white feminist theologians can use the work of Black female scholars because of the issues of appropriation and misappropriation. Today, not many people would say white scholars cannot use REM scholars' works, but the questions remain: how do they use it? And for what purposes? More careful study should be devoted to how race figures in REM scholars' work. We need to pay attention to the nuances of depiction about race in the works of Black scholars, such as James Cone and Delores Williams. We have yet to come up with methodologies to compare the deployment of race in theology across racial differences, such as in the work of Asian American theologian Rita Nakashima Brock and Latino theologian Roberto S. Goizueta.

Embodied scholarship that takes seriously race and racism in the history of the United States is daring and may be risky in some quarters. If one specializes on Asian American theology, the job market may be small and limited. Some professors on the tenure and review committee may think that this kind of theology is not *real* theology! Many REM students have been told that they should not work on more daring projects until they have received tenure. Intellectual gatekeeping is real and can produce the suffocating effect of self-censorship. Yet the most innovative and transformative scholarship has been done in spite of dangers, landmines, and potential attacks. In an interview, Edward Said surmised that he decided to write *Orientalism*, the foundational text in postcolonial theory, because of the constant disparity he felt between his experience as an Arab and the representations of the Middle East in arts and novels.[12] The book has created a new field and changed the humanities and social sciences. Toni Morrison's works have likewise changed the way we look at American literature. No one will read white American literature in the same way again after reading her book *Playing in the Dark: Whiteness and the Literary Imagination*.[13] Following their examples, theologians need to speak truth to power and craft works that embody the spirit of their own people.

Transformative Pedagogy

The #ScholarStrike movement requires professors to examine not only what we teach but also how we teach. In the past, there was an emphasis of creating a safe space in the classroom. A "safe space" is an environment in which people feel comfortable expressing themselves without the fear of attack and ridicule.[14] But the assumption that there is a safe space for everyone is not true. Black Lives Matter makes us aware that Black people are safe nowhere—not when they go to a convenience store (Trayvon Martin), jog (Ahmaud Arbery), or sleep in their own beds (Breonna Taylor). The illusion that an artificial safe space can exist in the classroom apart from the students' daily experiences seems disingenuous and far-fetched.

Furthermore, transformative learning does not happen when one stays in one's comfort zone without engaging in difficult dialogues. Thus, there has been a shift in academic circles to advocate for creating brave spaces over safe spaces. While a safe space emphasizes support, a brave space requires courage because it recognizes differences and holds each person accountable, which may be uncomfortable. According to Brian Arao and Kristi Clemens, a brave space within the classroom includes five elements: (1) controversy within civility, (2) owning intentions and impacts, (3) challenge by choice, where students have the option to step in and out of challenging conversations, (4) respect, and

(5) no attack.¹⁵ Schools have adopted the term "brave spaces" and use these five elements in their attempt to describe what "an achievable space of inclusivity and challenging dialogue looks like."¹⁶

Professors would need to develop skills and strategies to help turn their classroom into a brave space. I would like to share several examples from my classroom. Like many professors, I provide students with guidelines for multicultural/multiracial dialogue in my first class. In teaching a course on spirituality, I brought a drum from Indonesia and as I played the drum, I invited the students to join me by tapping on the table as if they were playing a drum too. We created different beats, sounds, and rhythms. I asked students to listen to the polyrhythmic beats and said that in this class they had to learn to listen to different beats simultaneously and not just their own.

This exercise proved to be providential, for soon an argument broke out early in the class. I was using the metaphor of sports to talk about spiritual discipline and exercise. A white student mentioned how American football players have to develop discipline and finesse their skills to succeed. A Black student took offense and said that Black football players were used and exploited by white owners who reap plenty from them. In this potentially conflictual situation, I helped the students to see that these two students were talking on two different levels. If the player is Black, the white student referred to how the player's work ethic and discipline help him to overcome racism at a personal level. The Black student focused on the corporate dimension of football and she emphasized racism at the institutional level. I reminded them of the drum exercise they had done and that they had to train their ears to listen to both voices. Learning to listen, refraining from jumping to conclusions, and being comfortable with different opinions are important steps to move toward creating brave spaces.

In another class on liberation theology, we read James Cone's *God of the Oppressed* and discussed his idea of the Black Christ.¹⁷ I knew that the concept of the Black Christ would be problematic for some white students for several reasons. First, the historical Jesus was a Jew from Nazareth and not Black. Second, the idea that Christ is Black will push the white students out of their comfort zone because they would have to reckon with race in Christology. Third, if Christ is Black, wouldn't God be partial toward Black folks? What about the white people!?

In a Wabash Center workshop, I learned to use debate as a teaching tool. So I asked for volunteers to join a debate in the class where we would discuss the Black Christ with one team arguing for the concept of the Black Christ while the other argued against it. I even promised a prize for the winning team! I also said students who were not participating in the debate would speak from the floor to support either team. The format of the debate was very successful. It was a lighthearted approach for an otherwise heavy and charged topic. Most importantly, students were given permission and were even invited to disagree with James Cone without being labeled as racists. They could assume a different persona in the debate in defense of a certain position, which might be different from that of their own. They also needed to obey the rules of the debate and treat the opposing team with respect. Thus, students could analyze the different positions without getting into personal attacks.

Sometimes what happens in the classroom cannot be forecast or controlled. In a systematic theology class, I have divided the students into small groups and given each group a newsprint and some markers. I asked them to come up with an image or metaphor for the relation between Christ and empire. Afterward, I asked each group to present what their group had come up with. They presented Jesus as the lamb and the crucifixion, among other images. I left the class feeling that the day was quite successful.

Sometime after the class, an international student brought to my attention that she was in a group with white students. A white student said something to the effect that the exercise was difficult for non-English speakers because the idea of a metaphor is difficult for them. The international student felt offended because the white student had assumed that her English was not good enough to understand.

This incident reminds me of the importance of clarifying the differences between intent and impact in the creation of brave spaces. First of all, the white student needs to examine whether he had intended to demean or embarrass the international student. It is easier to deal with a situation when a person has the wrong intention. The teacher can challenge the student's stereotypes and point to biases or ignorance. It is trickier to deal with a situation in which good intention produces negative impact. In this case, the white student might think he was expressing support and empathy for the international student and had no idea that he was hurting his classmate's feelings. He would be very surprised to find out that the international student was offended. In this situation, it is important for the white student to own that his words have created negative impact. It is equally important to create an atmosphere in the classroom for the international student to share her feelings so that both sides can learn from the situation. But the demand to constantly educate white students is very exhausting. Thus, white students need to educate themselves about microaggressions and other problematic behaviors. They can form study and support groups to learn and model anti-racist behaviors.

In another example, I did not expect a white female student to burst into tears in a class on Feminist Theology from the Global South I taught some years ago. I was discussing the plight of women in the Global South under the multiple oppressions of sexism, classism, racism, colonialism, and religion. I thought this was quite common sense, especially for a liberal and progressive divinity school. But a very privileged woman began to cry. When I asked why she cried, she replied that she felt guilty because she was not aware of the terrible situation in which her sisters in the Global South lived. I was taken aback because I had anticipated some students would cry if we were discussing trauma, rape, or war crimes. Since I did not anticipate a student crying in that class, I was ill prepared to respond on the spot.

Robin DiAngelo's book *White Fragility: Why It's So Hard for White People to Talk about Racism* helps me understand the larger context and meaning of white tears, especially those of white women. White fragility refers to the anger, fear, and guilt white people feel when their white identity and racial worldviews are challenged. She writes, "Though white fragility is triggered by discomfort and anxiety, it is born of superiority and entitlement. White fragility is not weakness per se. In fact, it is a powerful means of white racial control and the protection of white advantage."[18] She has a chapter on white women's tears, particularly those shed in cross-racial settings. DiAngelo says these tears are problematic because when a white woman cries over certain aspects of racism, people rush to comfort and attend to her. In a particularly subversive move, "racism becomes about white distress, white suffering, and white victimization."[19]

Robin DiAngelo reminds us to pay attention to emotion and affect in dealing with racism. In leading racial sensitivity training, she asks white participants who are moved to tears to please leave the room.[20] But this may not be reasonable or feasible in a classroom context. As a teacher, I can acknowledge the discomfort the white student feels and move on, without putting her at the center of attention. After the class, I can talk to her one-on-one if needed so she will not take up precious class time. The incident also reminds me of the emotional labor of REM students when racism is brought up in class. On the one hand, they have to deal with their own pain and frustration as minorities. On the other hand, they have to manage their emotional reactions to white students. White students may think "we are dealing with your issue" and even shed white tears. It is important to acknowledge and honestly talk about the emotional labor of

REM students at the beginning of the class, especially when there are only a few in the room. REM students will also need to have their own safe spaces to process their emotions and feelings.

Conscientious Assessment

A transformative pedagogy must address the politics of assessing students of diverse racial and cultural backgrounds. On the one hand, I have heard complaints from REM students that they are not graded fairly by their professors. On the other, I also hear from professors who say that REM students cannot write well. The politics of writing deserves our attention since writing is the dominant form of assignments in the humanities. Some of the REM students, especially Black students, come from churches and cultural contexts that value oral performance over writing. Because of racism and classism, REM students may not graduate from colleges with rigorous academic standards. They may not have the academic preparation and writing skills for graduate schools. They finish college without learning how to write, because their professors do not demand much from them for fear of being accused of racism. But it is precisely *because of* racism that REM students are not held to the same standards. It is often easier for a professor to give a student a barely passing grade than an "F." But we are not serving the churches and the wider society by lowering the standards. In accepting these students, theological schools have the responsibility to commit to their success by providing the help they need, such as a supportive writing center and peer tutoring.

The politics of assessment also involves asking the challenging question of whether REM scholars are helping to enforce white academic standards while serving willingly as gatekeepers. Are there color-blind "academic standards," given the long history of white hegemony in higher education? Citing Black women seminarians' experiences with theological writing in predominantly white schools, Black scholar Zandra L. Jordan writes,

> The teaching and evaluation of writing in any discipline are not arbitrary activities but rather ethical decisions shaped by the instructor's racialized, classed, and gendered epistemologies. Whether conscious or unconscious, professors make moral choices – what knowledge to assume, what readings to foreground, what kinds of writing to assign, what writing conventions to teach, what criteria to evaluate, what discourses to reward, what conversations to engage – that impact student success.[21]

Jordan suggests that professors interrogate their pedagogical praxis and criteria for assessment, asking questions such as: whether their assignments assume certain prior knowledge and privilege some students; whether the criteria of assessment invite or preclude diverse approaches; whether complexity of ideas is valued over grammar and style; whether we scaffold written assignments to help students better understand the requirements; and whether we provide opportunities for students to employ their own languages and interpretative practices in meaningful ways.[22] These interrogations are critically important, given what I experienced as the gulf between the cultural ethos of Black churches and that of predominantly white schools.

Jordan's questions about the ethics of evaluation also apply to the assessment of international students, for whom English is a second or third language. These students may have great ideas but they may not have the language skills to express them. Some of them may not come from an academic culture in which plagiarism is an important topic and a taboo. Lucretia Yaghjian, who has taught and tutored theological students about writing for twenty-five years, suggests that professors: initiate students into the writing conventions of their theological discipline; include alternative modes of discourse by encouraging cultural and pedagogical diversity in writing assignments; offer in-class writing workshops to explain the professor's expectations; and work collaboratively with writing tutors.[23] These recommendations will benefit all students and not just international students.

Conclusion

Most REM faculty have received their advanced graduate degrees from predominantly white institutions. They have negotiated the power structures and navigated the landmines of white academic institutions. They can provide unique insights and guidance to REM students who are new to the academic environment. The REM students would likely consult REM professors whether or not that REM professor is their advisor. This additional work and the emotional toll associated with this kind of work are not counted as regular faculty workload or responsibilities. A REM professor is expected to serve as a bridge between REM students and the school. When a critical racial incident occurs, they may be called upon to help resolve the conflict, whether they have the training to do so or not. The national reckoning of racial injustice provides a *kairos* moment to reflect on the institutional structure, curriculum, and culture of theological education. Embodied scholarship, transformative pedagogy, and conscientious assessment need to be practiced across the board and receive institutional support. It cannot be done in one or two classes or adopted only by REM professors. The ecology of teaching and learning must change to meet the challenges of Black Lives Matter.

Notes

1. Skylar Mitchell, "What You Need to Know about the #ScholarStrike and What It Means to Protest during a Pandemic," *CNN*, September 1, 2020. https://www.cnn.com/2020/09/01/us/professors-plan-protest-scholar-strike-trnd/index.html.
2. Patricia O'Connell Killen and Eugene V. Gallagher, "Sketching the Contours of the Scholarship of Teaching and Learning in Theology and Religion," *Teaching Theology & Religion* 16, no. 2 (2013): 115–22.
3. The syllabi can be found at the Wabash Center Website, https://www.wabashcenter.wabash.edu/syllabi-topic/Theology/.
4. William A. Dyrness, "Listening for Fresh Voices in the History of the Church," in *Teaching Global Theologies: Power and Praxis*, ed. Kwok Pui-lan, Cecelia González-Andrieu, and Dwight S. Hopkins (Waco, TX: Baylor University Press, 2015), 29.
5. Toni Morrison, "The Unspeakable Things Unspoken: The Afro-American Presence in American Literature," The Tanner Lectures on Human Values, University of Michigan, October 7, 1988, 136, https://tannerlectures.utah.edu/_resources/documents/a-to-z/m/morrison90.pdf.
6. This is the title of Toni Morrison's Tanner Lectures.
7. Ibid., 135.
8. Ibid., 136.
9. Willie James Jennings, *The Christian Imagination: Theology and the Origins of Race* (New Haven: Yale University Press, 2010).
10. Kwok Pui-lan, "Touching the Taboo: On the Sexuality of Jesus," in *Sexuality and the Sacred*, ed. Marvin M. Ellison and Kelly Brown Douglas (Louisville, KY: Westminster John Knox Press, 2010), 119–34.
11. Morrison, "Unspeakable Things Unspoken," 136.
12. Edward Said, "Edward Said on Orientalism," YouTube, https://www.youtube.com/watch?v=fVC8EYd_Z_g.
13. Toni Morrison, *Playing in the Dark: Whiteness and the Literary Imagination* (Cambridge, MA: Harvard University Press, 1993).
14. For the different definitions of "safe space," see Brian Arao and Kristi Clemens, "From Safe Spaces to Brave Spaces: A New Way to Frame Dialogue Around

Diversity and Social Justice," in *The Art of Effective Facilitation: Reflections from Social Justice Educators*, ed. Lisa M. Landreman (Sterling, VA: Stylus, 2013), 138.
15 Ibid., 143–49.
16 Diana Ali, "Safe Spaces and Brave Spaces: Historical Contexts and Recommendations for Student Affairs Professionals," NASPA Policy and Practice Series, Issue 2, October 2017, 7–8. https://naspa.org/images/uploads/main/Policy_and_Practice_No_2_Safe_Brave_Spaces.pdf.
17 Janes H. Cone, *God of the Oppressed*, rev. edn. (Maryknoll, NY: Orbis Books, 1997).
18 Robin DiAngelo, *White Fragility: Why It's So Hard for White People to Talk about Racism* (Boston: Beacon Press, 2018), 2.
19 Ibid., 134.
20 Ibid., 131.
21 Zandra L. Jordan, "Clarity and Creativity as Womanist Ethics for Teaching and Evaluating Theological Writings," *Teaching Theology & Religion* 22, no. 4 (2019): 256.
22 Ibid., 263.
23 Lucretia B. Yaghjian, "Pedagogical Challenges in Teaching ESOL/Multilingual Writers in Theological Education," *Teaching Theology & Religion* 21, no. 3 (2018): 173.

Bibliography

Ali, Diana. "Safe Spaces and Brave Spaces: Historical Contexts and Recommendations for Student Affairs Professionals." NASPA Policy and Practice Series, Issue 2, October 2017. https://naspa.org/images/uploads/main/Policy_and_Practice_No_2_Safe_Brave_Spaces.pdf.

Arao, Brian, and Kristi Clemens. "From Safe Spaces to Brave Spaces: A New Way to Frame Dialogue Around Diversity and Social Justice." In *The Art of Effective Facilitation: Reflections from Social Justice Educators*, edited by Lisa M. Landreman, 135–50. Sterling, VA: Stylus, 2013.

Cone, James H. *God of the Oppressed*, rev. edn. Maryknoll, NY: Orbis Books, 1997.

DiAngelo, Robin. *White Fragility: Why It's So Hard for White People to Talk about Racism*. Boston: Beacon Press, 2018.

Dyrness, William A. "Listening for Fresh Voices in the History of the Church." In *Teaching Global Theologies: Power and Praxis*, edited by Kwok Pui-lan, Cecelia González-Andrieu, and Dwight S. Hopkins, 29–43. Waco, TX: Baylor University Press, 2015.

Jennings, William James. *The Christian Imagination: Theology and the Origins of Race*. New Haven, CT: Yale University Press, 2010.

Jordan, Zandra L. "Clarity and Creativity as Womanist Ethics for Teaching and Evaluating Theological Writings." *Teaching Theology & Religion* 22, no. 4 (2019): 253–68.

Killen, Patricia O'Connell, and Eugene V. Gallagher. "Sketching the Contours of the Scholarship of Teaching and Learning in Theology and Religion." *Teaching Theology & Religion* 16, no. 2 (2013): 107–24.

Mitchell, Skylar. "What You Need to Know about the #ScholarStrike and What It Means to Protest during a Pandemic." *CNN,* September 1, 2020. https://www.cnn.com/2020/09/01/us/professors-plan-protest-scholar-strike-trnd/index.html.

Morrison, Toni. "The Unspeakable Things Unspoken: The Afro-American Presence in American Literature." The Tanner Lectures on Human Values, University of Michigan, October 7, 1988. Available online: https://tannerlectures.utah.edu/_resources/documents/a-to-z/m/morrison90.pdf.

Morrison, Toni. *Playing in the Dark: Whiteness and the Literary Imagination.* Cambridge, MA: Harvard University Press, 1993.

Pui-lan, Kwok. "Touching the Taboo: On the Sexuality of Jesus." In *Sexuality and the Sacred*, edited by Marvin M. Ellison and Kelly Brown Douglas, 119–34. Louisville, KY: Westminster John Knox Press, 2010.

Said, Edward. "Edward Said on Orientalism." YouTube, https://www.youtube.com/watch?v=fVC8EYd_Z_g.

Yaghjian, Lucretia B. "Pedagogical Challenges in Teaching ESOL/Multilingual Writers in Theological Education." *Teaching Theology & Religion* 21, no. 3 (2018): 162–76.

9

The Magic or Midrange Reflection

Molly H. Bassett
Georgia State University

Beginning with Midrange Reflection

When I began teaching Religious Studies at Georgia State University (Atlanta, GA), I adopted RELS 3270, "Survey of World Religions," a course I had neither taught before nor ever taken. Generous colleagues loaned me textbooks and recommended readings. I began to piece together a week-by-week study. I assigned a book that included excerpts from primary texts and black and white images that kept it affordable. That fall, I spent many evenings drafting lectures and creating PowerPoint presentations each of which I enthusiastically presented about thirty-six hours later.

I organized the class as you might expect. Sessions focused on particular topics came together in familiar clusters of religious traditions. After the requisite week spent orienting students by introducing bracketing and a list of famous definitions of "religion," we studied Indigenous religious traditions before launching into the "big five" (plus a few). Each class meeting began with prewriting exercises aimed at helping students process what they had read and prepare for the exams. The exams had multiple-choice questions and prompts for short-answer essays. For the most part, students seemed to get what they expected: a tour around the world of religions that was not too hard and not too easy. For my part, it left something—a lot, really—to be desired.

As I worked through the class, I began to identify issues with the way I taught it and with the survey format. For example, it was impossible to know why students selected incorrect multiple choice answers. Practical issues like this one came up in the context of broader pedagogical issues, including managing "objectivity" in the study of many religious traditions at a diverse and international university. Asking students to "bracket" their own thoughts, feelings, and beliefs increasingly felt like an inadequate and unrealistic mode of teaching and learning. I wondered if we could agree on a way to learn about religions that felt more authentic and could be of more use in conversations and life outside the classroom. Bear in mind that these questions (and others) arose in a survey of world religions, a course students demand and decolonialists deplore. I found myself, as many of us have, at the beginning of a career in teaching doing the best I could to make it work. I could see the raw edges of my class, and so I searched for help. I applied to a year-long early-career workshop.

A few months later, a dozen or so of us convened around a circle of tables adjacent to a bar of snacks, hot coffee, and cold fizzy waters. The workshop leaders encouraged us to reflect on our budding careers while simultaneously reassuring us that we were doing some things well. We discussed teaching, research, publishing, promotion, and tenure. The workshop leaders created time and space for us to reflect on specific courses and particular assignments. We looked at successful teaching techniques each of us had developed. In small and large groups, we talked about what made the tactics work well and how we might adapt them to other contexts. Our conversations ranged from the details of syllabi to the classes we wanted to offer someday. We also learned about the different contexts in which we were teaching: public and private, R1 and liberal arts, state schools and theological settings, large institutions and small. We talked through the audiences for various types of writing, like research publications, grant proposals, and tenure dossiers. I began to understand more about university administrative structures at the same time I was puzzling over challenges in my own class. I should add that it was not all work. We took time to relax and exercise. We talked about our families, our animal companions, and our aspirations. It was a formative experience. Although it felt magical, it was not magic. It was midrange reflection.

This I learned much later.

Starting Scholarship on Teaching and Learning

Over the course of the year-long workshop, I started the slow process of identifying the issues related to the survey course and how I might address them. For example, I felt stuck with multiple-choice and short answer exam assessments. They did not provide enough information on how or why students (mis)understood information, but I was not able to take on teaching writing to prepare students for essay exams or research papers. I reflected on the pros and cons of different forms of assessment. Multiple-choice exams are difficult to write well, and they offer little insight into student comprehension. They are, however, quick and easy to grade. By contrast, when students write essays, they can elaborate on points or describe their own reasoning. However, writing essays takes practice, and for many students, it also requires a measure of comfort and confidence as a writer. Providing students with feedback on writing is a significant investment of time. I started thinking about how to combine the best features of the two types of assessment. Eventually, I tried incorporating short written justifications into multiple-choice exams. I began keeping informal notes on what worked well (and didn't). Student feedback was positive, and so I decided to invest more time in the approach.

    I applied for and received Institutional Research Board approval to gather data on student justifications for multiple choice answers. I completely redesigned my exams. Beside each multiple-choice question, I included an empty box in which students explained the approach they took in selecting a response. I asked students to explain why (reasons, connections) and how (process) they selected an answer. They earned points for selecting the correct answer and full credit if their response explained their thought process and understanding of the material.[1] However, students could earn partial credit for missed questions if they explained the thinking behind their response. This process prompted students to think about their thinking, and it provided me with some insight into what went right or wrong in teaching and learning. I was able to respond with tailor-made feedback to students that supported their learning even after they had completed the exam.

    This work evolved into a formal project. I applied to a writing the scholarship of teaching and learning colloquy. In the supportive environment of the colloquy, I wrote a research-based article on how creating space for students' metacognition, or thinking about thinking, on selective-response exams might support their learning. The writing colloquy felt a lot like the early-career workshop had, although the goals were different. Everyone in this group was developing a scholarly project on teaching, and our common work focused on small-group support and accountability. As a large group, we discussed what scholarship on teaching and learning (SoTL) is and began thinking through its role in our teaching and research. Unlike the kinds of research published by education professionals, subject-area experts in specific fields, like Religious Studies, research and publish scholarship on teaching and learning (SoTL). The discipline of SoTL was new to me, but in many ways, writing SoTL was a natural outcome of learning how to reflect on my teaching.

Sketching the Contours

Patricia O'Connell Killen and Eugene V. Gallagher begin "Sketching the Contours of the Scholarship of Teaching and Learning in Theology and Religion" by introducing Ernest Boyer. Boyer's work in *Scholarship Reconsidered* (1990) launched renewed interest in scholars' engagement in teaching and learning.[2] "Boyer's proposal," they write, "opened up a space within which inquiry into one's teaching practice on the part of those who were experts in their discipline but not in education, could, even should, be considered scholarship."[3] In "Sketching," Killen and Gallagher take up questions related to the content and boundaries of SoTL in religious studies and theology. (On the off chance you have made it this far in this book and have not yet read their article, mark your place here, and go read it.) Killen and Gallagher draw on work by Maryellen Weimer and other experts to consider the "contours" of SoTL in religious studies and theological studies. Echoing these colleagues, they emphasize that the most successful SoTL research bridges the particularities of a specific classroom in a given field with observations that are transferrable to more general conversations among scholar-teachers.

Killen and Gallagher identify "clusters" or types of SoTL in religious studies and theology through a review of articles in *Teaching Theology and Religion*, which was first published in 1997. "Our intent," they note, "is to describe, analyze, and classify the scholarship of teaching and learning as it is emerging at a particular site of intellectual inquiry."[4] They go on to explain:

> Our orienting conception is that in any scholarship there exists a set of assumptions that guide writers in framing fruitful questions and lines of inquiry and in discerning areas of focus worth a scholar's attention. These are generative assumptions, generative in that they offer potentially fruitful openings and ways into problems, questions, and situations that result in new knowledge or deeper understanding that is, at least potentially, generalizable and translatable into other settings.[5]

I read "Sketching" the first time in preparation for the writing colloquy, and early in the group process, the leaders asked us to identify which generative assumption guided our project. Killen and Gallagher identify six: "show and tell," classroom practice; "personal/confessional/vocational," person of the professor; "unified field theory," purposes and politics of teaching; "philosopher's stone," pedagogies and theories; "resources in the field," practical possibilities of the field; and "field is the problem," problematic conventions for teaching and research.[6]

My own project fell squarely into the first category, that of classroom practice, as my idea to adapt forms of assessment proceeded from my practice (of) giving exams. Over the project's development, I attempted to craft "stronger form" of this type of SoTL by explaining the teaching and institutional contexts in which I identified the issue—a less-than-ideal form of assessment—and created a solution. In the article, I share example questions along with stronger and weaker student responses. I also situate the exam format in the broader context of teaching critical thinking skills by explaining how the justifications elicit metacognition—thinking about thinking—from students and exploring how metacognition can enhance and deepen learning. Writing the article prompted me to research critical thinking, selective-response exams, and metacognition and to reflect upon what worked well (and didn't) in a way that might prove transferrable to other instructors' classes. The support and structure of the colloquy—and the advice and encouragement of its leaders—facilitated the challenging work of reflection.

Reading, Reflection, and Rest

I read "Sketching" and Killen's "Midrange Reflection: The Underlying Practice of Wabash Center Workshops, Colloquies, and Consultations" (2007) most recently in preparation to write this essay. Where "Sketching" describes the form and function of SoTL, "Midrange Reflection" offers an introduction to the work involved in effective and engaging SoTL. The introduction Killen articulates is less an overview than a meeting: "Reader," she says, "meet reflection." "Reflection," she explains:

> begins when one pauses and ponders. Pausing gathers and refocuses attention .... Pondering involves a quality of attention that is alert, open, patient, expectant, and sustained. It allows the 'whom' or 'what' on which one's attention is focused to retain its own integrity, to be 'other,' even an other that one does not understand. Further, a pondering attention is unshackled from the chorus of premature judgments and anxieties that block both creative and analytical thought.[7]

Pondering is a curious activity. It reminds me of flow, but there seems to be more intention involved in pondering. Less happenstance. Because the work of reflection requires awareness, patience, openness, expectations, and energy, it takes (up) space. It requires place, too. While it is possible to make space nearly anywhere, place is purposeful. Place for pondering needs to be set apart from familiar distractions, obligations, and responsibilities: email notifications, laundry in the dryer, a chance encounter with a talkative colleague, a dog who needs a walk, an optional webinar, or a child asking for a snack. Whether in person (as workshop leaders) or through their writing, Killen and Gallagher create space and place for pondering, and when the judgments and anxieties arise—as they inevitably will and do—Killen reintroduces readers to reflection. She reminds us that "pondering expresses a seemingly contradictory quality of non-intrusive affective connection combined with intellectual distance that is described in many studies of creativity."[8] Eat a chocolate, sip a cup of coffee, or go for a walk.

Reflecting on teaching involves a back-and-forth movement from the particularities of a single incident, assignment, class, curriculum, or career to a broader field in which colleagues may find a technique, approach, or pedagogy instructive. Killen, in her explanation, draws on Gallagher's unpublished thoughts (likely archived on a sticky note):

> Midrange reflection on teaching and learning lifts out from the particularities of a concrete teaching incident the issues, themes, questions, approaches, procedures, and so forth, that have the potential, thus identified to be of general relevance in other situations of teaching and learning, though they would need then to be adapted not just adopted to other, equally particular contexts.[9]

In my experience, midrange reflection can function at different scales. Here Killen (with Gallagher) describes a broad scale. The scholar-teacher reflects on a single event in teaching and learning in a way that makes the event instructive for a broad readership. Midrange reflection can function in smaller-scale contexts, too. For example, faculty colleagues can engage in midrange reflection when they discuss curriculum changes, departmental student learning objectives, or mission statements. While my own experience leads me to believe this, I see colleagues working this way, too.

Applying the Learning

In "Teaching in Contexts: Designing a Competency-Based Religious Studies Program," Jenna Gray-Hildenbrand and Rebekka King demonstrate the potential for midrange reflection to shape teaching and learning. Gray-Hildenbrand and King "lift out" specific aspects of their context and field of study as they describe the curriculum they developed for majors in Religious Studies at Middle Tennessee State University.[10] Their competency-based curriculum pairs "religious literacy (or content knowledge) with disciplinary-based skills."[11] They explain the importance of considering their institutional context, including the students they teach and the institution's strategic goals. With their context and students in mind, they prioritize a holistic approach (teaching, programming, and mentoring) that supports students learning how "to speak academically about religion."[12]

In addition to aligning with institutional objectives, Gray-Hildenbrand and King develop the program's definition of "competency" in conversation with relevant teacher-scholars in Religious Studies. In particular, they engage scholars focused on religious literacy and the public understanding of religion, and they do this with two aspects of competency in mind: content and method. Drawing on Gallagher's "Teaching for Religious Literacy," Gray-Hildenbrand and King emphasize that "religious studies faculty must do more than offer basic information."[13] They quote Gallagher's emphasis on knowledge and application:

> To be literate about religion, one needs to know something about religious dynamics, mechanics, and processes – the how of religion. A clear understanding of both the what and the how is necessary to grasping the *why* of religion – why human beings have persisted in this mode of behavior, even as it has imposed extraordinary demands on them and as frequently brought them to tears as to joy.[14]

Knowing something about religions facilitates students' learning about how religions function, which can lead to students understanding the complex (and sometimes perplexing) obligations of religions, as well as the everyday and extreme experiences they offer. Gallagher cautions that this advice—teaching religious literacy qua competency—should be considered in light of the instructor's institutional context. In particular, he advises, "Teach the students you have, not the ones you wish you had."[15]

If it seems to be an ouroboric example, it is. Gray-Hildenbrand and King learn from "Religious Literacy," a product of Gallagher's midrange reflection on the subject. Then through their own process of reflection, including pausing to consider MTSU students and pondering the program's potential objectives, they develop an innovative and comprehensive major in Religious Studies. Their midrange reflection moved from close analysis of their experiences with students in their institutional context to more general ideas and observations about their program's components and goals. As Killen notes, "Midrange reflection builds toward bridging from an insightful interpretation of a particular event to future particular teaching situations."[16] Even if Gray-Hildenbrand and King had not shared their thinking and process in *Teaching Theology and Religion*, their collaborative midrange reflection happened. They bridged individual experiences with insights from the field to create a competency-based program that serves their students' needs, fits their institutional context, and incorporates research-based theories and practices from Religious Studies.

All that to say that midrange reflection need not be limited to SoTL. Issues pop up in faculty careers and departments all the time, and "issues are pivot points for midrange reflection."[17] Killen explains that "issues are pivot points precisely because they connect persons, field, institution, larger context, and the dynamic process of teaching and learning."[18] When an issue arises, then, midrange reflection can offer a process for its consideration and potential resolution. (See Killen 147–8, or call a consultant.) Most importantly, "The structure of midrange reflection opens possibilities for hospitality to the self and others, and so to a community that recognizes and exists in and through difference."[19] This, dear reader, is the magic. Midrange reflection is intentional and purposeful thinking about thinking, including both teaching and learning:

> Midrange reflection, like the skilled teaching it is intended to promote, provides the artful balance of challenge and support that propels both learning and the cognitive and personal development of new and experienced faculty, while at the same time respecting their integrity and freedom. Its practice is an act of integrity and resistance at a time and in a culture that increasingly misunderstands and undervalues the liberating power of the life of the mind.[20]

Those are Killen's words, not mine. I'll stick with, "Midrange reflection is the magic." It fits on a sticky note.[21]

Notes

1. See Molly H. Bassett, "Teaching Critical Thinking without (Much) Writing: Multiple-Choice and Metacognition: Teaching Critical Thinking," *Teaching Theology & Religion* 19, no. 1 (January 2016): 28–37, https://doi.org/10.1111/teth.12318.
2. Patricia O'Connell Killen and Eugene V. Gallagher, "Sketching the Contours of the Scholarship of Teaching and Learning in Theology and Religion: Sketching the Contours," *Teaching Theology & Religion* 16, no. 2 (April 2013): 107, https://doi.org/10.1111/teth.12020.
3. Ibid., 108.

4 Ibid., 114.
5 Ibid., 114–15.
6 Ibid., 115–20.
7 Patricia O'Connell Killen, "Midrange Reflection: The Underlying Practice of Wabash Center Workshops, Colloquies, and Consultations," *Teaching Theology & Religion* 10, no. 3 (July 2007): 144, https://doi.org/10.1111/j.1467-9647.2007.00342.x.
8 Ibid.
9 Ibid.
10 Ibid.
11 Jenna Gray-Hildenbrand and Rebekka King, "Teaching in Contexts: Designing a Competency-Based Religious Studies Program," *Teaching Theology & Religion* 22, no. 3 (July 2019): 192, https://doi.org/10.1111/teth.12495.
12 Ibid., 195.
13 Ibid., 199.
14 Eugene V. Gallagher, "Teaching for Religious Literacy," *Teaching Theology & Religion* 12, no. 3 (July 2009): 208, https://doi.org/10.1111/j.1467-9647.2009.00523.x.
15 Ibid., 212.
16 Killen, "Midrange Reflection," 145.
17 Ibid., 146.
18 Ibid.
19 Ibid., 148.
20 Ibid., 148.
21 My deep thanks to Eugene Gallagher, Carolyn Medine, Tom Pearson, Swasti Bhattacharyya, and Martha Stortz, who led the pre-tenure workshop and writing colloquy in which I participated. While Patricia O'Connell Killen was not a member of those meetings, her ideas were often in the room with us. I greatly appreciate colleagues who read drafts of this essay, including Nathan Springer.

Bibliography

Bassett, Molly H. "Teaching Critical Thinking without (Much) Writing: Multiple-Choice and Metacognition: Teaching Critical Thinking." *Teaching Theology & Religion* 19, no. 1 (2016): 28–37.

Gallagher, Eugene V. "Teaching for Religious Literacy." *Teaching Theology & Religion* 12, no. 3 (2009): 208.

Gray-Hildenbrand, Jenna and Rebekka King. "Teaching in Contexts: Designing a Competency-Based Religious Studies Program." *Teaching Theology & Religion* 22, no. 3 (2019): 192.

Killen, Patricia O'Connell and Eugene V. Gallagher. "Sketching the Contours of the Scholarship of Teaching and Learning in Theology and Religion: Sketching the Contours." *Teaching Theology & Religion* 16, no. 2 (2013): 107.

Killen, Patricia O'Connell. "Midrange Reflection: The Underlying Practice of Wabash Center Workshops, Colloquies, and Consultations." *Teaching Theology & Religion* 10, no. 3 (2007): 144.

Part Two

Persona

10

Overcoming Fears of a Normative Valence

Susan Marks
New College of Florida

Through the depth of their own teaching, Gene Gallagher and Patricia Killen helped me to understand the interaction of teacher, students, and course material in a shared place created by this interaction. In doing so, Patricia and Gene gave me the tools to solve small problems with individual lessons as well as larger ones concerning an entire course. For me the biggest problems have long involved how to teach when there is a normative valence. I served as a congregational rabbi before returning to school in order to earn a PhD. In that earlier role, the congregation had hired me in some sense to offer a normative message. Nevertheless, in most cases I still often chose to present the wisdom of the sources so that each person might wrestle on their own. This preference became more pronounced as I became a teacher of religion in a public institution in a land that has guaranteed freedom of religion, and where students of many different backgrounds took my courses, so there were no shared, authoritative, sources.

In studying with Gene and Patricia, I did not so much change this perspective, as learn a greater understanding and respect for the dynamic relationship of teacher, student, and content. This perspective importantly revealed a relationship that was resilient enough to allow for an occasional normative message without becoming brittle or broken. Or in other words, when the teacher and the students had a true voice, a normative note need not be abusive so much as one more source to consider. The most dramatic revelation of this new understanding occurred shortly after I finished my Fellowship with the Wabash Center for Teaching and Learning in Theology and Religion. I use the term "dramatic" because it involved revising a course that I had had no intention of revisiting. That course was "Judaism and Ecology," which I taught once and quickly shelved, expecting never to return to it.

The Challenge

I began to plan "Judaism and Ecology" because it reflected deeply held passions of mine, with no real sense of what it would look like as a course. I had long been devoted to environmental studies. I had considered declaring as a Biology major when I first went to college, and much later flirted with the idea of doing a Judaic Studies dissertation involving these issues, before finding other directions. So it was that when I arrived at New College, I took the opportunity to revisit environmental studies once again, as a teacher of Religion. New College of Florida, a small, public, Liberal Arts College on Sarasota Bay, with eager, talented, students and a vibrant Environmental Studies program, seemed like the perfect place to offer such a course. I found a book that had essays that interwove Jewish and environmental ideas, *Judaism and Ecology: Created World and Revealed World*.[1] I focused half the course on explorations of Conservation, especially the halachic principle in Jewish law that "you shall not destroy," built upon Deuteronomy 20.19, "in your wars against a city ... you shall not destroy its trees ...." Students wrote their first paper analyzing the beginnings of the development of this principle. The other half examined ideas related to Creation, and at the end of the course students did their own research project investigating a Jewish or interfaith organization that focused on an environmental issue. I have very few memories of the first time I taught this course. The students seemed to have a good time, but the readings I had chosen were too narrowly focused and seemed to me less accessible than I had hoped. I felt that I was trying to steer a runaway horse. When the course finished I thought of hiding under my bed and never coming out. Since I had other courses on my plate (courses that did not elicit these feelings), I looked the other way and let this experiment disappear into the past. Ultimately I was fairly successful at that, at least for a while. That was 2005.

Then in 2008 two things happened. I was a Wabash Fellow, studying with Gene, Patricia, and other wonderful Wabash teachers, learning about the teaching context and myself as a teacher. In addition, a student spoke to me of that earlier course. This student had studied with me for four years. She had concentrated in Religion and was finishing up her Senior Thesis on the Montanists. She offered an enthusiastic success story for our Religion program. I was talking with her, as one does, about past and future: What had she valued at New College? What were her plans? One of her answers floored me: her favorite course had been "Judaism and Ecology," which she had taken as a first-year student. She asked me why I hadn't offered it again.

Recognition of the Challenge: Why Had I Stopped Offering "Judaism and Ecology"?

I don't recall how I answered my student at that moment, or how much I even answered myself. But I heard her, and the question stayed with me. As I began to consider her question I realized that some of my feeling of being out of control had to do with the normative aspects of this course. I came to understand that I was more comfortable teaching early Judaism and Christianity and the careful reading of texts, highlighting a range of interpretive possibilities. This course felt like I had to teach a "right answer," after all, it was not okay to destroy the planet. My fear of taking a normative voice and bullying someone into thinking something they did not want to think made me eager to avoid this course. Nevertheless, here was my student who did not sound bullied. To listen to her speak of the course I had not forced monolithic answers on anyone. She had gone on from this course to a deeper study of Religion. Perhaps there was more here than I had understood. After all, would I really want to miss out on such students in the future?

What to Do About It

With my Wabash teachers in the back of my mind, it was easier to decide that my fears did not have to govern my teaching. I was looking at what Patricia would later call "Key challenges, opportunities, and goals," as she directed a panel of scholar-teachers to reflect upon their teaching.[2] She summed up, "All of you were trying to get the students connected to the material, in terms of its inherent interest, in terms of its connection to their lives. You were doing so in an effort to engage the students in the material and in a preliminary way in the scholarly tasks. Is this a fair take on your presentations?"[3] And even if her words were directed to the scholars in the panel, they describe the situation I understood myself to be in. The "challenges" I knew (and had feared), but, I realized through the words of my former student that connecting my teaching to environmental studies was not only a challenge, but was also still a goal. All of a sudden it appeared to be an opportunity as well. Students might sign up for this course because of its "inherent interest" to them, and because they recognized a possible "connection to their lives." Here were students who shared my passion for environmental studies and were willing, even eager, to embrace the materials of Religion that spoke of this passion.

During my time studying at Wabash I had come to learn more about the dynamic relationship within a classroom. As Gene summed up, "we are always caught in a triangular relationship between our roles as scholar-teachers, the material that we choose as the object of our attention, and the audience to whom we wish to communicate our ideas and opinions about that material."[4] I had run from this course because I did not trust myself or the materials that I had chosen. But, looked at this new way, I trusted my students and this relationship. If I could tweak the materials and relax into that trust, then "Judaism and Ecology" could possibly work for more students in the future.

Revisiting My Design of the Intellectual Experience

Some of the chapters in *Judaism and Ecology: Created World and Revealed World* had been too challenging for my students, relying too much on knowledge they did not yet possess. But not all essays were equally problematic. Some had worked. And the assignments had worked. I grew more selective in assigning chapters to read. And I added an additional book, *Ecology and the Jewish Spirit: Where Nature and the Sacred Meet*, with shorter, friendlier pieces that offered a good complement to the first book.[5] I also scouted out additional materials. Two of my Wabash cohort, Kate Blanchard and Kevin O'Brien had authored, *An Introduction to Christian Environmentalism: Ecology, Virtue, and Ethics*.[6] This proved a wonderful offering to Christian students discovering more interest in Religion than they had previously thought, and who were wondering whether Christianity had anything to teach in this area.

The organization of the course still made sense. It had good bones, focusing on Conservation as it appears in Jewish law and upon Creation. Using the book, *Ecology and the Jewish Spirit: Where Nature and the Sacred Meet*, allowed me to develop more of a focus on Time and on Activism. We considered religious time, the insights of calendar, and holy days, and particularly ideas developed by Abraham Joshua Heschel in *The Sabbath: Its Meaning for Modern Man*.[7] Heschel explores the idea that after God's six days of work, with the seventh God rested and called this Sabbath day "holy," emphasizing that the first entity named holy was not a person or a place, but rather a sanctified time. From this recognition he leads his readers to reflect upon the importance of resting, of "being" rather than always achieving. This provides a needed antidote to consumer culture, an idea with significant environmental importance. A focus on activism could also be developed from the voices of the authors who offered responses to the environmental crises. They spoke of their challenges and successes, each in a different way. And the icing on the cake came when Everett Gendler, an important Jewish environmental activist (appearing in *Ecology and the Jewish Spirit*), arrived in Sarasota a few years later. In response to my invitation, Everett came and spoke with my class, and has continued to do so each time I taught it. My class always adored his stories of how he made the relationship between the earth and Judaism come alive. He also offered them insights into how his embrace of Judaism allowed him to continue as an environmental activist year after year.

In addition to revisiting my own curriculum, I also plugged further into the Environmental Studies program at New College and into the Jewish calendar. I learned that the Introduction to the Environmental Studies was always offered in the Fall, so Spring would be the best time to teach my course. I realized that if I thought of this as a Spring course, then Tu B'shvat, the new year festival of the Trees, offered a ready-made beginning. Mystics in the land of Israel in the sixteenth century designed a seder meal around eating and reflecting upon many different fruits, being especially cognizant of their mystical associations. Here was a class session for the first week, for the asking. In addition, my scholarly work has been heavily involved with the Meals in the Greco-Roman World Seminar of the Society of Biblical Literature, so meals are a sweet spot for me. We could sit down together for a meal, outside, in January in Florida. What better way to establish a shared place, a teaching context? We could move from there back to our classroom having already begun to forge a shared space within which we could learn together to consider what Judaism and Religion could offer those of us who have a passion for the environment.

And from that time on, I have taught this course regularly. I came to recognize that the discomfort with the normative aspects of this course did not necessarily go away completely, but that when I began to recognize this fear, I could recall the dynamic relationship of myself as teacher, my students and the material we shared, as Gene and Patricia had taught me to understand. Somehow this "Judaism and Ecology" course might never feel in control. It often whooshed in directions that I could not quite anticipate. But on the whole it worked. I have over and over again been grateful for the students I meet in that course, who I would otherwise likely not have met. In 2008 we were not quite in the present focus on STEM-fields-above-all-else, but since then it has certainly proved a boon to have a course that could appeal directly to students who would otherwise take mostly sciences. I am awed by the commitment to biology or public policy or various other aspects of environmental studies that so many of these students exude, and feel better about the world knowing they are heading forth to help protect our beleaguered planet. And I have even had other students who started out taking this course and later wrote their Senior Thesis with me, realizing that what they really wanted was further study of Religion.

Conclusion

With the help of my Wabash teachers, I learned that by trusting the teaching context I could overcome an area of real doubt, and even fear. I could provide myself with a more nuanced understanding of how a classroom worked and thus better situate the inner voice that worried that I was misusing my position when I taught in a normative voice. In understanding the ideas shared by Patricia and Gene I could learn to count on the resilience of the relationship that I developed with my students. I could teach of environmental activism, and of the ways that religious traditions might nurture activism. Ultimately I could find ways of sharing my love of the outside world with my students. I could do this knowing that for many of them I was mostly offering a new way to consider something they already cared about, and possible new avenues to delve into, while others might hear something else. But in any case, the students had an important say in what they heard in the course. I had learned to trust the places they found all on their own, within our shared explorations. Secure in this knowledge of my students, myself as teacher, my teaching context, and a revised intellectual design of the course, I could resurrect a course I had earlier abandoned.

Postscript

And that would have been the final word, except that with the arrival of the recent global pandemic we all suddenly found ourselves teaching on Zoom. With everyone sheltering in place, there could be no shared meal, no Tu B'Shvat seder outdoors in order to establish our shared place. In fact, the shared teaching context suddenly had become a checkerboard of squares on a screen. And yet the students were still keen, knowing what they wanted. Their passion for the environment, and curiosity about Judaism or Religion, based on relatively little knowledge, meant they were still willing to learn despite the hurdles. Since we could not celebrate a shared meal, or eat different kinds of fruits together, I had each student decide upon a fruit during the first class meeting (the session before our virtual seder). They chose among fruits with skins, with pits and with small seeds only, which, according to the rabbi-mystics, could be mapped onto different spiritual states. I asked each student to reflect upon the fruit they had chosen, and in the next class session share a memory, a song, a drawing, something about this fruit, that we then wove into our virtual meal celebration. And with that we were off to yet another iteration of "Judaism and Ecology," with fears of my normative voice balanced by my trust in the teaching relationship that existed between me and my students.

Notes

1. Hava Tirosh-Samuelson, ed., *Judaism and Ecology: Created World and Revealed World* (Cambridge: Harvard University Press, 2002).
2. Patricia O'Connell Killen, Madeline Duntley, Constance Furey, W. Clark Gilpin, and Horace E. Six-Means, "Teaching the History of Christianity: Critical Themes and Challenges," *Teaching Theology & Religion* 12, no. 3 (2009): 258.
3. Ibid., 262.
4. Eugene V. Gallagher, "Teaching Outside the Classroom," *The Council of Societies for the Study of Religion Bulletin* 30, no. 2 (2001): 43.
5. Ellen Bernstein, ed., *Ecology and the Jewish Spirit: Where Nature and the Sacred Meet* (Woodstock VT: Jewish Lights, 2000).
6. Kathryn D. Blanchard and Kevin J. O'Brien, *An Introduction to Christian Environmentalism: Ecology, Virtue, and Ethics* (Waco, TX: Baylor University Press, 2014).
7. Abraham Joshua Heschel, *The Sabbath: Its Meaning for Modern Man* (New York: Farrar, Straus and Giroux, 1984 (1951)).

Bibliography

Bernstein, Ellen. *Ecology and the Jewish Spirit: Where Nature and the Sacred Meet.* Woodstock VT: Jewish Lights, 2000.

Blanchard, Kathryn and Kevin J. O'Brien. *An Introduction to Christian Environmentalism: Ecology, Virtue, and Ethics.* Texas: Baylor University Press, 2014.

Gallagher, Eugene V. "Teaching Outside the Classroom." *The Council of Societies for the Study of Religion Bulletin* 30, no. 2 (2001): 42–5.

Heschel, Abraham. *The Sabbath: Its Meaning for Modern Man*. New York: Farrar, Straus and Giroux, (1951).

Killen, Patricia O'Connell, Madeline Duntley, Constance Furey, W. Clark Gilpin, and Horace E. Six-Means. "Teaching the History of Christianity: Critical Themes and Challenges." *Teaching Theology & Religion* 12, no. 3 (2009): 258–286.

Tirosh-Samuelson, Hava. *Judaism and Ecology: Created World and Revealed World*. Cambridge: Harvard University Press, 2002.

11

A Vulnerable Persona: Wrestling with the Legacy of Jean Vanier

Reid B. Locklin and Andrea Nicole Carandang
St. Michael's College, University of Toronto

In his short essay, "Cultivating a Teaching Persona," Jay Parini draws a parallel between writing fiction and developing a *persona*, a "mask" or deliberate pattern of self-presentation cultivated for the purpose of teaching.[1] "It involves artifice," he writes, "and the art of teaching is no less complicated than any other art."[2] These masks are not pure fabrications, of course. The best teaching *personas* emerge organically from the *personas* of our own mentors, and we cultivate them to help us encounter, challenge, and empower the students who pass into and out of our care over the course of a teaching career. At the same time, every mask carries some peril. In addition to facilitating effective teaching, a carefully constructed *persona* can also disguise or channel destructive forces of insecurity, competition, domination, and even narcissism. Most of us who teach at a college or university—particularly those who carry the privilege of tenured faculty status, along with gendered or racialized privilege—will find ourselves navigating both kinds of mask, those masks that empower others and those masks that merely hide our more destructive compulsions and desires. Confusingly, these are sometimes the same mask.

This dynamic manifests itself well beyond the borders of higher education. In this essay, we consider a specific *persona* that deeply impacted both of us, as teachers and learners: the celebrated public philosopher Jean Vanier (1928–2019). Vanier was most well-known for founding the international L'Arche movement, a network of intentional living communities built around their "core members," persons with severe mental and physical disabilities. Vanier was widely revered, particularly in Canada and France, as a "living saint" and a prophet of the transformative power of weakness and vulnerability.[3]

Vanier was also, it turns out, a perpetrator of sexual abuse. Shortly after his death in 2019, after a multi-year investigation, L'Arche International concluded that their founder had sexually abused at least six adult, non-disabled women in the context of spiritual direction.[4] The *persona* of this revered figure was, it turns out, just a mask.

Or was it?

In this essay, we re-examine the *persona* of Jean Vanier with specific reference to the international community-engaged learning (CEL) organization he founded in 2000, Intercordia Canada. For over a decade, a course offered in partnership with Intercordia Canada became the premier social justice initiative of the Christianity and Culture program at St. Michael's College, in the University of Toronto, running continuously from 2005 to 2017. The program's most distinctive element was an emphasis on student's weakness, vulnerability, and dependence in three-month international service placements. This distinctive focus set the program apart from other CEL programs focused on service or vocational training. In retrospect, after the revelations about Vanier, this emphasis also became newly problematic. Can intentional vulnerability be saved, as an ideal of community-engaged learning and of teaching and learning more broadly? In order to explore this question, we first offer a self-reflective, critical examination of the program, across its history at St. Mike's; then we turn to vulnerability itself, as a risky, but still worthy educational ideal.

We decided to conduct this enquiry as a dialogue between friends with different perspectives on the program. Locklin served as coordinator of Intercordia throughout its life at St. Michael's College; Carandang participated in the program as an undergraduate student in 2014–15 and served as program assistant for the following two years. We have continued to collaborate on several projects after this, notably an initiative related to the Truth and Reconciliation of Canada that emerged indirectly from Intercordia.[5] Importantly for the present essay, the Intercordia program was the basis of Locklin's first contact with Patricia Killen, as editor of *Teaching Theology and Religion*. In 2010, he published an article on Vanier and the distinctive approach of Intercordia in the journal.[6] This would become one of Locklin's most widely cited articles. It also paved his way to join wider conversations in the Scholarship of Teaching and Learning in Theology and Religion, with Patricia and Gene as primary interlocutors. It seems appropriate to take a conversational approach here, as a tribute to Patricia and Gene's own fruitful dialogue,[7] as well as their shared commitment to reflective dialogue itself as a practice of teaching and scholarship.

A Fragile Foundation? "Intercordia" and Its Discontents

Locklin

The Intercordia program, and its pedagogy of vulnerability, was deeply formative for me as a new faculty member at St. Mike's. I was hired in 2004. One early morning that same fall, as I was making instant oatmeal in the office kitchenette, I ran into an oddly familiar, older man. "And who are you?" he asked, with a vague smile. I quickly found myself in conversation with Jean Vanier, as he waited for a meeting with the college principal. Soon I was also having conversations with the principal and the executive director of the recently founded Intercordia NGO. A year and a half later we launched the course and sent the first group of students to placements in Nicaragua, Honduras, Ecuador, and Ghana.

The motto of Intercordia was, "Seeing the World through the Eyes of the Heart," and at its height the NGO facilitated CEL experiences for courses in theology, religious studies, or sociology at universities across Canada. These three-month summer placements were arranged with grassroots organizations in Latin America, Africa, and Ukraine, as well as at selected L'Arche communities in North America. In a recorded interview, Vanier insisted that, although these were selected as places of "poverty and pain," student participants would undertake their placements "not essentially to do something, but to be – that is to say, to discover the culture that is there, to discover the beauty of that culture, so then the persons of Intercordia … they are changed, more than what they can do for others."[8] Stated differently, the program aimed to broaden students' imaginative understandings and to foster relational solidarity. Expectations that they would provide assistance for those in need or gain professional experience were strictly subordinated to a specific vision of personal transformation.

In our work with Intercordia at St. Michael's College, we took these broader goals very much to heart. Students completed an intense academic seminar on social justice and development theory in the winter term, reflected with a partner throughout their placement, and wrote a final integration paper. In the application and interview process, each student was asked to reflect on an experience of weakness or failure; and we pressed questions of vulnerability throughout the academic and experiential components of the course. I personally became convinced that the vision of Vanier and the broader L'Arche movement was importantly countercultural. My commitment was such that, when the Intercordia NGO unexpectedly suspended its operations in 2014, I continued to offer the program under a new name. When I launched a research project with students to reconsider the Catholic mission of St. Michael College in conversation with our library's special collections and archives, moreover, I placed the most hope in the L'Arche Fonds, which featured public lectures and retreats by Vanier.[9]

In retrospect, I am puzzled by my own naiveté. While I continue to hold L'Arche and the colleagues who led Intercordia in high respect—it was they who first reached out to make sure I knew about the Vanier revelations in 2020—it also seems clear that there were warning signs. In the first year, for example, I found myself objecting strongly to Vanier's book *Finding Peace*,[10] insisting to my then co-instructor that we use something else in future years.[11] I convinced myself that I was mainly annoyed by Vanier's prose style. Years later, colleagues at the University of Toronto Centre for International Experience raised concerns about what they perceived as an intrusive mentorship style provided by Intercordia staff during students' placements. I convinced myself that this testified to our countercultural approach. Then there were issues raised by several of my more perceptive students, who posed serious, critical questions to Vanier as a moral theorist. I welcomed such criticism in principle, of course, and I convinced myself that this was the expected result of a successful academic seminar. After 2020, however, all of these moments came back to haunt me. Had I been missing signs of an abusive culture all along? Did Intercordia actually embody a different ethos than the one I imagined, the ethos of a founder who knowingly exploited weakness and vulnerability to abuse persons in his spiritual care?

One of those perceptively critical students, who continued as a facilitator for the final two years of the program at St. Mike's, was Andrea Nicole Carandang.

Carandang

I participated in the Intercordia program in 2014–15; this fulfilled a lifelong dream of serving marginalized populations internationally. As I learned more about the program during our training sessions, I found myself especially attracted to its focus on vulnerability, which was emphasized particularly in the sharing of "life stories" by student participants. These training sessions took place in seminar format outside of the regularly scheduled classes taught by Reid, and were facilitated by students who had completed the program in earlier years together with representatives from Intercordia.

We had just completed the first seminar when my peers and I received an email from the Intercordia, stating that they were suspending operations for a year. This meant that we would be unable to go on our international placements.

Reid gave us the option of continuing with the course, and finding our own placements. A handful of students, including myself, opted to continue. The placements that we chose that year varied—some were able to partner with an international NGO, while others, like myself, opted to stay in Canada and work with a local organization.

In the academic component of the course, Reid assigned a variety of theorists and social justice advocates for the students to engage. We read the works of Amartya Sen, John Borrows, Dorothy Day, bell hooks, and Paulo Freire, before concluding with Jean Vanier's *Becoming Human*. Prior to reading Vanier, I found that each author presented their own view of how to address social injustice through a variety of lenses. When I read *Becoming Human*, at the end of the course, I saw themes that were appealing to me. He spoke about the need to recognize one's common humanity to build communities, for they can foster "love, openness and compassion for others."[12] These communities can nourish and strengthen connections between people, allowing them to share their hopes and fears with each other, which then leads to a growth in love.[13] The sharing of hopes and fears through stories can help one accept oneself as one is, along with experiencing freedom from inner hurts.[14] These ideas helped me articulate my own experiences with the communities that I am part of, for these communities have helped me start on my own healing process from the traumas in my life.

As attractive as I found this vision, however, I ultimately felt it was too utopian and was not enough for addressing structural injustice. Vanier's vision does not address the roles of large institutions in perpetuating harm, or in encouraging the vision of community that he so strongly believed in. "We may be different in race, culture, religion, and capacities," writes Vanier in *Becoming Human*, "but we are all the same, with vulnerable hearts, the need to love and be loved, the need to grow, to develop our capacities, and to find our place in the world."[15] This is a beautiful vision, but it also feels a bit too simple.

A Question of Vulnerability

Carandang

Despite these reservations, my experience of the Intercordia program—and particularly of the placement—was indeed one of profound vulnerability. I completed my placement for this course at a Canadian middle school that served inner-city, at-risk youth. The placement was the first time that I had ever lived away from home, which in itself involved a lot of growing pains. My time at the school also involved being able to be open to the tasks that they asked for me to complete that day. Some days, I worked with teachers to help them with the lessons they were teaching that day. Others, I was baking in the kitchen or organizing the library. I had to be open and faithful to addressing whatever needs the school had that day. The vulnerability required of me did lead to a sense of belonging in the school community. What love I gave to the tasks I had to complete, I received back in abundance. As I reflected on my experiences, I thought that Vanier would be able to perfectly articulate all that I was going through, and I chose to re-read *Becoming Human* upon my return to Toronto, in preparation for my final integration paper.

To my disappointment, I found it inadequate. As mentioned above, Vanier does not adequately address the need to respond to the harms perpetuated by social structures. This question was especially important for my work at the school, for most of the students at the school were Indigenous. While I was working at the school, the Truth and Reconciliation Commission of Canada released its final report. The Truth and Reconciliation Commission of Canada was created as a result of a 2007 legal settlement between survivors of the Indian Residential School System, the Canadian state, and the churches that ran the schools. Over the course of six years, the Commission traveled all over Canada to hear from Indigenous peoples' experiences of residential schools. The goal of the Commission was to highlight the truth of the residential school history as a way of moving Canadian society toward reconciliation. In other words, "[n]ow that we know about residential schools and their legacy, what do we do about it?"[16] The Final Report also includes ninety-four Calls to Action, addressed to all parts of Canadian society, to encourage every person in Canada to take action in light of the findings on residential schools. These two factors meant that there needed to be an attempt to articulate the role of social structures in perpetuating injustice, and how these structures can be transformed to prevent the further perpetuation of harms.

When I became a facilitator of the program, I was still interested in vulnerability, despite my own criticisms of Vanier. As aforementioned, "life stories" were part of the training facilitated by Intercordia, and I had found it lifegiving to share my own story and to hear the stories of my classmates. This, along with the experience of having to find new placements and the struggles that came with that helped us form a community. I thus decided to encourage future participants to share their life stories within future training sessions. However, the bonds were not as strongly formed in the latter years of the program. Though students were willing to share their life stories, I was never sure of whether it led to the same connection that was formed with my peers and me. Looking back, it feels like an attempt to force vulnerability to build community, rather than letting community form organically. While vulnerability was important to my experience of Intercordia, it seemed to become a smaller part of the experience of future students as they prepared for their placements.

Locklin

There were a couple of substantive changes in the program in its final years, both of which may bear on Andrea Nicole's observations and the broader question of vulnerability. First of all, after the loss of our NGO partner in 2014–15, we worked to identify new recruitment strategies and new sources of financial support. As a consequence, we also attracted students from a wider range of disciplinary perspectives, and this in turn changed the character of their student cohorts. Second, the process of student formation became removed from the institutional culture that had grown around Vanier. To provide one concrete example: although we asked the same questions about experiences of failure and vulnerability in the application interviews that we had been asking since 2006, it made a difference that I was conducting those interviews with a former student and a Student Life officer, rather than with a community partner shaped by the charism of L'Arche. Vulnerability was still central to the curriculum, but Vanier himself became more like just another seminar reading, rather than the *raison d'être* of the program.

With the wisdom of hindsight, it seems like it should have strengthened the program to shed some of the influence of Vanier. But, as revealed in Andrea Nicole's reflections, there was also a sense of loss—loss of profound mutual vulnerability, loss of a spontaneous, unforced sense of community. Why? Andrea Nicole and I have already alluded to some possible reasons. But I think this also invites at least some reflection on the intrinsic complexity of Vanier himself.

Natalie Wigg-Stevenson has brought out some of this complexity in a 2020 article for *Sojourners Magazine*. Wigg-Stevenson notes that Vanier's profound insights about the power of weakness and his formation as a sexual predator both appear to have originated with his Dominican mentor, Fr. Thomas Phillippe.[17] It was at the invitation and prompting of Phillippe that Vanier initiated the first experiments that led to the creation of L'Arche; in the same period, Phillippe and other members of his own intentional spiritual community, at the L'Eau Vive theological institute, were crafting an elaborate spiritual ideology to justify their practices of psychological and sexual abuse. Phillippe was thus Vanier's "spiritual father" in creating vibrant spiritual communities, and also in exploiting spiritual authority to perpetrate abuse. Vanier fully embodied both elements of this formation, from the early years of L'Arche in the 1960s right up to his death at age ninety. "The Vanier who abused women was not a fallen saint, succumbing to the temptations and opportunities afforded by his rising fame," writes Wigg-Stevenson. "This was who he had been all along: a man exquisitely and terribly attuned to the vulnerabilities of others."[18]

For Wigg-Stevenson, the deep ambiguity of Vanier's public and private *persona* redirects our attention to the deep ambiguity of desire, especially the pursuit of the holy. Desire was also the subject of a correspondence between Vanier and the postmodern theorist Julia Kristeva in 2009. This correspondence centered around Vanier's claim that the primary "motivation" and "secret" of L'Arche's flourishing is simply "pleasure," the pleasure of embodied souls joined in community through mutual weakness.[19] Kristeva raised concerns about what such a claim might imply about protecting the vulnerable against projection or domination by caregivers. "In psycho-analytic terms," writes Carolyn Whitney-Brown, Kristeva "questions whether Vanier is aware of how pleasure is linked with desire in all its multiple and ambiguous dimensions such as narcissism, or even masochism and sadism."[20] Vanier responded to the critique by appealing directly to the actual, concrete lives of L'Arche communities, including moments of difficulty, mutual transformation and comic joy.

The instinct, reading this exchange in the wake of the L'Arche report in 2020, is simply to take Kristeva's side in this debate and perhaps to discard Vanier's vision in search of fairer shores. But matters are never quite so simple. There *is* a wisdom in L'Arche, a wisdom deeply rooted in Vanier's insights about vulnerability, mutual relationship and love, a wisdom that eludes reduction to the language of clinical psychology. This wisdom eventually won Kristeva over to Vanier's side, at least on Whitney-Brown's reading of the exchange.[21] But Kristeva was also fundamentally correct to insist that even the most holy wisdom could be deployed to manipulate, dominate, and destroy—as in fact it was deployed by Vanier.

And this, in turn, presses the central question of our reflection in this essay. Is there any way to separate the authentic wisdom, still embodied at the grassroots level in L'Arche communities throughout the world, from its distorted, destructive foundation in the public and private *persona* of Jean Vanier? Is there any way to preserve vulnerability, in other words, as the basis of community and as an educational ideal?

Carandang

One way to think about vulnerability in the classroom is by widening the conversation to include the full range of thinkers that Reid had my classmates and me read for his class. In looking at the list of thinkers and reviewing my own integration essay, I realized that both Paulo Freire and bell hooks also mention the importance of vulnerability—Freire implicitly and bell hooks explicitly.

Freire, in *Pedagogy of Solidarity*, highlights the importance of taking risks as part of the creation of knowledge. He argued that educators need to encourage risking, and that "a desirable consequence of risking is committing mistakes. The educator must then be prepared to work with risk and to deal with mistakes in a positive, encouraging and challenging way."[22] In reading this, I realize that there is a sense of vulnerability required for the teacher and student to create a space where risk-taking, and the consequence of making mistakes, is welcomed and encouraged.

This aspect of risk-taking is also discussed by bell hooks, in *belonging: a culture of place*, but through the lens of anti-racist work. This risk-taking occurs within the building of communities that transcend differences. Doing this requires "an ethic of relational reciprocity," where, she writes "all things do not need to be equal in order for acceptance and mutuality to thrive."[23] She argues that this is "a more constructive and positive foundation for the building of ties that allow for differences in status, position, power and privilege whether determined by race, class, sexuality, religion or nationality."[24] How is this made possible? hooks argues that it is accomplished through vulnerability by all parties, which allows for "the possibility of recognition, respect, and mutual partnership."[25]

Many of these ideas resonate with what Vanier wrote in his book. He wrote that entering into personal relationships with those "on the fringes of society" allow us to be able to "look more critically at our own culture."[26] Furthermore, communities are places where people "can serve and create, and, most importantly, where they can love as well as be loved."[27] This is done through the formation of relationships. While I agree with what Vanier wrote, I find that he does not talk about how much of a risk it is to try and form communities that transcend differences to allow for "acceptance and mutuality to thrive."[28] Both hooks and Freire find ways of integrating vulnerability into their writings in a way that is conducive to the transformation of society.

What I find striking about the idea of vulnerability as based on an ethic of relational reciprocity and mutuality is that it seems to be what is necessary for universities and churches to respond to the Calls to Action of the Truth and Reconciliation Commission of Canada. Vulnerability is necessary here in order to recognize the harms done through the residential school system, and create partnerships and commitments that move toward reconciliation between Indigenous and non-Indigenous peoples in Canada.

Vulnerability is first seen in the need to recognize the harms done through residential schools, which includes apologizing for the role that the institutions may have had to play in perpetuating these harms and making necessary reparations for these harms. From July 24 to July 30, 2022, for example, Pope Francis visited cities in Alberta, Quebec, and Nunavut. Calling his Apostolic Journey a "penitential pilgrimage," Francis apologized for the Church's role in the residential school system after visiting the former site of the Ermineskin Indian Residential School in Maskwacis, Alberta. Vulnerability, as hooks describes it, is necessary to be able to enter into a relationship that allows for recognition, respect and mutual partnership. There was vulnerability within the Church and the Pope to recognize the hurt the Church has committed toward Indigenous peoples and to apologize for what was done. However, vulnerability is also necessary to continue the hard work of reconciliation, which includes ongoing education about the residential school system and the injustices still faced by Indigenous peoples, as well as working toward reparations.

For universities, Freire's encouragement of risk-taking seems to be the most salient, though communities of reciprocity as hooks explains still plays a key role. Calls to Action #62–65 of the Truth and Reconciliation Commission are focused on education for reconciliation. Risk-taking here is necessary, in that trial and error will be part of what it means to incorporate Indigenous pedagogies and knowledges into post-secondary education. Any errors made must then be addressed in consultation with appropriate Indigenous parties and corrected as soon as possible, which also demonstrates the need for these initiatives to be done in communication with Indigenous peoples. This thus requires communities of partnership and reciprocity to make sure that this work—and correction when necessary—is possible.

Moving Forward—In Ordinary Vulnerability

Carandang

I have seen the importance of vulnerability even in my own personal commitments to reconciliation in Canada. After the discoveries of the unmarked graves at the former Kamloops Indian Residential School in the summer of 2021, I created a reading plan for *What We Have Learned*, one of the reports published by the Truth and Reconciliation Commission of Canada.[29] I knew that it was a risk creating this plan, because I was not sure of how it would be received by those who would see it, or whether it would be a fruitful exercise for those seeking to learn. However, I knew that it was through education that the work of reconciliation can take place, so I shared the plan, along with the insights that I was learning on my social media accounts, hoping to spark conversation and reflection among those who would see it. By putting the reading plan out into the world, and being vulnerable in my call on those in my network to read along with me, I hoped to encourage vulnerability among those who would read it to enter into the history of residential schools.

Through the process of sharing my insights about this reading plan, I received two types of responses. The first were from those who were seeking resources to learn more about the residential school system in Canada, who were encouraging and willingly shared the resource I had created. The second—albeit a minority—response was from those who were critical of what I was doing, and were uncomfortable with the truth that the Catholic Church played a role in the residential school system. I found this minority critical response to be rather difficult, because it is through coming to terms with this truth, and finding ways of repairing and perhaps recreating relationships between the Church and Indigenous peoples and nations that reconciliation can happen. While there were many who were willing to embrace the vulnerability of entering into the discomfort of accepting the Church's role in the residential school system, there were others who found this very difficult.

Locklin

Andrea Nicole's reading plan, and the different responses she received, reveals something important about vulnerability: namely, that vulnerability may just be the ordinary situation of anyone engaging questions of justice and attempting to build authentic community. One radio documentary about Jean Vanier is titled, "How to Do Ordinary Things." This documentary took its inspiration from Vanier's claim that "Love doesn't mean doing extraordinary or heroic things. It means knowing how to do ordinary things with tenderness."[30] Vanier's insight, perhaps, was his willingness to identify vulnerability as our ordinary human condition, disclosed powerfully in those whose vulnerabilities are most evident and profound. His willingness to exploit vulnerability to gratify his own desires—if not of persons with disabilities, so far as we know, nevertheless of those who placed themselves in his care—was also tragically ordinary, as we have all learned too well in the era of #MeToo.

Freire and hooks, as Andrea Nicole has brought out, also see vulnerability as an ordinary feature of human living, with an important difference. For both of them and beyond them, in the documents of the Truth and Reconciliation Commission of Canada, there is no vulnerability in general. Ordinary vulnerability is always vulnerability to someone or something: vulnerability to the ordinary process of knowledge-creation, vulnerability across boundaries of difference as an ordinary practice of community. In each case, critically, voluntary or intentional vulnerability also implies some form of accountability: to Indigenous peoples enduring the continuing trauma of cultural genocide, to those who have been racialized or marginalized, and ultimately to reality itself. If vulnerability is the ordinary human condition, then it is this ordinary vulnerability, negotiated in structures burdened by legacies of domination, not the highly idealized, spiritualized vulnerability that so often characterized the rhetoric and *persona* of Jean Vanier.[31]

Looking back, I see now that I anticipated something like this conclusion in my 2010 article, which was also my first connection with Patricia Killen. In this article, somewhat surprisingly, I pushed back on the pedagogy of vulnerability advanced by Intercordia. Instead, I suggested that we gain more by emphasizing the civic and academic objectives of a CEL course like Intercordia. And we do this

> ... even if we may also expect that students' most transformative learning will follow less from their success at achieving these objectives than from the uncomfortable insights that come to light when, at least in the terms set for them by the dominant society, they inevitably and providentially fail.[32]

Ordinary vulnerability, on this reading, represents the inevitable result of striving to do good, and failing, and rejoining the ranks of humanity as a result. Vanier did not invent or bestow the power of such vulnerability. He noticed it and gave it a distinctive language, for good and for profound ill. And so, perhaps, the real task of educators—and the fragile *personas* we each construct—is to embrace such ordinary vulnerability in our lived teaching practice, rather than to indulge the grander constructions of a thinker, and predator, like Jean Vanier.

Notes

1. Jay Parini, "Cultivating a Teaching Persona," *Chronicle of Higher Education*, 5 September 1997, https://www.chronicle.com/article/Cultivating-a-Teaching-Persona/99957, Retrieved August 14, 2021.
2. Ibid.

3 Quotation from Natalie Wigg-Stevenson, "When a Trusted Spiritual Leader Turns Out to Be a Sexual Predator," *Sojourners Magazine* 49, no. 7 (2020), https://sojo.net/magazine/july-2020/when-trusted-spiritual-leader-turns-out-be-sexual-predator, accessed September 4, 2021. A good example of the high regard in which Vanier was held can be found in a 2016 Canadian Broadcasting Company documentary, re-released to honor his passing as Ideas, "Remembering Jean Vanier: The Rabbit and the Giraffe," May 7, 2019, *CBC Radio*, https://www.cbc.ca/radio/ideas/remembering-jean-vanier-the-rabbit-and-the-giraffe-part-1-1.3755882, accessed August 31, 2021.
4 Stephen Posner and Stacey Cates-Carney, "Letter to the Federation of L'Arche," February 22, 2020, *L'Arche USA*, https://www.larcheusa.org/news_article/letter-of-stephan-posner-and-stacy-cates-carney-to-the-federation-of-larche/, accessed August 14, 2021.
5 For more information on this continuing initiative, see *Teaching and Learning as Treaty Peoples*, https://treatylearning.ca/, accessed August 31, 2021. Carandang will discuss the Truth and Reconciliation Commission in more detail below.
6 Reid B. Locklin, "Weakness, Belonging and the 'Intercordia Experience': The Logic and Limits of Dissonance as a Transformative Learning Tool," *Teaching Theology & Religion* 13, no. 1 (2010): 3–13.
7 See especially Patricia O'Connell Killen and Eugene Gallagher, "Sketching the Contours of the Scholarship of Teaching and Learning," *Teaching Theology & Religion* 16, no. 2 (2013): 107–24.
8 Quoted in Locklin, "Weakness, Belonging and the 'Intercordia Experience,'" 4.
9 See the website, http://www.reasoningforourhope.ca/.
10 Jean Vanier, *Finding Peace* (Toronto: House of Anansi Press, 2003).
11 It was Jean Vanier, *Becoming Human* (Toronto: House of Anansi Press, 1998).
12 Ibid., 55.
13 Ibid., 56.
14 Ibid., 99–100, 135.
15 Ibid., 153.
16 Truth and Reconciliation Commission, *Honouring the Truth, Reconciling for the Future: Summary of the Final Report of the Truth and Reconciliation Commission of Canada* (Toronto: James Lorimer and Company, 2015), v–vi.
17 Wigg-Stevenson, "Trusted Spiritual Leader."
18 Ibid.
19 The following conversation is based on the exposition in Carolyn Whitney-Brown, *Tender to the World: Jean Vanier, L'Arche, and the United Church of Canada* (Montreal & Kingston: McGill-Queens University Press, 2019), 162–6 (quotation at 163).
20 Ibid., 163.
21 Ibid.,166. Whitney-Brown's study was published in 2019, before the details of Vanier's abuse became widely available.

22. Paulo Freire, with Ana Maria Araújo Freire and Walter de Oliveira, *Pedagogy of Solidarity* (Walnut Creek, CA: Left Coast Press, 2014), 39.
23. bell hooks, *Belonging: a culture of place* (New York and London: Routledge, 2009), 87.
24. Ibid.
25. hooks, *Belonging*, 88.
26. Vanier, *Becoming Human*, 95.
27. Ibid., 11.
28. hooks, *belonging*, 87.
29. Truth and Reconciliation Commission of Canada, *What We Have Learned: Principles of Truth and Reconciliation* (Winnipeg: Truth and Reconciliation Commission of Canada, 2015), https://ehprnh2mwo3.exactdn.com/wp-content/uploads/2021/01/Principles_English_Web.pdf, accessed September 4, 2021. For more information on the reading plan and its context, see Andrea Nicole Carandang, "Starting Over and Taking Action," *Insight Out*, University of St. Michael's College, https://stmikes.utoronto.ca/news/insightout-starting-over-and-taking-action, accessed September 4, 2021.
30. Ideas, "How to Do Ordinary Things," September 2, 2014, *CBC Radio*, https://www.cbc.ca/radio/ideas/jean-vanier-how-to-do-ordinary-things-part-1-1.2914058, accessed August 31, 2021.
31. On this point, see especially Wigg-Stevenson, "Trusted Spiritual Leader."
32. Locklin, "Weakness, Belonging and the 'Intercordia Experience,'" 12.

Bibliography

Carandang, Andrea. "Starting Over and Taking Action." Available online: https://stmikes.utoronto.ca/news/insightout-starting-over-and-taking-action.

Freire, Paulo, Ana Maria Araújo Freire and Walter de Oliveira. *Pedagogy of Solidarity*. California: Left Coast Press, 2014.

hooks, bell. *belonging: a culture of place*. New York and London: Routledge, 2009.

"How to Do Ordinary Things." *CBC Radio*, September 2, 2014. Available online: https://www.cbc.ca/radio/ideas/jean-vanier-how-to-do-ordinary-things-part-1-1.2914058.

Killen, Patricia and Eugene Gallagher. "Sketching the Contours of the Scholarship of Teaching and Learning." *Teaching Theology & Religion* 16, no. 2 (2013): 107–24.

Locklin, Reid. "Weakness, Belonging and the 'Intercordia Experience': The Logic and Limits of Dissonance as a Transformative Learning Tool". *Teaching Theology & Religion* 13, no. 1 (2010): 3–13.

Parini, Jay. "Cultivating a Teaching Persona." Last modified September 5, 1997. Available online: https://www.chronicle.com/article/Cultivating-a-Teaching-Persona/99957.

Posner, Stephen and Stacey Cates-Carney. "Letter to the Federation of L'Arche." Last modified February 22, 2020. Available online: https://www.larcheusa.org/news_article/letter-of-stephan-posner-and-stacy-cates-carney-to-the-federation-of-larche/.

Reasoning for Our Hope: Catholicism and the Liberal Arts, from Newman to Nouwen. Available online: https://www.reasoningforourhope.ca/.

"Remembering Jean Vanier: The Rabbit and the Giraffe." *CBC Radio*, May 7, 2019. Available online: https://www.cbc.ca/radio/ideas/remembering-jean-vanier-the-rabbit-and-the-giraffe-part-1-1.3755882.

Teaching and Learning as Treaty Peoples. Available online: https://treatylearning.ca/.

Truth and Reconciliation Commission of Canada. *Truth and Reconciliation Commission, Honouring the Truth, Reconciling for the Future: Summary of the Final Report of the Truth and Reconciliation Commission of Canada*. Toronto: James Lorimer and Company, 2015.

Truth and Reconciliation Commission of Canada. *What We Have Learned: Principles of Truth and Reconciliation*. Winnipeg: Truth and Reconciliation Commission of Canada, 2015.

Vanier, Jean. *Finding Peace*. Toronto: House of Anansi Press, 2003.

Vanier, Jean. *Becoming Human*. Toronto: House of Anansi Press, 1998.

Whitney-Brown, Carolyn. *Tender to the World: Jean Vanier, L'Arche, and the United Church of Canada*. Montreal & Kingston: McGill-Queens University Press, 2019.

Wigg-Stevenson, Natalie. "When a Trusted Spiritual Leader Turns Out to Be a Sexual Predator." *Sojourners Magazine* 2020 49.7.

12

"Ungrading" and the Unmaking of Professorial Persona

Kathryn D. Blanchard
Alma College (emerita)

Introduction

Countless factors go into a teaching persona, only some of which are within an individual teacher's control. As Patricia Killen and Gene Gallagher note in their oft-cited piece, "Sketching the Contours of the Scholarship of Teaching and Learning in Theology and Religion," many teacher-scholars have wrestled with what to make of this. Attempts at scholarship of teaching and learning often begin with the "generative assumption" that *"the person of the teacher is crucial to the processes of teaching and learning,"* whether one sees a teacher's persona as a matter of authentic self-disclosure, truly indicative of something that goes on inside of them, or as a willful and skillful performance of selective revelation and concealment, a "mask" crafted by the teacher for particular purposes, particular audiences, particular times and places.[1]

As a fifteen-year veteran of full-time teaching, I would never presume to define "persona" once and for all, or to adjudicate the validity among various scholarly definitions. To paraphrase an old religious joke, if you ask two teachers, you'll get three opinions. I will reflect here on just one almost universal—and universally-hated—aspect of every teacher's persona: the role of grader. No matter how hard we might try to weed distrust and control issues out of our teaching, the act of assigning grades haunts our best efforts. Thanks to the educational systems in which we find ourselves, almost no teacher can escape this role or the way it shapes persona. What would avoiding grading altogether do to "the person of the teacher"? Could "ungrading" help "unmake" the authoritarian aspects of it? And would this unmaking be genuinely helpful?

What Is Ungrading?

The practice of "ungrading" came to my attention through the writings of author and filmmaker Jesse Stommel.[2] His prescription was refreshingly direct: "If you're a teacher and you hate grading, stop doing it."[3] *Hey,* I thought in response, *I hate grading! Can I really stop doing it?* It's not that I don't enjoy reading students' thoughts; I often do. It's rather that I dislike the creeping sense that assigning grades is a cheap substitute for whatever it is I'm *supposed* to be doing. Ideally I should be helping students create, as Alfie Kohn writes, "a culture of vibrant intellectual discovery," through well-crafted curriculum, pedagogy, and assessment methods.[4] Grading signifies a lack of trust in the effectiveness of those methods, and at the same time a desire to maintain control; it is a neon light declaring that we the teachers are still the bosses of students' educations, regardless of how students feel.

Grading is, moreover, not a given, but a historical and cultural tradition that may or may not have arisen from a desire to motivate students to do their best work. Perhaps predictably, grading has become "a mechanism for coercion—rewards, but also punishments, with bad grades meant to serve as a socializing source of shame."[5] The most charitable argument is that grading provides feedback to students, letting them know where their work stands in comparison to others', in clearer terms than written or spoken words might convey. But the power of grades doesn't stop in the classroom. For this feedback to be used by outside entities to rank and predict future work, it has to be standardized, like a type of "currency" that stays with students through time and space. In short, "Letter grades do several different things, none of them well, and the result undermines student learning."[6]

For me personally, the worst part is the feeling that I am policing students, forcing them to do things they don't want to do, which takes much of the joy out of teaching. This feels especially wrong when dealing with young adults (mostly ages 18 to 22) who are ostensibly in my classroom voluntarily. I want them to learn happily, not see religious studies as an unpleasant chore. I want them to enjoy the feeling of surprise when they realize something about the world they hadn't known before, or when they discover their own capacity for mind-blowing new thoughts. And I want them not to worry about whether their enjoyment will translate into a letter that impresses. I can still remember the almost physical sensation of my college brain making new connections, within itself and to the world around me. Why would I want to do anything that might hinder students' capacity for that kind of intellectual excitement?

The gospel of ungrading seeks to set us all free—teachers and students alike. Stommel's foundation is: "Start by trusting students."[7] It is a sign of the thoroughness of my indoctrination that, after decades of experience as a student and teacher, this came as such a revolutionary idea. In the fall of 2019, I realized there was very little to lose from a failed experiment. I had tenure. I almost exclusively taught general education courses rather than specialized upper-level seminars. The lone religious studies grade on any given student's transcript was not likely to unfairly make or break their GPA. Even for my few religious studies majors, one semester of self-determined grades couldn't really harm them. There seemed to be low risk to my relaxing about grades, while the potential benefits seemed promising. So I joined the ranks of other teachers inspired to stop grading.[8]

Ungrading, Take One: Fall 2019 (before the Pandemic)

I decided to go all in, incorporating ungrading into all three of my fall courses, for introductory and upper-level students, "one-and-doners" and majors alike. To offer structure, I provided a two-tiered list of assignments. There were a few larger assignments, including essays, exams or quizzes, and minimum attendance, which were "required" for any student who wanted to assign themselves a passing grade. I also provided other assignments, such as individual or group presentations, podcasts, films, campus events, and so on, which were "optional" for those students who were motivated to learn more or who really wanted to feel they had *earned* As. I held office hours for students who wanted to talk, offered regular written feedback on small and large assignments, and required a final meeting with me at the end of the term so they could talk to me directly about the semester grades they were assigning themselves.

The end-of-term opinion surveys confirmed the sense I had gotten along the way that responses to this arrangement were mixed. A few saw it as a major strength of the course. "The non-grading really made the class more enjoyable and made it a lot easier to learn the material from our own perspectives, rather than focusing on memorization;" and "it allows students to take an individualized approach to learning. There was personal growth and gains made and acknowledged throughout the course;" and best of all, "The class was not stressful." For some students, not worrying about grades made it easier to enjoy learning about religions.

But even more students expressed dislike. In my large introductory course (thirty-five to forty students), the comments expressed unease about not knowing exactly where they stood, even though they were assigning their own grades. "Not a fan for the self-grading aspect of the course," wrote one, "because I am someone who usually follows rules to a T and understands exactly how to get the grade that I want and I did not completely understand that in this course." Similarly, "having the no grade policy was a little weird. I had no idea where I was in the course," and "I would much rather know where I stand throughout the semester." At least a few seemed to fear the final exit meeting with me: "I really do not like having to argue why I should get a good grade." Most bluntly, "the class structure was awful." Many of the commenters expressed a wish for more traditional course trappings like quizzes and "real" grades, either for their own peace of mind, or to "force" them or their classmates to do more work.

Another family of complaints I heard was more common among upper-level students, and had to do with the fact that the course "wasn't very challenging," or that it didn't demand enough work. Although I had offered detailed instructions on how to prepare *thoroughly* for class, as well as countless "optional" ways to do more than just the minimum, few students seemed to exert themselves. I can hardly blame them for prioritizing their time, but when asked to motivate themselves, many can't be bothered or literally don't know how, and I had not provided a long enough runway. Understanding the academic culture they bring to learning is part of what it means to cultivate "a deep respect for students," and I should have known better.[9]

Despite students' mixed reactions (and when don't students have mixed reactions?), ungrading was almost perfect *for me*. I felt overwhelming relief in not having to assign letter grades. I learned that what makes grading so odious is how bad it makes me feel. It is toxic, putting me on the defensive against disgruntlement. As a way of protecting myself, my comments are often harsher than necessary just to provide cover. When not assigning grades, I found reading thirty-five essays to be virtually painless; I wasn't filled with the usual dread.[10] I also found it easier to be fully present with students, whether in class or in meetings. Instead of readying for a fight, I could focus on listening and being more humane. I could be there *for them* instead of having to protect myself or some abstract standard of academic rigor. One student who was having a particularly hard semester thanked me, after a meeting about excessive absences, "for just being a nice person." I'm not always a nice person, but when I am, it might be because I am less stressed than usual.

Another benefit is illustrated by the fact that I heard not a single complaint about final course grades. When students get to (or have to) talk with you face to face about the work they've done, the majority are quite honest and realistic in their assessments. I didn't have to cajole most of them into adjusting their grades downward; like Jesse Stommel, I found it more common to push overly humble students upward in their estimations. All in all, my first experiment in ungrading was a mixed success. It was an A+ for me, if only a B or C for the students. I planned to try again with adjustments to make it work well for a higher proportion of students.

Ungrading, Take Two: Fall 2020 (Amid the Pandemic)

I was on sabbatical in the spring of 2020 so was spared the chaos of suddenly pivoting to online teaching. Meanwhile I was myself completing an all-online, asynchronous degree, so the specter of remote teaching was not as mystifying to me as it was for some. My institution opted to have students living on campus and attending class face-to-face wherever possible, with countless adaptations and accommodations. Though conditions were far from ideal, I felt confident about supporting my students, remotely or up close, in whatever capacity they could manage in a time of collective trauma.

Again, I made ungrading part of all of my classes, and I tried hard to communicate more clearly the objectives behind this madness. Anticipating many cases of illness and quarantine, I offered half the class sessions in person, half synchronously online, and I made attendance entirely optional. I rejected "hyflex" models of teaching online and in person simultaneously as unsustainable. Students could live at home, take time off while sick, or learn from the safety of their dorms. I offered both in-person and online office hours. Ungrading was one component in my campaign to keep everyone's stress to a minimum, while "delivering the content" they were paying for—religious studies knowledge and skills, as well as a personalized education where your teacher pays attention to your individual work and knows your name (however difficult with masks on and cameras off).

Given the utter strangeness of the semester, it is perhaps not surprising that most students had nothing at all to say in their opinion surveys about ungrading. Those who did were consistently negative and made clear that they did not fully understand ungrading despite my best efforts. "The grading scale is stressful. It needs to be more clearly outlined that extra credit assignments aren't 'optional' and do count against you if they aren't completed." "Explain the grading process in detail at the beginning of the term." "I think it would be helpful for the optional assignments to improve your grade, and the not optional assignments be the baseline. Extra credit assignments should not account against you." "The amount of extra work was overwhelming at times." These commenters (who filled out these evaluations the week before they had their final meetings with me) were still under the impression that their final grades were in my hands and would be based on standard points and "extra credit," a term I had studiously avoided using. My students again demonstrated "that they've been essentially indoctrinated into habits of mind that might not be so useful when it comes to actual learning," and I had again failed to un-indoctrinate them.[11]

Even as students noted ungrading as a weakness of my courses, many students still had overall positive feelings about their experiences. "Dr. Blanchard allowed us to speak our minds in a judge-free zone. I think that she really did a great job accommodating people in this hard time. I loved the way she ran her class." "The course is set up for you to really learn and understand the material." "We had plenty of time to complete the assignments. Dr. B. responded to emails promptly, which I appreciated. We had many different opportunities to earn points for our overall grade." "Dr. Blanchard is amazing and works well with students, making the course work more fun." "Was very enthusiastic about teaching." "Flexible and engaging material. The course gives you a chance to learn about what interests you in a topic." "This was a perfect class that was challenging but not overwhelming." In giving myself permission not to grade, I believe I was better able to play a helpful role for students learning in a disappointing and stressful semester. By taking myself out of the role of enforcer, I saved my precious energy for preparing lectures, leading discussions, reading their writing, and offering as much feedback, compassion, and encouragement as they could ask for. I could position myself "more as a coach than as a judge."[12]

The heaviest cost of ungrading for me personally was having to assign high final grades to students who had done little or nothing all semester. There were many more of these in 2020 because I could not require face-to-face meetings. As much as I tried not to, I felt angry that they wanted credit for work they hadn't done. Some students held their ground, others backed down, but neither result made me feel good about trying to talk them into a grade closer to the one *I* thought they deserved. It caused me great anxiety to feel I was letting students lie to themselves, and I saw my well-intentioned ungrading attempt being corrupted by the student-as-consumer model. At a basic level, the whole ungrading process did not feel wholly authentic to me. I felt I was "playing at" being a progressive instructor, trying on a persona that didn't quite fit, at least not in my current context and not without laying much more ground work. "We can't simply take away grades without re-examining all of our pedagogical approaches," Stommel rightly notes, "and this work looks different for each teacher, in each context, and with each group of students."[13]

No Take Three: Winter 2021

Exhausted from 2020, and having decided to leave my job at the end of the academic year, I accepted defeat and took a student's advice to "Do grading differently." I switched to a points-based "choose your own adventure" system that students more readily understood, with a mix of possible assignments and due dates.[14] My rationale was twofold: to give students a greater sense of control over their grades (they could easily keep a running tally of points and keep going until they reached the threshold of the grade they wanted), and to free myself from anxiety around the final grade meetings at the end of the term. While this predictably led to some students doing most of their work in the last weeks of the semester, it nevertheless prevented failure among those willing to put in at least some effort. Responses this time were overwhelmingly positive: "I love the way Dr. Blanchard had this class set up as a point system rather than a percentage system. I think it really made it personal for each student to choose how they got their points and I enjoyed that." "I like how our grade is points based, and not percentage based. This really helped me not focus so much on my grade, rather what I was learning and the importance of it." "Loved the choose your own adventure."

More importantly, this method also came closer to having the desired effect of *aligning students' perceptions of my teaching persona with the persona I was going for*: not an enforcer, but an enabler and encourager. The more relaxed I was about grades, the more relaxed they could be about learning. Sample comments reflected this: "I really appreciated how much feedback was given on the assignments. … Getting feedback makes it seem like the assignments were actually important to the instructor as well." "[S]he really focuses on you learning the material rather than quizzing you or testing your knowledge." "Dr. Blanchard … greatly respects students' time and other commitments. She pays attention and genuinely cares about her students and their well-being, and allows you to build your grade in this class based off of what YOU want to take on."[15] In short, these students seemed to see me the way I wanted to be seen.

It still wasn't perfect. Several students skipped one or more of the major assignments which were specially designed to meet course goals, and instead did an abundance of small-point assignments, which were worthwhile but not as carefully targeted to particular outcomes. At worst, I had one student who plagiarized on a major assignment and still somehow managed to get an A in the class by doing enough other assignments—an eventuality I had failed to anticipate or guard against in the syllabus language. Inadvertently I fostered a mindset of "gaming the system" through a continued "misplaced focus on accumulating points rather than on learning."[16] This was a significant failure on my part. But at the end of the term I didn't have to explain grades to anyone. Students knew exactly how many points they had earned, so they sent me not a single complaint email (and really, isn't that every professor's dream?).

Conclusion

I wish I had discovered ungrading earlier in my career so that I'd had more time to figure out how to make it work well. On principle, I really wanted to be a professor who practices ungrading; in practice, I needed a lot more help. But I can at least be grateful that it came to me when it did, near the final stages of my unmaking as a religious studies professor. Letting go of the illusion of control over students' grades also helped me learn to accept my lack of control over bigger things happening in my institution and higher education more broadly.

I think every instructor should try ungrading at least once. Our best teaching requires courage and self-awareness, and ungrading can teach us a lot about ourselves and our personas. It can act like a mirror, and we may not like what we see. I didn't like seeing a teacher who was suspicious of students and self-righteous in my work ethic, and knowing these tendencies is a step to dealing with them. Even though ungrading wasn't a total win, it was an important experiment and step toward unmaking a persona that I needed to outgrow.

Stommel argues that "grades are not a good measure of learning, that they inhibit intrinsic motivation, and that they create a competitive environment between students and hostile relationships between students and teachers."[17] I would add that competition and hostility also inhibit *our* intrinsic motivation for *teaching*. No one goes into teaching because they want to give good grades to smart kids or stick it to bad students. We teach because of love—we loved our teachers, we love learning, and we are excited to share the love with others. To do ungrading well is extremely labor intensive and requires internal and external resources I didn't have, and I have great respect for those who succeed with it. But I don't think professors who ultimately decide against it need to feel inadequate. Teaching the students we have, while being the people we are, resists any universal solution. As long as we are thinking critically, being self-reflective, and putting student learning first, good teachers can come to a variety of conclusions about grading and ungrading.

Notes

1 Patricia O'Connell Killen and Eugene V. Gallagher, "Sketching the Contours of the Scholarship of Teaching and Learning in Theology and Religion," *Teaching Theology & Religion* 16, no. 2 (April 2013): 115–16. Emphasis original.
2 Jesse Stommel, "How to Ungrade," Blog (March 11, 2018): https://www.jessestommel.com/how-to-ungrade/.
3 Ibid. See also Beckie Supiano, "Forget Grades and Turnitin. Start Trusting Students," *Chronicle of Higher Education* (October 27, 2019): https://www.chronicle.com/article/forget-grades-and-turnitin-start-trusting-students/; Colleen Flaherty, "When Grading Less Is More," *Inside Higher Ed* (April 2, 2019): https://www.insidehighered.com/news/2019/04/02/professors-reflections-their-experiences-ungrading-spark-renewed-interest-student.
4 Alfie Kohn, "Foreword," in *Ungrading: Why Rating Students Undermines Learning (and What to Do Instead)*, ed. Susan D. Blum (West Virginia University Press, 2020): https://www.alfiekohn.org/article/ungrading/.
5 Jack Schneider, "Pass-Fail Raises the Question: What's the Point of Grades?" *New York Times* (June 25, 2020): https://www.nytimes.com/2020/06/25/opinion/coronavirus-school-grades.html.
6 Ibid.
7 Jesse Stommel, "Why I Don't Grade" (October 2017): https://www.jessestommel.com/why-i-dont-grade/.
8 For example, Beckie Supiano, "Grades Can Hinder Learning. What Should Professors Use Instead?" *Chronicle of Higher Education* (July 19, 2019): https://www.chronicle.com/article/grades-can-hinder-learning-what-should-professors-use-instead/; Maha Bali, "Ungrading My Class—Reflections on a Second Iteration," *Chronicle of Higher Education* (March 20, 2018): https://www.chronicle.com/blogs/profhacker/ungrading-my-class-reflections-on-a-second-iteration.
9 Sara Goldrick-Rab and Jesse Stommel, "Teaching the Students We Have, Not the Students We Wish We Had," *Chronicle of Higher Education* (December 10, 2018): https://www.chronicle.com/article/teaching-the-students-we-have-not-the-students-we-wish-we-had/.

10 Maha Bali, "Reflections on Ungrading for the 4th time," *Reflections Allowed* Blog (March 23, 2019): https://blog.mahabali.me/pedagogy/reflections-on-ungrading-for-the-4th-time/.
11 Rachel Toor, "The Controversial but Useful Practice of 'Ungrading' in Teaching Writing," *Chronicle of Higher Education* (April 2021): https://www.chronicle.com/article/why-to-use-ungrading-when-you-teach-writing.
12 Blum, cited in Toor.
13 Jesse Stommel, "Grades are Dehumanizing; Ungrading Is No Simple Solution" (June 2021): https://www.jessestommel.com/grades-are-dehumanizing-ungrading-is-no-simple-solution/.
14 Like Theresa MacPhail, I was secretly trying to get them to think by writing, in whatever medium might motivate them: "Tell Me a Smart Story: On Podcasts, Videos, and Websites as Writing Assignments," *Chronicle of Higher Education* (April 9, 2019): https://www.chronicle.com/article/tell-me-a-smart-story-on-podcasts-videos-and-websites-as-writing-assignments/. I also followed Catherine Denial's lead on final assignments: "The Unessay" (April 26, 2019): https://catherinedenial.org/blog/uncategorized/the-unessay/.
15 Full disclosure: NOT all students were so enamored of my persona! One particularly disgruntled student thought I was "immature" and "unprofessional" and made excessive fun of Catholics in my Reformation class.
16 Susan D. Blum "Why Ungrade?: An excerpt from Susan D. Blum's forthcoming book *Ungrading*," Booktimist (March 2021): https://booktimist.com/2020/03/20/why-ungrade-an-excerpt-from-susan-d-blums-forthcoming-book-ungrading/.
17 Stommel, "Grades are Dehumanizing."

Bibliography

Bali, Maha. "Ungrading My Class—Reflections on a Second Iteration." *Chronicle of Higher Education* (March 20, 2018). Available online: https://www.chronicle.com/blogs/profhacker/ungrading-my-class-reflections-on-a-second-iteration.

Bali, Maha. "Reflections on Ungrading for the 4th Time." *Reflections Allowed Blog* (March 23, 2019). Available online: https://blog.mahabali.me/pedagogy/reflections-on-ungrading-for-the-4th-time/.

Blum, Susan D. "Why Ungrade?: An Excerpt from Susan D. Blum's Forthcoming Book Ungrading." *Booktimist* (March 2021). Available online: https://booktimist.com/2020/03/20/why-ungrade-an-excerpt-from-susan-d-blums-forthcoming-book-ungrading/.

Denial, Catherine. "The Unessay" (April 26, 2019): https://catherinedenial.org/blog/uncategorized/the-unessay/.

Flaherty, Colleen. "When Grading Less Is More." Inside Higher Ed (April 2, 2019). Available online: https://www.insidehighered.com/news/2019/04/02/professors-reflections-their-experiences-ungrading-spark-renewed-interest-student.

Goldrick-Rab, Sara and Jesse Stommel. "Teaching the Students We Have, Not the Students We Wish We Had." *Chronicle of Higher Education* (December 10, 2018). Available online: https://www.chronicle.com/article/teaching-the-students-we-have-not-the-students-we-wish-we-had/.

Killen, Patricia O'Connell and Eugene V. Gallagher. "Sketching the Contours of the Scholarship of Teaching and Learning in Theology and Religion." *Teaching Theology & Religion* 16, no. 2 (April 2013).

Kohn, Alfie. "Foreword," *Ungrading: Why Rating Students Undermines Learning (and What to Do Instead)*, edited by Susan D. Blum (West Virginia University Press, 2020). Available online: https://www.alfiekohn.org/article/ungrading/.

MacPhail, Theresa. "Tell Me a Smart Story: On Podcasts, Videos, and Websites as Writing Assignments." *Chronicle of Higher Education* (April 9, 2019). Available online: https://www.chronicle.com/article/tell-me-a-smart-story-on-podcasts-videos-and-websites-as-writing-assignments/.

Schneider, Jack. "Pass-Fail Raises the Question: What's the Point of Grades?" *New York Times* (June 25, 2020). Available online: https://www.nytimes.com/2020/06/25/opinion/coronavirus-school-grades.html.

Stommel, Jesse. "Why I Don't Grade." (October 2017). Available online: https://www.jessestommel.com/why-i-dont-grade/.

Stommel, Jesse. "How to Ungrade." Blog (March 11, 2018). Available online: https://www.jessestommel.com/how-to-ungrade/.

Stommel, Jesse. "Grades Are Dehumanizing; Ungrading Is No Simple Solution" (June 2021). Available online: https://www.jessestommel.com/grades-are-dehumanizing-ungrading-is-no-simple-solution/.

Supiano, Beckie. "Grades Can Hinder Learning. What Should Professors Use Instead?" *Chronicle of Higher Education* (July 19, 2019). Available online: https://www.chronicle.com/article/grades-can-hinder-learning-what-should-professors-use-instead/.

Supiano, Beckie. "Forget Grades and Turnitin. Start Trusting Students." *Chronicle of Higher Education* (October 27, 2019). Available online: https://www.chronicle.com/article/forget-grades-and-turnitin-start-trusting-students/.

Toor, Rachel. "The Controversial But Useful Practice of 'Ungrading' in Teaching Writing." *Chronicle of Higher Education* (April 2021), Available online: https://www.chronicle.com/article/why-to-use-ungrading-when-you-teach-writing.

Tennis, Anyone?

Joanne Maguire
University of North Carolina, Charlotte

Game, set, match. Class, semester, career.

Metaphors for teaching abound. None are perfect, but one is particularly pervasive and problematic: teaching is a vocation. This high-minded framework of "calling" overlooks and undervalues the hard intellectual and physical labor teaching requires. Vocation language seems to make success in teaching seem ineluctable and somehow natural rather than the result of years of concerted effort and practice. This essay suggests that a game of tennis is a more useful metaphor for teaching, as it captures the work, the practice, and the sheer "feel" for the elements of the game that can only come from being both physically and intellectually in it, for any who are inclined to play. The essence of the metaphor, moreover, works as a corrective because it captures the joy of playing with ideas. It also accounts for the exhaustion and exhilaration, which are well-earned, rather than dismissing them as part of the inevitable sacrifices and rewards that result from being called or chosen.

In tennis, your opponent and the ball and the racquet all teach you how to play, repetition after repetition. Almost anyone can play but not everyone can play well. Each rally poses new angles and new approaches, although you've soon also seen them all, in some way, before. You can know the rules but still be surprised. Most teachers enter the profession knowing enough to play a decent game, because they've been spectators (and even on the court, as teaching assistants) for years. They know the rules and etiquette, the basic moves, and they know, at least in theory, how a game might go. But they learn—game after game, set after set—to serve better, to return more accurately, and to be the last one to hit the ball in the court, at least sometimes. A good player adapts to sameness and difference day after day, year after year, even when it's hot and sunny and simply exhausting. Even when, at times, an opponent seems disengaged. Even when nobody reads the syllabus. Even when a strategic lob falls just out of bounds.

Metaphors Matter

Teaching is _____. Of the possible words that could fill that blank, many will be metaphors. Metaphors creep into our language so often that we barely notice them, and some scholars have argued we cannot even think without them.[1] That kind of claim, made popular by George Lakoff and Mark Johnson and repeated often since *Metaphors We Live By* was originally published in 1980, is perhaps overstated, but there is little doubt that metaphors both reflect and shape behavior.[2] Thinking of teaching as transmission, facilitation, or catalysis shapes the way we design curricula and classes.[3] Thinking of a teacher as the "sage on the stage" or the "guide on the side" or a tour guide or a coach helps us structures courses and pedagogical approaches. Thinking of teachers as gardeners, artists, craftspeople, or doctors likewise shapes and is shaped by our approach to our subjects and our students.[4] Thinking of students as vessels to be filled, such as in the banking model derided by Paulo Freire, structures curricula and drives school design. Thinking of schools as factories turning out products based on specifications for the market, or as businesses that must attract consumers and satisfy them, deeply shapes expectations and behavior. Thinking of schools as storage facilities, holding cells for age-segregated groups of people unready for the "real world," helps define teachers' and students' roles within school walls.[5] Some metaphors, when imposed, can be awkward, while similar metaphors, when chosen, can seem uniquely apt.[6]

But what if we think of teachers and students as playing a game, which most can learn and some can excel at? What if good teaching is more about technique and practice than about being chosen to do a particular thing for somewhat mysterious reasons? What happens to our understanding of teaching if we shift our metaphors to the realm of play and away from theology?

Vocation as a Problem

Rarely does one speak of a person who is called to management or who puts heart and soul into custodial work or whose "authentic self" enables the production of computer programs. We don't speak of individuals "called" to coal mining.

And yet teachers are encouraged to understand their work as part of a calling, and, in some ways, a higher calling.[7] This is not without consequence. The word "calling" is from "vocation," a Latin word with deep religious—specifically Christian—roots and resonance.[8] To follow a vocation was to be called away from the "real world" to another, more inward, path devoted to higher pursuits. Those called away were rarely women or laborers: they were those who could, due to the work of others, choose something different. Although those in Christian monastic orders had to do some work for sustenance, connecting that work with either profit or pride were strictly forbidden. This monastic ideal faded a bit in the sixteenth century and beyond, when Protestant theology encouraged individuals to mundane work as divine calling, in which profit if not always pride were embraced.[9] Considering one's job a vocation continues to bear both the positive and negative weight of its original meaning, with the negatives including expectations of self-sacrifice, lack of agency, selfless dedication and service, and even exploitation. A calling may come from without or from within; either way, it is urgent, it is hard to refuse, and it can come with heavy baggage. Infusing some divine calling into one's worldly work assumes chosenness, and chosenness is exclusive. In short, there can be significant moral weight to claiming vocation for teaching.

Some might argue that "vocation" as used today is a secular holdover, like "profession," that has shed its Christian roots. That might be true in some ways, as the use of "vocational" to describe students' approach to education seems far more oriented to the practicality than to service. Yet as Brent Davis rightly notes in *The Inventions of Teaching: A Genealogy*, "… contemporary discussions of teaching rest on sedimented layers of vocabulary that have never been completely dissociated from the sensibilities that gave rise to them."[10] This is borne out in studies of pre-service and in-service K-12 teachers' self-understanding in relation to their work, and it haunts much of the literature devoted to instilling a sense of service and selflessness into teaching. Those sources tend to embrace vocation as an unalloyed positive. For instance, an edited volume titled *Metaphors We Teach By: How Metaphors Shape What We Do in Classrooms* explores religious metaphors in education, but the authors do so without much questioning of the status quo and within a heavily religious framework.[11] The chapter on "Metaphors for Teaching" includes metaphors such as servant, moral friend, and covenanter.[12] One chapter on "Princesses and Superheroes: Metaphors that Work against Wholeness" is attentive to the ways metaphors can shape unhealthy realities, but that sort of insight does not extend to possibly burdensome views of teachers as those who are at the behest of a calling.[13] In each of these sources as well as many others, framing teaching as a vocation is positive, a door to freedom and a fulfillment of authentic selfhood, as shown particularly in the work of Parker Palmer.[14] Like many metaphors, it seems to work well for those for whom it resonates.[15]

And yet there is a dark side to this naïve positive spin. Zygmunt Bauman is perhaps best at calling attention to the privilege of claiming a vocation. As he notes in *Work, Consumerism and the New Poor,* academia is classed as an "elevated" profession, involving "good taste, sophistication, discernment, disinterested dedicated and a lot of schooling."[16] Academia is not anything like, say, coal mining or sheet metal work. As such, it is classed with other work assumed to be fit for the elite. He writes, "Work that is rich in gratifying experience, work as self-fulfilment, work as the meaning of life, work as the core or the axis of everything that counts, as the source of pride, self-esteem, honour and deference or notoriety, in short, work as vocation, has become the privilege of the few; …"[17] Bauman goes on to assert that thinking of one's work as a vocation "carries enormous risks and is a recipe for psychological and emotional disaster."[18] One can extend his critique to show that the notion of vocation in any line of work serves as a gatekeeper against those who might, say, be intellectually or for other reasons drawn to the work rather than "called"—or born—to the work.[19] Vocation is centered on the self but is somehow also selfless, because those who are called often claim they would do the labor even if they were not paid, as such elevated work contains its own intrinsic rewards. It is no accident that teachers are often underpaid and overworked.

The negative impact of theological metaphors might be most problematic for those in humanities disciplines.[20] Theological metaphors are as common to humanities pedagogy as business metaphors are to academic administration literature. For instance, a review of recent literature on the status of the humanities paints teachers as expected to tend to or even battle for the "impoverished" or lost souls of students or of the soul of higher education itself. For some, this mission is salutary and meaningful; for others, as the rise of academic "quit lit" illustrates, the gatekeeping of and prevalent myths around vocation and soul saving can be deal breakers: It is a short step from calling to mission, and this is where "vocation" seems to ask too much, particularly of those who do not see their work in that way. To put it bluntly, vocation indicates privilege as well as chosenness. It also potentially marks one as open to being underpaid, overworked, and undervalued (and responsible for saving a field). Claiming teaching a vocation rather than a job is a convenient way to cover up profit motives for institutions while exhausting those who do the hard physical and intellectual labor of teaching.

Finally, teaching as vocation allows observers and teachers themselves to overlook the importance of practice and technique and continual learning. Teaching as play forefronts personal agency and opens the door to many different types of talent. Thinking about teaching as a game where your eye is on the ball and the ball is in your court can encourage teachers to step onto the court each day, ready to play and to improve based more on the actual context of the court and the variables of the game than on a presumption of chosenness inherent in vocation language.

Enter Tennis

Some metaphors for teaching come from sports or games, and to speak of teachers as players or athletes is never far from the mark.[21] There are several ways this sort of metaphor works as a corrective to vocational language. For instance, athletes are not expected to be chosen but to play with skill and grace and to follow the rules. Athletes might have talent or strengths that make them good fit for a game, but rarely is their sport considered a calling, perhaps, in part, because a sport is rarely a lifelong endeavor. Injury, age, and competition can all cut short any professional athletic career; teachers are assumed to be called and in it for the long haul. There are valid reasons to reject sports metaphors for teaching, particularly when they are adopted to encourage productivity metrics and competition.[22] Yet it seems that the game of tennis, if not the sport, works well for this exercise in rethinking teaching metaphors.

Why tennis? Why not civil engineering or sex?[23] The metaphor has flaws, of course. Tennis can be perceived as elitist, as can higher and private education, and ableist. But it's open to all in most community parks, and it requires minimal equipment. Some people are really bad at it, however much they practice. Others, having played wireball on the streets as a child, come to the game with some skills. But if we take seriously the notion that metaphors shape the ways we act and think in "surprising, hidden, and often oddball ways," then we might do well to attend to how teaching is, at its best, a game, with tennis as a test case.

The etymology of the word speaks volumes: "tennis" comes from the Old French *tenez*, meaning take, receive, or hold. Originally, a server would shout "*Tenez!*" when serving to an opponent.[24] This image of an opening mirrors that of many classroom engagements: "Take," says the teacher. "Receive."

"Hold." But send it back so I can send it back to you with different angles and another spin. The one-on-one nature of a singles tennis game better captures what happens between teacher and student, even in a packed classroom. Some students won't hit a shot back, however gently served. Some are decent servers but don't show much follow through. Others have clearly played a few games, but on a different surface and with other players. Some watch the ball bounce and let it go, while others furiously chase every ball that falls in the court (and even those that are out of bounds). The basics remain the same: the rules, the boundedness of a single court, the relative expertise and finesse of the players, the etiquette, and the subtleties of the game when played again and again with the same players.

Tennis also requires intense focus in the moment, because game play is fast. Overanalysis can mean paralysis. It requires quick decisions, the ability to pivot when needed, and the ability to handle stress. Anyone can pick up a racquet and a ball, but not everyone can understand at once how to handle the many changing but predictable-within-the-context variables. That comes with time. As David Foster Wallace notes in his ode to tennis,

> Given a net that's three feet high (at the center) and two players in (unrealistically) fixed positions, the efficacy of one single shot is determined by its angle, depth, pace, and spin. And each of these determinants is itself determined by still other variables – i.e., a shot's depth is determined by the height at which the ball passes over the net combined with some integrated function of pace and spin, with the ball's height over the net itself determined by the player's body position, grip on the racket, height of backswing and angle of racket face, as well as the 3-D coordinates through which the racket face moves during that interval in which the ball is actually on the strings.[25]

This passage depicts tennis as a game of physics involving many but not infinite variables. If we replace the physics with pedagogical elements, we see the many but not infinite variables in an undergraduate classroom:

Given a syllabus that includes five books and a selection of primary sources and a teacher and a student, the efficacy of a single pedagogical approach is determined by its angle, depth, pace, and spin. And each of these determinants is itself determined by still other variables—that is, a class' depth is determined by its level combined with some integrated function of context and discipline, with teacher and student success itself determined by their positions and assumptions, preparation, connection of ideas and theories, as well as the classroom space through which the ideas move …

This maps well onto the complexity of any given class on any given campus on any given day as well as the sweep of a teaching career. The beauty of tennis, for Foster, arises from the mix of these changing variables, from the talents and technique of the players but also and importantly from repetition and difference within bounds. Tennis is challenging, often sweaty work filled with unconscious, in-the-moment responses to what the other player has done. The feel for the game improves the longer one plays on a given court or classroom. Put any good hard surface player on a grass or clay court and it will take them a bit to adjust. Context matters.

This metaphor shows how content and pedagogical technique, symbolized by the ball making its way back and forth due to effort on both sides, are in a constant state of being mastered on both sides. When it comes down to it, teachers send balls over the net to their students and hope they send them back, perhaps with added spin. Some balls never come back. Some are lets, just barely scraping by. Some are returned with accuracy and grace. Sometimes, even the best teacher is driven by frustration to quoting John McEnroe at Wimbledon: "You *cannot* be serious." Teaching is, in short, about technique and practice, not whether or not an authentic self is called to serve. It is about drive to improve, whether or not one is called to it. Any individual teacher's game, played over a career, also shows discrete improvements and major leaps over time. No player can work on all skills at once. Some are better at backhand, while others struggle to serve even one ace. Knowing the rules of the game is essential, and knowing how the opponent plays is important as well. One learns how to work with those contingencies to get into the zone.

In this replacement metaphor, then, each classroom session is a rally and each semester is a match, over which time both sides learn the moves of the other and learn to anticipate what is expected and what they can do with the bounds of the court. The derivative metaphors are many. Some shots are straight down the line; others are drop shots the receiver just can't reach. Some answers are straightforward volleys made without moving; others can take you across the court. Players will make unforced errors, perhaps more often than they'd like. The metaphor can be extended, to include team teaching (doubles); to class outlines written on a single Post-It note (baseline, sidelines, and service box); to a series of double faults when nothing quite seems to work (or the lingering death tiebreak). To think of a teaching career as a series of rallies that comprise games and games that comprise sets and sets that comprise matches (class, semester, career) is to reframe the job as one that is about both hard work and finesse, not privilege and some innate sense of chosenness. Just play each game as best you can and go home for a shower, a cold drink, and a good meal. That should be enough.

Notes

1 Raymond Williams, *Keywords: A Vocabulary of Culture and Society* (London: HarperCollins, 1976).
2 George Lakoff and Mark Johnson. *Metaphors We Live By* (Chicago: University of Chicago Press, 2003).
3 Ken Badley and Jaliene Hollabaugh, "Metaphors for Teaching and Learning," 2012. (*Faculty Publications–* School of Education, George Fox University. Paper 49). http://digitalcommons.georgefox.edu/soe_faculty/49, 52.
4 Sophie S. Park, et al. "Forum: Quilting as Metaphor for Theological Education," *Teaching Theology & Religion* 22, no. 2 (2019): 143–58.
5 The education world has long been interested in its own metaphors. See, for instance, H. Kliebard, *Curriculum and Evaluation* (Berkeley: McCuthen Publishing, 1977), and A. M. Martinez, N. Sauleda, and L. G. Huber, "Metaphors as Blueprints of Thinking about Teaching and Learning," *Teaching and Teacher Education* 17 (2011): 965–77. One fundamental study is Stanley D. Ivie, *On the Wings of Metaphor* (San Francisco: Caddo Gap Press, 2003).

   See also T. Patchen and T. Crawford, "From Gardeners to Tour Guides: The Epistemological Struggle Revealed in Teacher-Generated Metaphors for Teaching," *Journal of Teacher Education* 62, no. 3 (2011): 286–98, and C. Rosaen and S. Florio-Ruane, "The Metaphors by Which We Teach: Experience, Metaphor, and Culture in Teacher Education," In *Handbook of Teacher Education: Enduring Questions in Changing Contexts*, ed. M. Cochran-Smith, S. Feiman-Nemser, and D. J. McIntyre (New York and London: Routledge, Taylor and Francis and the Association of Teacher Educators [ATE], 2008), 706–31. Finally, see an interesting taxonomy in David D. Chen, "A Classification System for Metaphors about Teaching," *Journal of Physical Education, Recreation, and Dance* 74, no. 2 (February 2003): 24–31.
6 See, for instance, Amy Carr and John K. Simmons, "Between Guru and Deceiver? Responding to Unchosen Metaphors in the Religious Studies Classroom," *TTR* 13, no. 2 (2010): 156–68; Emily O. Gravett's "'Who Am I?': The Biblical Moses as a Metaphor for Teaching," *Teaching Theology & Religion* 18, no. 2 (2015): 159–69; and Kim Paffenroth's "The Best Teacher Is Like a Famous Mage Everyone Knows—Just Not Any of Your Favorites," *Teaching Theology & Religion* 20, no. 3 (2017): 257–62.
7 The use of the "higher calling" seems reflexive and unconsidered in many works. See, for instance, Scott C. Beardsley, *Higher Calling: The Rise of Nontraditional*

Leaders in Academia (Charlottesville, VA: University of Virginia Press, 2017) and Johanna Hakala, "The Future of the Academic Calling? Junior Researchers in the Entrepreneurial University," *Higher Education* 57, no. 2 (2008): 173–90; and Andrew T. Kemp, ed. *Dignity of the Calling: Educators Share the Beginnings of Their Journeys* (Charlotte, NC: Information Age Publishing, 2019).

8   For a general overview, see Herbert A. Applebaum, *The Concept of Work: Ancient, Medieval, Modern* (New York: State University of New York Press, 1992). An interesting collection of texts about work can be found in Gilbert C. Mailaender, ed. *Working: Its Meanings and Its Limits* Ethics of Everyday Life Series. South Bend, IN: Notre Dame University Press, 2000.

9   Jane Dawson, "A History of Vocation: Tracing a Keyword of Work, Meaning, and Moral Purpose," *Adult Education Quarterly* 55, no. 3 (May 2005): 220–32.

10 Brent Davis, *The Inventions of Teaching: A Genealogy* (New York: Taylor & Francis, 2004). Available online: https://ebookcentral.proquest.com/lib/uncc-ebooks/reader.action?docID=335503.

11 Ken Badley and Harro Van Brummelen, *Metaphors We Teach By: How Metaphors Shape What We Do in Classrooms* (Eugene, OR: Wipf & Stock, 2012).

12 Tim Wineberg, "Metaphors for Teaching," in *Metaphors We Teach By* ed. Badley and Van Brummelen (Eugene, OR: Wipf & Stock, 2012), 32–51.

13 Allyson Jule, "Princesses and Superheroes: Metaphors That Work against Wholeness," in *Metaphors We Teach By*, ed. Badley and Van Brummelen, (Eugene, OR: Wipf & Stock, 2012), 109–19.

14 Parker J. Palmer. *The Courage to Teach: Exploring the Inner Landscape of a Teacher's Life*, 20th Anniversary Edition. 1st edn. (San Francisco, CA: Jossey-Bass, 2007). See also Eila Estoa, Raija Erkkila, and Leena Syrjla, "A Moral Voice of Vocation in Teachers' Narratives," *Teachers and Teaching: Theory and Practice* 9, no. 3 (2003): 239–56.

15 For an interesting interpretation of Weber on scholarly work, see Chad Wellmon's "The Scholar's Vocation" in *Aeon*. https://aeon.co/essays/weber-diagnosed-the-ills-of-the-modern-university-and-prescribed-the-cure. Accessed November 27, 2020.

16 Zygmunt Bauman. *Work, Consumerism, and the New Poor* (Buckinghamshire, UK: Open University Press, 1998), 33.

17 Ibid., 35.

18 Ibid.

19 On this, see the work of Robert V. Bullough, Jr., "Exploring Personal Teaching Metaphors in Preservice Teacher Education," *Journal of Teacher Education* 42, no. 1 (1991): 43–51 and "Personal History and Teaching Metaphors: A Self-Study of Teaching as Conversation," *Teacher Education Quarterly* 21, no. 1 (1994): 107–20. See also Anne E. McEwan, "Do Metaphors Matter in Higher Education?" *Journal of College and Character* 8, no. 2 (2007): 1–8. doi: 10.2202/1940-1639.1166.

20 David S. Cunningham, ed. *Vocation across the Academy: A New Vocabulary for Higher Education*. Published to Oxford Scholarship Online, January 2017. doi: 10.1093/acprof:oso/9780190607104.001.0001. The most relevant essay here is that by Mark U. Edwards, "Religion, Reluctance, and Conversations about Vocation." doi: 10.1093/acprof:oso/9780190607104.003.0013.

21 Evan H. Offstein and Christopher P. Neck, "From 'Acing the Test' to 'Touching Base': The Sports Metaphor in the Classroom," *Business Communication Quarterly* 66, no. 4 (2003): 23–5.

22 Bourree Lam, "Against Sports Analogies at Work," *The Atlantic* June 17, 2016. https://www.theatlantic.com/business/archive/2016/06/sport-metaphors/487433/ and Bill Taylor, "Why Sports Are a Terrible Metaphor for Business," *Harvard Business Review*. February 3, 2017. https://hbr.org/2017/02/why-sports-are-a-terrible-metaphor-for-business?ab=at_articlepage_relatedarticles_horizontal_slot3.

23 Thor-André Skrefsrud, "Teachers as Intercultural Bridge-Builders: Rethinking the Metaphor of Bridge-Building," *Teaching Theology & Religion* 23, no. 3 (2020): 151–62 and See Teresa Delgado, "Metaphor for Teaching: Good Teaching Is Like Good Sex," *Teaching Theology & Religion* 18, no. 3 (July 2015): 224–32.

24 Tennis has monastic origins, as its ancestor was a game of handball played in monastic cloisters.

25 David Foster Wallace, "The String Theory," in *Esquire*, September 17, 2008. https://www.esquire.com/sports/a5151/the-string-theory-david-foster-wallace/, accessed September 17, 2021.

Bibliography

Applebaum, Herbert A. *The Concept of Work: Ancient, Medieval, Modern*. New York: State University of New York Press, 1992.

Badley, Ken and Harro Van Brummelen. *Metaphors We Teach By: How Metaphors Shape What We Do in Classrooms*. Eugene, OR: Wipf & Stock, 2012.

Badley, Ken and Jaliene Hollabaugh. "Metaphors for Teaching and Learning." *Faculty Publications—College of Education*, George Fox University. Paper 49. 2012. http://digitalcommons.georgefox.edu/soe_faculty/49.

Bauman, Zygmunt. *Work, Consumerism, and the New Poor*. Buckinghamshire, UK: Open University Press, 1998.

Beardsley, Scott C. *Higher Calling: The Rise of Nontraditional Leaders in Academia*. Charlottesville, VA: University of Virginia Press, 2017.

Bullough, Robert V., Jr. "Exploring Personal Teaching Metaphors in Preservice Teacher Education." *Journal of Teacher Education* 42, no. 1 (1991): 43–51.

Bullough, Robert V., Jr. "Personal History and Teaching Metaphors: A Self-Study of Teaching as Conversation." *Teacher Education Quarterly* 21, no. 1 (1994): 107–20.

Carr, Amy and John K. Simmons. "Between Guru and Deceiver? Responding to Unchosen Metaphors in the Religious Studies Classroom." *Teaching Theology & Religion* 13, no. 2 (2010): 156–68.

Chen, David D. "A Classification System for Metaphors about Teaching." *Journal of Physical Education, Recreation, and Dance* 47, no. 2 (February 2003): 24–31.

Davis, Brent. *The Inventions of Teaching: A Genealogy*. New York: Taylor & Francis, 2004.

Dawson, Jane. "A History of Vocation: Tracing a Keyword of Work, Meaning, and Moral Purpose." *Adult Education Quarterly* 55, no. 3 (May 2005): 220–32.

Delgado, Teresa. "Metaphor for Teaching: Good Teaching Is Like Good Sex." *Teaching Theology & Religion* 18, no. 3 (2015): 224–32.

Edwards, Mark U. "Religion, Reluctance, and Conversations about Vocation." In *Vocation across the Academy: A New Vocabulary for Higher Education*, edited by David S. Cunningham. Published to Oxford Scholarship Online, January 2017. doi: 10.1093/acprof:oso/9780190607104.001.0001.

Estoa, Elia, Raija Erkkila, and Leena Syrjla. "A Moral Voice of Vocation in Teachers' Narratives." *Teachers and Teaching: Theory and Practice* 9, no. 3 (2003): 239–56.

Gravett, Emily O. "'Who Am I?': The Biblical Moses as a Metaphor for Teaching." *Teaching Theology & Religion* 18, no. 2 (2015): 159–69.

Hakala, Johanna. "The Future of the Academic Calling? Junior Researchers in the Entrepreneurial University." *Higher Education* 57, no. 2 (2008): 173–90.

Ivie, Stanley D. *On the Wings of Metaphor*. San Francisco: Caddo Gap Press, 2003.

Jule, Allyson. "Princesses and Superheroes: Metaphors That Work against Wholeness." In *Metaphors We Teach By*, edited by Badley and Van Brummelen, (Eugene, OR: Wipf & Stock, 2012), 109–19.

Kemp, Andrew T. ed. *Dignity of the Calling: Educators Share the Beginnings of Their Journeys*. Charlotte, NC: Information Age Publishing, 2019.

Kliebard, H. *Curriculum and Evaluation*. Berkeley: McCuthen Publishing, 1977.

Lakoff, George, and Mark Johnson. *Metaphors We Live By*. Chicago: University of Chicago Press, 2003.

Mailaender, Gilbert C., ed. *Working: Its Meanings and Its Limits*. Ethics of Everyday Life Series. South Bend, IN: Notre Dame University Press, 2000.

Martinez, A. M., N. Sauleda, and L. G. Huber. "Metaphors as Blueprints of Thinking about Teaching and Learning." *Teaching and Teacher Education* 17 (2011): 965–77.

McEwan, Anne E. "Do Metaphors Matter in Higher Education?" *Journal of College and Character* 8, no. 2 (2007): 1–8. doi: 10.2202/1940-1639.1166.

Offstein, Evan H. and Christopher P. Neck. "From 'Acing the Test' to 'Touching Base': The Sports Metaphor in the Classroom." *Business Communication Quarterly* 66, no. 4 (2003): 23–5.

Paffenroth, Kim. "The Best Teacher Is Like a Famous Mage Everyone Knows—Just Not Any of Your Favorites." *Teaching Theology & Religion* 20, no. 3 (2017): 257–62.

Palmer, Parker J. *The Courage to Teach: Exploring the Inner Landscape of a Teacher's Life*. San Francisco, CA: Jossey-Bass, 2007.

Park, Sophie, et al. "Forum: Quilting as Metaphor for Theological Education." *Teaching Theology & Religion* 22, no. 2 (2019): 143–58.

Patchen, T. and T. Crawford. "From Gardeners to Tour Guides: The Epistemological Struggle Revealed in Teacher-Generated Metaphors for Teaching." *Journal of Teacher Education* 62, no. 3 (2011): 286–98.

Rosaen, C. and S. Florio-Ruane, "The Metaphors by Which We Teach: Experience, Metaphor, and Culture in Teacher Education." In *Handbook of Teacher Education: Enduring Questions in Changing Contexts*, edited by M. Cochran-Smith, S. Feiman-Nemser, and D.J. McIntyre. New York and London: Routledge, Taylor and Francis and the Association of Teacher Educators (2008), 706–31.

Skrefsrud, Thor-André. "Teachers as Intercultural Bridge-Builders: Rethinking the Metaphor of Bridge-Building." *Teaching Theology & Religion* 23, no. 3 (2020): 151–62.

Taylor, Bill. "Why Sports Are a Terrible Metaphor for Business." *Harvard Business Review*. February 3, 2017. https://hbr.org/2017/02/why-sports-are-a-terrible-metaphor-for-business?ab=at_articlepage_relatedarticles_horizontal_slot3.

Wallace, David Foster. "The String Theory." *Esquire*, September 17, 2008. https://www.esquire.com/sports/a5151/the-string-theory-david-foster-wallace/.

Williams, Raymond. *Keywords: A Vocabulary of Culture and Society*. London: HarperCollins, 1976.

Wineberg, Tim. "Metaphors for Teaching." In *Metaphors We Teach By*, edited by Badley and Van Brummelen, 32–51. Eugene, OR: Wipf & Stock, 2012.

Part Three

Place

14

Who Is in the Chair? The Professor Faces the Classroom

Arthur M. Sutherland
Loyola University Maryland

I learned much from the concept and practice hospitality of Patricia Killen and Eugene Gallagher while participating in workshops they led at the Wabash Center for Teaching and Learning in Theology and Religion. Killen's insistence that professors engage in "midrange reflection"[1] and Gallagher's guidance on how to create a welcoming space[2] are pillars in my professorate. For both Gallagher and Killen knowing the student is at the center of hospitable pedagogy.[3] I have now had several years to reflect on my experience, and I wish to build on the foundation I gained from them.

Hospitable pedagogy begins when the professor walks into the classroom at the start of the semester. Normally, the study plan for the next several months is fixed and sure. The syllabus outlines the intended topics, establishes a rhythm, and presents the tools a student will need to navigate through new terminology and unexplored theories. Most importantly, the syllabus aligns with the professor's learning objectives. Many professors will readily admit that syllabus design is the most exciting and fulfilling part of pre-semester activities. Even after twenty years of teaching, the feeling one has from the warm papers that click out of the copy machine in early September, so neatly collated and stapled, is akin to the comfort of puppies. There are of course numerous positions on the construction of syllabi. Drawing on a wide field of published articles, Blair Thompson concludes that the syllabus is a symbol of the teacher's persona that tells the sound of the course.[4] While Michael Woolcock reminds us, "Even the dullest lecturer can be an effective teacher when they give extended and thoughtful consideration to how and why their courses are set up."[5]

Although careful and deliberate syllabus construction is vital, one must also consider the range of students sitting in the classroom eagerly awaiting, or dreading, the arrival of the professor whose backpack is full of newly printed expectations. When the professor arrives and observes those sitting in the facing chairs, he or she can only conjecture what students are feeling. Some of them, ever eager and sitting at chair's edge, are anxiously plundering the internet looking for information about their teacher or texting former roommates whom they recall had the same professor three semesters ago. Some of them wandered into the room and are suddenly aware that this is not just the wrong day and the wrong section, but the wrong class altogether and are preparing themselves mentally for the embarrassment due them when they excuse themselves and grope for the exit. But students are only part of the story. The professor ought to also engage in self-examination. What ought to matter to the professor is understanding that good teaching goes beyond remembering that Aimee with two "ee's" is a different woman than Aimme with two "mm's." The professor's self-examination must include reflection on the attitudes and commitments that students bring with them into the classroom. This brief essay argues that professors need to recognize that who they face is more important than the well-constructed syllabus and its tidy rows of reading assignments. Simply put, the professor needs to ask each time they enter the classroom, "Who is the student sitting in the chair?"

Who Is in the Chair?

In my view, there are nine types of students in our classrooms; I will define each type and offer illustrations.

I Don't Want to Know. This student is in the classroom reluctantly. Perhaps the course is part of the college's liberal arts core or a public school's general education requirements. The student may be resentful that their time is being used in this way when other "more important" courses are on the dock, typically courses needed to complete a major. Thus, the subject matter is of no use to them; it is a frivolity at best and an irritant at worst. On the other hand, the student might be marginally interested in the course but resents or is begrudging toward the professor for reasons that include accent, personality, or social-political views. This subtype might be saying, "I don't want to know from you." In any case, the student's openness to learning is blocked by his prejudice.

I Don't Know That I Don't Know. Many students come into the classroom with previous experience with the subject matter but cannot appreciate that they have knowledge gaps and blanks. This happens quite often to me. Many of my students have had four, six, ten years of religion classes because they attended Catholic parochial schools. In their view, the material I intend to share with them is redundant. What could I possibly say that is new and different? This problem is most acute in the early days of the semester, which are often given over to orientation and ramping up rather than the discovery of new knowledge. The student has not yet encountered the complexity offered in a college course. In their mind, they have seen it all and done it all. It has never occurred to them that the course in religion they took in high school is not the same as their college course in theology.

I Don't Know. At this point on the continuum, the student is expressing either honesty or bewilderment. The student has never thought about the subject but is not resistant to learning. I'd be careful about saying that this student is a *tabula rasa*. Knowledge is cumulative and they may know more than they think they do. Yet we can certainly say that if the student takes a glance at the index or glossary of terms, an admission that they are rookies with this material is likely to follow. This does not make them feel good.

I Have Obstacles to Knowing. Blockades to knowing are constructed from many different materials. Some students are not able to afford class texts. Some have food and housing insecurity. Some are feeling the pull to change schools or majors or vocational commitments. Some are first-generation students and don't have a family member familiar with terms like office hours, academic advising, and credits. Some first-year students are fretful because attending my class on Tuesdays at 9:25 AM restricts their ability to support their family *now* no matter how many allurements are presented to graduating seniors by the tasseled shoe recruiters flown in by corporate to meet them in the career center.

I Compromise with Obstacles to Knowing. Many students will deal with obstacles by adopting an attitude of "I will just do the best I can." While this is admirable, it can mean that a student suffers in silence. An otherwise "A" student accepts becoming a "B" student because they are not able to consistently borrow the textbook or count on having a stable Wi-Fi connection at home. The professor, unaware of the leak in the bottom of the barrel, keeps pouring in water while the student uses more fingers to plug the holes. A few students will decide that "it is what it is" and simply decide to give up seeking a solution. Freedom to learn comes with a price, and this price is not always affordable.

I Am Removing Obstacles to Knowing. At this point of the continuum, we find students become creative and resilient. The student whose home is noisy and crowded may commit herself to waking up early and being first in line when the library opens its doors. The dyslexic student may seek diagnosis and support. Having been caught unprepared for yet another quiz, the student resolves emerges to yellow highlight each due date. This student is engaged with learning and taking action to face their problems head-on. This is a responsible and creative learner who is determined to succeed.

I Can Connect What I Know Now to What I Already Knew. When a student reaches this point, it is the beginning of transformative learning. In a class on Reformation theology, the student comes into the course knowing some rough facts about Martin Luther. But because of new information, they can appreciate how Luther's wedding to Katharina von Bora changed theological perspectives on marriage, the household, and children. As we consider this student, we are reminded of Jack Mezirow's theory that a student's engagement in critical reflection on their experiences leads to a transformation of perspective.[6]

I Can Make Creative Use of What I Know. The next stage of learning is experimental. The student is not just familiar with ideas, and not just able to make connections between ideas, but able to extend their learning into new fields.[7] To return to my example of the student learning about Reformation theology, Luther's marriage becomes the locus for inquiries into new lines of thought driven not just by the professor's enthusiasm but by a flowering intellectual curiosity. The question of "what if" starts to strike the learning bell. Moreover, the student stands at the opening of interdisciplinary learning. Luther's comment, "The Christian is supposed to love his neighbor and since his wife is his nearest neighbor, she should be his deepest love" can become an avenue for the student's self-driven dialogue between theology and psychology. This is the stage when thesis and argument emerge.

I Want to Know More. We have now reached the last student. My lectures, the ones that I thought were full meals, are for this student, just tasty snacks. They stay after class and corner me. Hunger and thirst impel the student into the library shelves for deeper nourishment. They start to push back against the received tradition. They become wary of the merely new. They want to dare assumptions and form judgments. Innovation and collaboration matter to them.

So What Do We Make of This?

If I am right, that the teacher in the classroom faces roughly nine types of learners, then some broad musing about how to interpret this assertion is important in creating a hospitable pedagogy. The students are guests and knowing their attitudes allows me to think about how to serve them.

The first item to consider is that a classroom does not have to have all nine types present. This is a simple enough observation. Indeed, depending upon the course level and the requirements for enrollment, the class mix could be skewed in one direction or another.

Second, all students, the best and the most recalcitrant, are dynamic. I must not forget the meaning of Heraclitus's river. The student has changed from when I talked with them last semester, last month, last week.

Third, I must as a teacher have appropriate tools at hand. Some students need a bop from my cudgel; others, the stroke of my feather brush.

Fourth, it does me no harm, and frankly some good, to meet with each student early in the semester. Admittedly, this is difficult for the largest classes. But for smaller classes, for first-year seminars, the type of early semester handout advocated by Maura Reynolds has the potential to do the teacher a world of good at the investment of a small amount of time. She describes her questionnaire, with unobtrusive questions like, "What were your favorite classes in high school?" and "What do you intend to accomplish in college?" and "What is your greatest academic concern?," as opportunities for an advisor (in this case the professor) to provide encouragement and support. Open-ended and relationship-building questions allow the professor "to walk alongside the student as good company."[8] When I shared these observations with a colleague, he added questions like "What would get you excited about learning?" and "How could this class be useful to you?" and "When you think about learning, what has made the difference for you?"[9]

Showing the Teacher's Home

My definition of hospitable pedagogy is analogical. Hospitable pedagogy is akin to inviting someone into your home. In this case, home is the teacher's classroom. Hospitable pedagogy consists of a series of actions that begins with greeting and concludes with sending. First, hospitable pedagogy takes full measure of what college catalogs typically call "course offerings." This list, maintained by the Records office, gives descriptions of the instruction available to students. No college, of course, offers every class, every semester, but the college is telling students what the provost, the dean, the chair, and the professor have all agreed to extend as possibilities. When students come into my classroom, I am offering my class in conjunction with dozens, if not hundreds, of other courses.

Second, when someone accepts my offer of hospitality to come into my home, I must open the door and let them inside. In hospitable pedagogy, "opening the door" means greeting students and letting them know that they are welcome to step inside my learning space. I must admit that I have never thanked a class for coming to me for instruction. But I must wonder how that small gesture would change the attitudes of the reluctant learner.

Third, a gracious host will typically invite their guests to explore parts of their home. Not all rooms, of course, but those spaces in the home where love, and warmth, and acceptance are natural. I might invite someone to view the pictures on my fireplace mantel. I take them to the garden. I might show off my library. Similarly, hospitable pedagogy welcomes students to explore the corners and contours of my plan of study for them. It lifts out why a reading matters before the assignment starts.

Fourth, the hospitable teacher will offer guests refreshments. In my view, this is done in the classroom by showing students how insights fit together to create something new. For example, it might be achieved by asking students to overlay the conversion experience of Malcolm X with the conversions of St. Paul and Jarena Lee. Perhaps this can be done, perhaps, by reviewing some internet trend that seems out the bounds of normal class activity, but with careful consideration yields interesting results. Asking, "Have you ever thought about?" brings relief to the course that is veering toward the mundane.

Finally, like the good host sending guests away at the end of their stay, the practitioner of hospitable pedagogy will consciously supply their students with sustenance for their journey. For example, each year I teach "Introduction to Theology." My university also requires that students take a second theology course to fulfill their core requirements. My introductory course is roughly divided into thirds: the Bible, the historical development of theological ideas, and some sort of contemporary theological concern. But in my view, my work is not done adequately if I have not spent some time engaging my student's imagination on what their second course could provide them beyond acquiring three more credits. It would be best if I selected a few electives and discussed how each can expand their excitement about what they learned from me.

In reflection on this essay, it now occurs to me that what holds hospitable pedagogy together is the ability of the teacher to engage a student's imagination. The difference between the student who says, "I don't want to know" and the student who says, "I want to know more" is curiosity. Without exception, every pen is picked up and every keyboard is clacked when I tell students, "This will be on the test." But very little of that statement moves the student away from simply compiling information and toward cultivating transformation. However, when I build into the course statements about how my knowledge became *useful to me*, both hands and minds are engaged. Many years ago, I had a professor of New Testament, Abraham Malherbe, who shared with me that the best class he ever had was a seminar in the Netherlands that examined the theology found in the critical apparatus of 1 Corinthians. This work involves examining manuscript fragments, the use of phrases and terms in early church history, and teasing apart what amounts to lexicographical fistfights. It seemed dreadfully dull to me at the time. I still don't have much use for it. But, his remark, an aside really, flush with remembered excitement, was an invitation to explore not what mattered to him, but to me. This is hospitable pedagogy and is illustrative of Killen and Gallagher's cross-campus appeal and explains why their courses were so heavily subscribed.

It seems somehow unfortunate that college students are not afforded a homeroom period like those offered in middle and high school. There is no place for them to regularly gather and converse. Considering this, making the classroom a place for hospitable pedagogy seems even more needed.

Notes

1   Patricia O'Connell Killen, "Midrange Reflection: The Underlying Practice of Wabash Center Workshops, Colloquies, and Consultations," *Teaching Theology & Religion* 10, no. 3 (2007).
2   Eugene V. Gallagher, "Welcoming the Stranger," *Teaching Theology & Religion* 10, no. 3 (2007).
3   Carolyn M. Jones Medine, "*Hospes*: The Wabash Center as a Site of Transformative Hospitality," *Teaching Theology & Religion* 10, no. 3 (2007).
4   Blair Thompson, "The Syllabus as a Communication Document: Constructing and Presenting the Syllabus," *Communication Education* 56, no. 1 (2007).
5   Michael J. V. Woolcock, *Constructing a Syllabus: A Handbook for Faculty, Teaching Assistants and Teaching Fellows*, 3rd rev. edn. (Providence, RI: Brown University, 2006), 9.
6   Jack Mezirow, *Transformative Dimensions of Adult Learning* (San Francisco: Jossey-Bass, 1991).
7   C. Susan Fostaty Young and Robert J. Wilson, *Assessment and Learning: The ICE Approach* (Winnipeg, Ontario: Portage & Main Press, 2000).

8   Maura Reynolds, "Advising Students through First-Year Transitions," in *Academic Advising and the First College Year*, ed. Jennifer R Fox and Holly E Martin (National Resource Center for The First-Year Experience and Students in Transition, 2017).

9   I wish to thank Drew Leder, of my university's philosophy department, for his fruitful conversation with me.

Bibliography

Fostaty Young, C. Susan, and Robert J. Wilson. *Assessment and Learning: The Ice Approach*. Winnipeg, Ontario: Portage & Main Press, 2000.

Gallagher, Eugene V. "Welcoming the Stranger." *Teaching Theology & Religion* 10, no. 3 (2007): 137–42.

Killen, Patricia O'Connell. "Midrange Reflection: The Underlying Practice of Wabash Center Workshops, Colloquies, and Consultations." *Teaching Theology & Religion* 10, no. 3 (2007): 143–9.

Medine, Carolyn M. Jones. "*Hospes*: The Wabash Center as a Site of Transformative Hospitality." *Teaching Theology & Religion* 10, no. 3 (2007): 150–5.

Mezirow, Jack. *Transformative Dimensions of Adult Learning*. San Francisco: Jossey-Bass, 1991.

Reynolds, Maura. "Advising Students through First-Year Transitions." In *Academic Advising and the First College Year*, edited by Jennifer R Fox and Holly E Martin, 45–8. Columbia, SC: National Resource Center for The First-Year Experience and Students in Transition, 2017.

Thompson, Blair. "The Syllabus as a Communication Document: Constructing and Presenting the Syllabus." *Communication Education* 56, no. 1 (2007): 54–71.

Woolcock, Michael J. V. *Constructing a Syllabus: A Handbook for Faculty, Teaching Assistants and Teaching Fellows*. 3rd rev. edn. Providence, RI: Brown University, 2006.

15

Finding Your Place on the Map

Rebekka King
Middle Tennessee State University

I open with three quotations:

Map Is Not Territory.
—Jonathan Z. Smith, "Map is not Territory" (1978)

"Get out the map, get out the map and lay your finger anywhere down. We'll leave the figuring to those we pass on our way out of town."
—Indigo Girls, "Get Out the Map" (1997)

"In your life, there are a few places, or maybe only the one place, where something has happened, and then there are all the other places, which are just other places."
—Alice Munro, "Face" (2008)

The first quotation, likely familiar to students and scholars of religion, if not overly so, is the notorious maxim from the study of religion's requisite celebrity, Jonathan Z. Smith. When employed in a classroom, we often evoke the idea that "map is not territory" to reassure our students and perhaps ourselves that the work we do in studying religion is something different from being religious.[1] We engage in the process of classification and categorization, which points to our subject matter and provides insight into its navigation. As metaphorical cartographers, we take comfort in a certain degree of physical and ideological distance from our study subjects.

In applying this metaphor to the classroom, we embrace the possibility of teaching our trade skills to students: initially outlining the familiar boundaries and coordinates to be followed by more complex instructions regarding the compilation of new or revised maps from existing ones. As Richard Ascough reminds us, while the work of map-making is not itself territory, it is territorial (2008: 69). We must therefore remain mindful of the different topographies, systems of classification, organizational hierarchies, and representational tactics drawn and legitimated by both religious adherents and the scholars who study them. In so doing, the question of who, how, where, and what constitutes the map is explicitly about negotiations of power. This premise stands out, obviously, in research and writing, but perhaps more importantly, in teaching and learning.

The second quote comes from a song by Emily Saliers of the Indigo Girls. It is likely recognizable to anyone who has been paying attention to the folk-rock music scene since the 1990s. The song speaks to the transitory quality of youth and happiness. It appears to advocate for a carpe diem approach to life—albeit thoroughly aware that such an approach is difficult to achieve and maintain. The song's protagonist reflects on friends who have departed to following enriching careers while she remains unsure of her next step. Despite this uncertainty, she continues on the journey, preferring its arbitrary nature to the settled life of "those they pass on the way out of town." While perhaps a stretch to apply to teaching scenarios, it reminds us of the transitory nature of the student experience within higher education.

The third quotation is possibly less well-known and certainly more personal. It comes from a short story by my favorite author, Alice Munro. Often celebrated as "Canada's Chekhov," Munro notably won the Nobel Prize for Literature in 2013 (Merkin 2004). While most of her stories focus on the lives and struggles of a mid-twentieth-century farming community in rural Ontario, Munro has an uncanny ability to capture in a few short pages a lifetime of emotions and memories in a way that feels familiar and almost universal despite the fact they relate the specific experiences of a fictional protagonist. In her short story "Face," published in the *New Yorker*, Munro's protagonist revisits the memories from his childhood after the death of his parents and his return to live at his childhood home. The act of recalling his childhood memories allows the narrator to finally understand the impact that otherwise happenstance events had on his adult life. Like many of Munro's stories, the protagonist's recollective detour brings insight into his present circumstances.

Each of these quotations speaks to a consideration of place and its representation through the media of memories and maps. In different ways, Sailers, Smith, and Munro invite us to linger over the question of place. Turning these quotations over in our minds, once clear concepts become more abstract with each consideration. Signifiers, it seems, only make sense in relation to another: finger to map, map to place, the *one* place to all the *other* places.

When I first set forward to write this essay, I anticipated taking "place" literally and offering a reflection on the importance of understanding one's local context and institutional structures when developing teaching styles and strategies. I had sketched out an essay that would offer some practical insight into thinking broadly about "place" in terms of regionalism, socio-economics, culture, and nationality. Then I began to review key works on teaching and learning by Patricia Killen and Eugene Gallagher. In two individually authored key works (discussed below), they introduce related concepts of "Gracious Play" (Killen 2001) and "Intellectual Hospitality" (Gallagher 2007). Neither concept is central to my argument, but both are central to my approach. In what follows, I want to play with the idea that place, emplacement, or finding one's place on the map might serve as a metaphor for thinking about the relationship between how we teach and how students receive it. The evocation of a map—which departs from Smith's intended meaning in ways that I hope he might appreciate—is particularly apt in our contemporary context, where the idea of what makes a map has radically changed. No longer painstakingly charted by trained cartographers, maps are now produced by satellites and revised with user-generated data from smartphones and GPS systems.

The Place Where Something Happened

Many of us can look back upon our own formative experiences in the classroom as the inspiration for our journeys in higher education and our desire to be educators. In an early *TTR* article reflecting on teaching as a vocation, Killen (2001) reminds us that when done well, teaching has transformative potential. In this essay, Killen urges caution and conscientious consideration of how such transformation occurs. She highlights not only its gains but also its potential losses.

What I love most about this article is how profoundly personal it is. Killen begins with a compelling description of her own undergraduate experience. Immediately we (the readers) are there with her as her cousin, en route to a camping trip, drops Killen off in front of the administrative building at Gonzaga University. Clutching a single suitcase in one hand and a used portable typewriter, Killen appears in a liminal space between the familiar world of family and something new and uncertain. As she continues, we are struck by the contrast between the young, unassuming Killen, first in her family to attend university, and her more sophisticated socialite classmates.

Those who have benefitted from Killen's mentorship over the years will recognize in this article the purposeful bridgebuilding that accompanies moments in which she shares personal recollections. Killen continues to paint a picture of her early college experiences. She describes how the world opened up in "books to read, ideas to consider, worlds to imagine, the life of the mind"

(Killen 2001: 3). Her recollection of how surprised she was to discover such strong connections between disparate courses and disciplines that cumulated in the classification of eras known as the Enlightenment, Romantic, or Colonial periods brought me back to my own similar experience as an undergraduate student. Instantly, I could recall the smell of the crisp winter air, the sound of the snow crunching under my boots, and even what I was wearing as I walked across the campus of Bishop's University and thought to myself, "modernity matters!"

Killen's anecdotes do more than offering a compelling hook. Her transformational experience is juxtaposed with observations of her students. She is quick to enumerate the differences between her generation and those she taught in 2001. Herein lies the value of taking the theme of place seriously. While we are wise to return to our roots and recollect our own early college experiences, we must not equate our students with ourselves.[2] Drawing on sociological literature from the era, Killen notes that the previous generation (her generation) was one in which "dwelling" was considered standard. In contrast, their successors were marked by a "seeker" consciousness with far fewer shared experiences and reference points.[3] The seekers "have spent their lives negotiating and constructing temporary and often fleeting and multiple families, friendship networks, institutional connections ... theirs is a world of loose connections and porous institutions" (Killen 2001: 6). For Killen, understanding these different starting points is essential for meeting students where they are.

With these generational differences at the forefront of her concern, Killen embarks on the work of true teaching and learning. Drawing from research by the psychologist of education Robert Kegan, Killen explains, "to ask students to learn anything is to ask them ... to 'leave home' and to do so not once but repeatedly. Our students come to us with furnished and familiar mental homes. When we ask them to think (which is what the university is about), we are asking them to go out of their minds" (Killen 2001: 4). As educators, we see the value in this venture. We recall its transformative potential in our lives and the lives of former classmates. However, it is crucial to remember that while we may sit at the other side of this transformation and remember it fondly as an edifying experience, this may not be the case for our students. Considering the differences between "dwellers" and "seekers," Killen observes that meaning-making is something the latter see as rare and precious, something in need of protection. Not something that they readily or enthusiastically wish to deconstruct.

My brief assessment of Killen's article side-steps its main argument, which encourages faculty to adopt a "gracious play" model to nurture these transformative moments. Certainly, I encourage the reader to review it in full.

Nevertheless, I find it fruitful to linger on the strategy by which she first invites us to return to the place and time of our own early college experiences. Killen writes,

> if we want to support our students, we must be willing to go through the mental and emotional gymnastics of remembering what it was like before we knew X or could do Y, not because our students are replicas of us, but because this exercise can focus and extend our awareness of the drama of courage, struggle, and even delight that we are privileged to encounter (dare I say midwife?) each time we walk into a teaching situation.
>
> (Killen 2001: 7)

In this way, Killen does something akin to what good storytelling does. She invites us to suspend disbelief and imagine ourselves in the protagonist's (or our student's) shoes—forging an empathetic connection that does not lose sight of difference.

This invitation to remember and return to our roots only works when we are aware of the different and diverse resources and experiences our students bring to the classroom. Those resources available to dwellers and seekers reflect generational differences—and we would be wise to expand this observation to think about how other demographic differences also impact our teaching and its reception. Returning to the theme of maps, along with remembering what it was like before "we knew X or could do Y," we need to visualize how we would learn both X and Y, not with the creased roadmaps of bygone days, but with current resources: GPS tracking devices, smartphones, and the integrated apps familiar to today's students.

Lay Your Finger Anywhere Down

Most of us are aware of the power of an old song to trigger memories. Unexpectedly, perhaps in line at the store or driving on the highway, a song from long ago will begin to play. Instantly, we are transported back through time and space. Anyone who has spent even a short period with Eugene Gallagher will note his propensity for evoking song lyrics in everyday conversations. At the end of the second summer for the 2015–16 Wabash Workshop for Early Career Religious Studies Faculty, Gallagher emailed our cohort a playlist with specific songs dedicated to each of us that reflected our "work, social location, personality, or, frankly, anything else that the committee could come up with."

I will leave it to the other members of my Wabash cohort to reflect on the significance of the songs assigned to them. My selection included, perhaps predictably, "Ridin' with the King" by Eric Clapton and B.B. King, "Tennessee Plates" by John Hiatt and the Goners, and "Every Breath You Take" by The Police (a nod to my ethnographic fieldwork). Setting aside the fast living and felonious lifestyle evoked by these songs, I suspect that Gallagher's referents were intended not as a commentary on my way of life as it was a nod to place. Specifically, a nod to my new home in Murfreesboro, Tennessee—a noteworthy transition from my northern roots in the Canadian provinces of Ontario and Quebec.

My work at Middle Tennessee State University is one of the greatest privileges and pleasures of my life. Along with my esteemed colleague, Jenna Gray-Hildenbrand, I was hired to develop a new religious studies major, the first of its kind, at a public university in Middle Tennessee.[4] Like the moves that many faculty make to new locations, it has required learning a new culture, context, and institutional structure.[5] Any move to any new institution requires flexibility and elasticity. Syllabi and assignments so carefully constructed in the context of one educational setting will inevitably fall short in another. The disciplinary maps, so painstakingly charted in graduate school, do not always serve as reliable guides once we find ourselves in the unfamiliar terrain of foreign classrooms and departments.

When it comes to teaching, anthropologist of religion James Bielo reminds us of the need to be "ethnographers in, of, and for our courses" (Bielo 2012: 206–7). While professors might be more used to speaking in the classroom, Bielo encourages us to use the ethnographic skills of listening and reflexivity to understand better our university, departmental, classroom, and enrollment contexts. To Bielo's point, we might add participant observation, textual analysis (of the faculty handbook and university policies), and the gathering of in-depth oral histories as essential methodologies for all junior faculty.

In my experience, the General Education curriculum served as the most notable novel terrain. The structure and philosophy of general education coursework were ideals I had not encountered in Canadian higher education. Nor was I familiar with the typical student appraisal of general education as, in many cases, composed of a series of courses that one had to navigate before the real learning in their programs of study could begin. In his seminal article on teaching religious literacy, Gallagher affectionately refers to these as "one and done" students. He argues that the need for the "one and done" students to develop critical thinking skills over content knowledge about religious traditions should be our primary goal. In other words, Gallagher warns against focusing too much on teaching the *what* of religion at the expense of the *how* and *why* (Gallagher 2009).

These observations parallel my experience at Middle Tennessee State University. Students often arrive in our introductory general education course, "Religion and Society," with a collection of knowledge about religion—curated from personal experiences, popular culture, high-school courses, and the ever-present opinions and sage advice of parents, pastors, and other authoritative figures. In general, they are aware that not all of their information is reliable, but they are uncertain about how to evaluate it properly. Indeed, many of them have enrolled in the course to gain more accurate descriptions of religious traditions in hopes of a quick substitution of outdated ideas with more advanced and amenable content knowledge. The challenge of teaching introductory courses as part of the general education curriculum is to encourage students to develop the critical thinking skills and methods of analysis that they can apply not only to the study of religious phenomena but throughout their programs of study (see also Gallagher and Maguire 2020).

The imperative to teach introductory courses focusing on developing critical thinking skills is likely applicable to faculty teaching in most contexts. As Forrest Clingerman and Kevin J. O'Brien note, these requirements are not limited to introductory courses at some institutions but often extend to upper-level and more advanced religious studies coursework (Clingerman and O'Brien 2015). Clingerman and O'Brien address the question of upper-level courses that satisfy general education requirements and frame their discussion around finding ways to do introductory work at a more advanced level. While only lower-division courses comprise the general education curriculum at MTSU, we find ourselves needing to situate our advanced level classes within the broader learning goals of a general education curriculum.

Elsewhere, Gallagher reminds faculty to "teach the students you have, not the ones you wish you had" (2009: 212; see also Gallagher 2007). Here Gallagher paraphrases an adage I have heard him repeat on multiple occasions from the 1971 hit song "Love The One You're With" by Crosby, Stills, and Nash. The majority of MTSU students are first-generation college students. Many come to college with expectations that their degree programs will connect concretely with their future careers. The institution is renowned for its signature degrees programs in Aerospace, Recording Industry Music, Concrete Management, and Criminal Justice. While an earlier version of myself might have envisioned a classroom full of students like myself, endlessly fascinated by abstract nuances of religion, my students are more interested in the practical application of their studies—something that has rubbed off on me.

In response, we have designed our religious studies major to fit as a second major alongside another major in diverse departments. When chatting with students and even more so with parents, we emphasize the pragmatism of studying religion. Rather than focusing on area, methods, or tradition-based studies, our curriculum focused on developing religious studies competencies. All courses are designated within one of these competencies and highlight knowledge and skills necessary for the study of religion but also applicable to programs and proficiencies necessary for other academic programs, future careers, and everyday life.

Concluding Remarks

In quite different ways, Gallagher and Killen remind us that we are not our students but that we should work diligently to understand them and identify points of connection. The religious studies program at MTSU anticipates the needs and aspirations of the students at MTSU—majors, minors, and one-and-done-ers—based on their feedback. I sometimes try to imagine how the college-age version of myself might have situated herself within its curriculum (I am of the generation that Killen describes as a "seeker" in contrast to her own "dweller" generation). I suspect that I would have been suspicious of the pragmatic language related to the competency model that I now so enthusiastically endorse.

This observation underscores what I hope is the larger thrust of this essay. Like students, faculty bring a set of expectations generated from previous experience, our particular studies, and the ever-present opinions and sage advice of mentors and colleagues. Such observations need to be in conversation with the experiences of and with our students. There is a challenge to teaching that requires us to recall our own student experience and remember what it was like before we knew what we now know. We must do so without conflating ourselves with our students. As much as we push our students to grow, we should remember to hold ourselves to the same expectations. The works by, insights from, and most importantly, lived examples of Killen and Gallagher serve as a pedagogical model. They invite us to remember and remap those places that shaped us and think about how we might draw new maps with our students.

Notes

1. Leslie Dorrough Smith likens our over-evocation of this phrase to peculiar rite of passage for scholars of religion (Smith 2019: 3–4).
2. Gallagher echoes Killen's point about meeting students where they are on a couple of noteworthy occasions. For example, in a 2007 *TTR* article, he likewise urges us to distinguish between ourselves and our students. He writes, "it is much more productive for teachers to assume that their students are *not like them*, either as the teachers are now or as they were themselves as undergraduates. That recognition of distance and dissimilarity should lead teachers to cultivate an ethnographic curiosity about the motley assortment that has assembled before them" (2007: 139).
3. It is worth noting that this essay has an uncanny foreboding to it. Published in the early months of 2001, Killen noted a lack of collective consciousness or shared reference points among her students. While the Challenger explosion was seen as something they held in common, they otherwise lacked major events "that marked them as an age cohort" (Killen 2001: 6). This observation, no doubt, radically changed a few months later when the September 11 attacks occurred. The nature of this irony feels even more striking twenty years later, as I write this chapter in the late summer of 2021, myself preparing to return to a physical classroom after seventeen months of remote and online learning in the midst of the coronavirus pandemic. I can't help but reflect on the "places" that have served as my classroom during this pandemic and of the "classroom" to which I return after three semesters of online and remote teaching.
4. Gray-Hildenbrand and I provide an overview and evaluation of this process in a 2019 article in *TTR* (see Gray-Hildenbrand and King 2019). We owe a significant amount of gratitude to Eugene Gallagher, who served as a Wabash consultant in the early days of planning our program and also mentored us in the process of writing this article.
5. For the sake of this essay, I will focus on the professional elements of this transition, rather than those related to politics, personal life, or perspiration (I do not think I will ever adapt to the heat and humidity of the Tennessee summers that start in mid-April and stretch on into October).

Bibliography

Ascough, Richard S. "'Map-maker, Map-maker, Make me a Map': Redescribing Greco-Roman 'Elective Social Formations,'" in *Introducing Religion: Essays in Honor of Jonathan Z. Smith*, edited by Willi Braun and Russell McCutcheon, 68–84. Sheffield: Equinox, 2008.

Bielo, James S. "Religion Matters: Reflections from an AAA Teaching Workshop." *Religion and Society: Advances in Research* 3, (2012): 203–8.

Clingerman, Forrest and Kevin J. O'Brien. "Teaching Introductory Upper-Level Religion and Theology Classes." *Teaching Theology & Religion* 18, no. 4 (2015): 326–42.

Gallagher, Eugene. "Welcoming the Stranger." *Teaching Theology & Religion* 10, no. 3 (2007): 137–42.

Gallagher, Eugene. "Teaching for Religious Literacy." *Teaching Theology & Religion* 12, no. 3 (2009): 208–21.

Gallagher, Eugene and Joanne Maguire. "Teaching Religion to Undergraduates in the 2020s: A Preliminary Reconnaissance." *The Wabash Center Journal on Teaching* 1, no. 1 (2020): 9–22.

Gray-Hildenbrand, Jenna and Rebekka King. "Teaching in Context: Designing a Competency-Based Religious Studies Program." *Teaching Theology & Religion* 22, no. 3 (2019): 191–204.

Killen, Patricia O'Connell. "Gracious Play: Discipline, Insight, and the Common Good." *Teaching Theology & Religion* 4, no. 1 (2001): 2–8.

Merkin, Daphne. "Northern Exposures." *The New York Times Magazine.* October 24, 2004. Available online: https://www.nytimes.com/2004/10/24/magazine/northern-exposures.html.

Smith, Leslie Dorrough. "'If I Had a Nickle for Every Time ... ': Thinking Critically about 'Data,'" 1–6 in *Constructing "Data" in Religious Studies: Examining the Architecture of the Academy.* Sheffield: Equinox, 2019.

16

Mise en Place: Efficiency and Ethics in the Practice of Teaching

Tina Pippin
Agnes Scott College

Mise en place, the French culinary term for "put in place" or "everything in its place," is considered an essential ritual by top chefs. Many chefs consider mise en place a spiritual practice; the late Anthony Bourdain called it "his religion."[1] The founder of the culinary site Hedley & Bennett, Ellen Bennett, is a prime example of this "exactly standard of organization." She organizes her kitchen from countertops to drawers to refrigerator. For Bennett: "Knowing there's a zone for everything makes it easier to just go and find."[2] This philosophy of planning calls for pre-arranging the ingredients and equipment to ensure a level of control and creative flow to the cooking process. Gathering, organizing, assembling, and producing are what Dan Charnas calls "clean work," that he describes as "prep, process, and presence."[3] There is a certain Zen-nature to this "clean work" that calls for a clean, organized space in which to focus on the craft of cooking. Work is thought through, organized ahead of time, grounded in culinary theory.

The metaphor for culinary organization seems fitting in a reflection on the work of Eugene Gallagher and Patricia O'Connell Killen. Their focus on preparation, setting, outcomes, and process leads to new understandings of the good "work" of teaching. I had the privilege of being a participant in their first Colloquy on Writing the Scholarship of Teaching and Learning in Theology and Religion in 2009–10 at the Wabash Center. It was at this workshop that I learned the inner workings of SoTL and the value of organized planning and deep research in the field of educational theory.

How kitchens are set up efficiently by the really good chefs is like their SoTL workshop I experienced. Mise en place would be their template for SoTL around "generative assumptions," "Classroom Practice," "Person of the Professor,"

"Purposes and Politics of Teaching," "Pedagogies and Theories," "Practical Possibilities of the Field," and "Problematic Conventions for Teaching and Research."[4] Each of these assumptions, in their weaker and stronger forms, leads to "more sustained thinking and writing about what is going on."[5] Their method intends to be revelatory about the inner workings of the teaching process by exploring a classroom incident or pedagogical question.

In each case, the classroom and pedagogical practices are the starting points for research into teaching. For example, the teacher's self-knowledge and narrative is a step toward a more critical investigation of issues of specific pedagogical moments and broader conversations. Gallagher expressed the gist of the method: "I think what you're talking about here is taking our disciplinary scholarship and 'SoTL-izing it.' If you take this disciplinary knowledge seriously, it has real implications for teaching. My task can be to tease out the implications, to point out how this should be affecting curriculum design, course design, and teaching in the classroom."[6] By "SoTL-izing" the discussion, a brighter light is shone on the theory and practices that shape a classroom experience. This transparency can then lead to deeper assessment of the teaching and learning practices and outcomes, and lead to positive revision and change.

Building on Ernest Boyer's work, and in mise en place fashion, Charles E. Glassick, Mary Taylor Huber, and Gene I. Maeroff, in their book, *Scholarship Assessed: Evaluation of the Professoriate*, identified six markers of scholarly work, including the scholarship of teaching. According to them, scholarly work should have: "1. Clear goals; 2. Adequate preparation; 3. Appropriate methods; 4. Significant results; 5. Effective presentation; 6. Reflective critique."[7] In a similar vein, Patricia Killen offers a useful concept of "midrange reflection" that has guided the Wabash Center's teaching workshops: "Midrange reflection is a particular kind of reflection, but first and foremost it is reflection. Reflection involves slowing down the meaning-making or interpretive process to look again at an event, for example a particular incident from one's teaching, and at the categories, assumptions, and theories by which one has made or failed to make plausible sense of that event."[8] She invites the teacher to "ponder" their pedagogical practices in an open and sustained way. Killen defines the term further: "Midrange reflection on teaching and learning lifts out from the particularities of a concrete teaching incident the issues, themes, questions, approaches, procedures, and so forth, that have the potential, thus identified, to be of general relevance in other situations of teaching and learning, thought they would need then to be adapted not just adopted to other, equally particular contexts."[9] She names two skills required for midrange reflection: "(1) the ability to identify issues and (2) the ability to design sequences of questions and intellectual activities that promote reflection on those issues."[10] Discovery of new pedagogical approaches and solutions is through design and reframing of the event in the classroom.[11] Both Killen and Gallagher emphasize the importance of community (and the incredible hospitality of the Wabash Center) in midrange reflection and SoTL. What are some ways, with critical theory and social justice pedagogies, to push the boundaries of this conversation?

What Would Freire Say about SoTL?

I want to begin with some ways critical pedagogies have been used in writing on SoTL. For example, Suzanne Grant and Fiona Hurd show "how reflective teaching and experiential learning can be used to incorporate critical pedagogy into the SoTL" in their management courses. They focus on the students' reality in an exercise of students drawing their "career" and reflecting throughout the semester on their ideas and motivations.[12] Following the work of Laura Servage,[13] Grant and Hurd offer a critique of SoTL practices that view students as neoliberal subjects and, quoting Servage, "'entrepreneurial learners' who conceptualize education primarily for its use value."[14] The critique lies mainly with streams of neoliberal embeddedness in SoTL that see students and classrooms as research subjects for assessment. Servage summarizes her critique: "I wish to illuminate the ways in which the humanistic and progressive aspirations of improved teaching, so central to SoTL, serve in many ways to advance higher education's deepening implication in the advancement of the twin forces of neoliberal policy and flexible capitalism."[15] Further, she argues that "it is all too easy for SoTL to succumb to the busnocratic rationality ... by equating good teaching with commodifiable outcomes, such as technical competence in pedagogy or high student grades."[16] Each of these authors call SoTL to account not only by offering a metacritique of connections with neoliberal capitalism in higher education, but also by instead centering the stories and experiences of their students, connecting these experiential narratives with the course material and student-set goals.

The use of experiential learning in SoTL in religious studies has been illustrated by Fred Glennon[17] and Barbara Patterson[18] in their links in an upper-level ethics class (Glennon) and a religious studies internship course (Patterson). Both Glennon and Patterson connect students in concrete and reflective ways to social justice organizations and issues. For example, Glennon outlines the pedagogical principles of a social justice approach:

- First, all education is value-laden and political.
- Second, learning about social justice must begin with students' prior learning and experiences.
- Third, when it comes to social justice active learning is better than passive learning; doing is better than receiving.
- Fourth, the quality of the experience is critical to the learning that takes place.
- Fifth, in teaching and learning about social justice, the learner should be actively involved in shaping the purpose and direction of the learning that takes place.
- Sixth, in the case of teaching and learning about social justice, a praxis (action-reflection) model provides a more qualitative experience for learning about social justice than reading about social justice.[19]

In this way SoTL is able to link "the word with the world," and supply students with the responsibility to appropriate theory and critical thinking with/in community partner organizations.

Taking a step further, multicultural educator Laura Rendón addresses the traditional framework of higher education as a way to deconstruct the status quo. She calls the structure "privileged agreements governing the present pedagogical dreamfield." The agreements are as follows:

1. the agreement to privilege intellectual/rational knowing
2. the agreement of separation
3. the agreement of competition
4. the agreement of perfection
5. the agreement of monoculturalism
6. the agreement to privilege outer work
7. the agreement to avoid self-examination[20]

Rendón invites us to resist the traditional "banking model" of education, and to challenge and change these Western, patriarchal, hierarchical ways of teaching and learning. She calls her pedagogical theory/practice *sentipensante* (sensing/thinking) pedagogy with the following goals:

> To create a new teaching and learning Dreamfield that is intellectual (i.e., includes high standards of academic achievement, allows students to engage in

problem solving and critical thinking, engages multicultural perspectives, etc.) and spiritual (i.e., honors our humanity; instills a sense of wonder, sacredness, and humility in our college classrooms; respects and embraces alternative cultural realities; involves social change and healing; and connects faculty and students in meaningful ways) ....[21]

Rendón is asking us to rethink and reconstruct the systems of oppression in our educational spaces toward the dream of "the liberating, socially just classroom" in which personal narratives and identities, critical consciousness, problem-solving, reflection, compassion, and activism are key.[22] Rendón's model of sentipensante pedagogy is a useful model for extending SoTL toward a social justice, and student-centered, approach. She begins with a central question of heart and mind that guides her work: "What is the experience of creating a teaching and learning dream (pedagogical vision) based on wholeness and consonance, respecting the harmonious rhythm between the outer experience of intellectualism and rational analysis and the inner dimension of insight, emotion, and awareness?"[23] Rendón shifts the investigation in SoTL to a consideration of the whole person as the starting point. She also adopts Freire's emphasis on freedom, hope, and the dream of a democratic society.

The words that guide liberating approaches to SoTL are instructive in identifying the methodological approaches. They include: personal, relational, systemic, transdisciplinary, responsive, reflective, democratic, cooperative, collaborative, communal, consonate, whole, participatory, engaging, mutually transparent, accountable, questioning, resisting, dissenting, decolonizing, abolitional, activist, just, mindful, transformational, sustaining, validating, inclusive, integrative, illuminating, renewing, and healing. These ways of thinking about SoTL involve co-planning of teachers with students, centering the subjects, experiences, and knowledges of the class.

These words are certainly utopic. They also extend the current discourses on SoTL toward problem-posing education for social change. Freire contends, "Education is the practice of freedom—as opposed to education as the practice of domination."[24] Against the banking method of the teacher inserting knowledge and correct answers into passive, empty student vessels, Freire advocated that the way to freedom was with problem-posing education in which students and teacher investigate their world: "The students—no longer docile listeners—are not critical co-investigators in dialogue with the teacher .... The role of the problem-posing educator is to create; together with the students, the conditions under which knowledge at the level of the *doxa* [belief] is superseded by true knowledge, at the level of the *logos* [reason, plan]."[25] In other words, liberatory pedagogy is thus dialogical and "reading the word and the world" (Freire and Macedo). As Freire states, "To speak a true word is to transform the world."[26] The "true word" is the word of the experience of, conscientization of, and future visions of a just world by and with the oppressed.

What Freire's dialogical approach offers SoTL is an expansion of the dominate model offered by the main SoTL journals[27] and texts.[28] One example of Freire's dialogical thinking about research in teaching is in the area of student-faculty partnerships. For example, John Peters and Leoarna Mathias imagine a Freirean student-teacher partnership and point out "the tension between liberation and domestication" that exists with an uneven distribution of power.[29] They remind us that "it is important that we maintain awareness of the challenge we are undertaking and the powerfully domesticating forces operating against any form of educational practice which unsettles the established order."[30] As they name the neoliberal traps for this liberatory work, the authors turn their focus on the Freirean concept of shared hope in the transformative potential of these partnerships. "The Freirean idea of partnership is human, emotional, and romantic, in the sense of investing the educational relationship with our hopes and dreams for each other. It emphasizes the collegial and social mobility and empowerment for particular individuals."[31]

Conclusion

A Freirean approach to SoTL involves planning, although it is a more open-ended approach. In its most controlled version, traditional guidelines for SoTL focus on a question from the professor that is to be assessed and "solved" by the research on students. Freire asks us to consider the ideological and political context in which students problem-pose. The generative questions are asked with students in partnership, with social justice as an underlying principle.

In the spectrum of SoTL there are few Freirean voices. A dialogical design of SoTL is a more open invitation—to critical reflection of the process and pedagogy and also critical consciousness. The "contours" that Killen and Gallagher sketch out show the necessity of pedagogical research in teaching and learning in theology and religion. They have given us the valuable raw materials, and more, for pedagogical research. Bringing in more voices in critical pedagogies and social justice teaching only enriches the traditional SoTL method.

Working clean is not a Freirean approach. There is much resistance to shared power and partnership with students and with community partners in civic engagement, even if the research—and practice—overwhelmingly prove its success. Delving into the metacontext of SoTL involves facing the ideological commitments that are often at odds with social justice teaching and democratic education. It also means confronting some of the basic premises of SoTL to create, in Rendón's term, a "Dreamfield" of a more just world.

Mise en place makes imminent sense and is an orderly process that leads to clarity and student success. And I think Freire would argue that the traditional SoTL methods are too teacher-centered and driven. With a Freirean method the focus shifts from teacher-driven to student-partnered research in order to identify and raise consciousness about oppression and injustice, both in the traditional classroom and outside of in the world. Freire argues for "methodological exactitude" and rigor,[32] as he also advocating a transgressive pedagogy—one that crosses the boundaries of the hierarchies of knowledge and experience, honors and respects the students, and connects the subject/word with the world. He states, "What ought to guide me is not the question of neutrality in education but respect, at all costs, for all those involved in education."[33] Thus students and faculty are both "cultural workers," together, in the struggle for freedom, sharing a meal prepared by all.[34]

Notes

1. Dan Charnas, *Work Clean: The Life-Changing Power of Mise-En-Place to Organize Your Life, Work, and Mind* (New York, NY: Rodale, 2016), xi. See also, Dan Charnas, "For a More Ordered Life, Organize Like a Chef," NPR Morning Edition (August 11, 2014). Available online: https://www.npr.org/sections/thesalt/2014/08/11/338850091/for-a-more-ordered-life-organize-like-a-chef, accessed August 26, 2021. See also: D. S. Weisberg, et al., "Mise en Place: Setting the Stage for Thought and Action," *Trends in Cognitive Sciences* 18, no. 6 (2014): 276–8.
2. Janelle Zara (April 3, 2019), "How to Organize Your Kitchen Like a Professional Chef," *The New York Times*. Available online: https://www.nytimes.com/2019/04/03/t-magazine/kitchen-organization.html, accessed on September 1, 2021.
3. Charnas, *Work Clean*, viii.
4. Patricia O'Connor Killen and Eugene Gallagher, "Sketching the Contours of the Scholarship of Teaching and Learning in Theology and Religion," *Teaching Theology and Religion* 16, no. 2 (2013): 115–19.
5. Ibid., 114.

6 Thomas Pearson, Kwok Pui-lan, and Eugene Gallagher, "Conversations on the Scholarship of Teaching and Learning", *Wabash Center Journal on Teaching* 1, no. 2 (2020): 69. See also: Emily O. Gravett, (2016), "The Scholarship of Teaching and Learning in Religious Studies," *Journal of the American Academy of Religion* 84, no. 3 (2016): 589–616.

7 Charles E. Glassick, Mary Taylor Huber, and Gene I. Maeroff, *Scholarship Assessed: Evaluation of the Professoriate* (San Francisco, CA: Jossey-Bass, 1997), 25. See also Ernest L. Boyer, *Scholarship Reconsidered: Priorities of the Professoriate*, Princeton, NJ: The Carnegie Foundation for the Advancement of Teaching. Carnegie Academy for the Scholarship of Teaching and Learning (CASTL) Higher Education (Stanford, CA: Carnegie Foundation, 2020); Available online: http://archive.carnegiefoundation.org/scholarship-teaching-learning.html, accessed August 25, 2021.

8 Patricia O'Connor Killen, "Midrange Reflection: The Underlying Practice of Wabash Center Workshops, Colloquies, and Consultations," *Teaching Theology and Religion* 10, no. 3 (2007): 107–24.

9 Ibid., 144.

10 Ibid., 145.

11 Ibid., 148.

12 Suzanne Grant and Fiona Hurd, "Incorporating Critical Pedagogy into the Scholarship of Teaching and Learning: Making the Journey Alongside Our Students", *International Journal for the Scholarship of Teaching and Learning* 4, no. 2 (2010): 1.

13 Laura Servage, "The Scholarship of Teaching and Learning and the Neo-Liberalization of Higher Education: Constructing the 'Entrepreneurial Learner,'" *The Canadian Journal of Higher Education* 39, no. 2 (2009): 25–44.

14 Grant and Hurd, "Incorporating Critical Pedagogy," 2; quoting Servage, "The Scholarship of Teaching and Learning," 25.

15 Servage, "The Scholarship of Teaching and Learning," 27.

16 Ibid., 38.

17 Fred Glennon, "Experiential Learning and Social Justice Action: An Experiment in the Scholarship of Teaching and Learning", *Teaching Theology and Religion* 7, no. 1 (2004): 30–7.

18 Barbara A.B. Patterson, "Ethnography as Pedagogy: Learning and Teaching in a Religion Department Internship Class", *Teaching Theology and Religion* 6, no. 1 (2003): 24–36.

19 Glennon, "Experiential Learning," 31–3.

20 Laura I. Rendón, *Sentipensante (Sensing/Thinking) Pedagogy: Educating for Wholeness, Social Justice, and Liberation* (Sterling, VA: Stylus, 2009), 26.

21 Ibid.

22 Ibid., 105–9.

23 Ibid., 160.
24 Paulo Freire, *Pedagogy of the Oppressed*, 30th Anniversary Edition (New York: Continuum, 2007), 81.
25 Ibid.
26 Paulo Freire and Donald Macedo, *Literacy: Reading the Word and the World* (New York: Routledge, 2016), 87.
27 *International Journal for the Scholarship of Teaching and Learning; International Journal of Teaching and Learning in Higher Education; Journal of the Scholarship of Teaching and Learning; Journal of Excellence in College Teaching; Teaching and Learning Inquiry.*
28 A few of the main texts on SoTL include: Nancy L. Chick, ed. (2018), *SoTL in Action: Illuminating Critical Moments of Practice* (Sterling, VA: Stylus, 2018); Nancy L. Chick, *The SoTL Guide*, Available online: https://nancychick.wordpress.com/sotl-guide/, accessed on September 1, 2021; Cathy Bishop-Clark and Beth Dietz-Uhler, *Engaging in the Scholarship of Teaching and Learning: A Guide to the Process, and How to Develop a Project from Start to Finish* (Sterling, VA: Stylus, 2012); Regan A. R. Gurung and Beth M. Schwartz, *Optimizing Teaching and Learning: Practicing Pedagogical Research* (Malden, MA: Wiley-Blackwell, 2008); Mick Healey, M. (2018), *Students as Partners in Learning and Teaching in Higher Education: A Selected Bibliography*, www.mickhealey,co.uk/resources, accessed on September 9, 2021; Pat Hutchings, Mary Taylor Huber, and Anthony Ciccone, *The Scholarship of Teaching and Learning Reconsidered: Institutional Integration and Impact* (San Francisco, CA: Jossey-Bass, 2011); Kathleen McKinney, *Enhancing Learning through the Scholarship of Teaching and Learning: The Challenges and Joys of Juggling* (Boston, MA: Anker, 2017).
29 John Peters and Leoarna Mathias, "Enacting Student Partnership as Though We Really Mean It: Some Freirean Principles for a Pedagogy of Partnership", *International Journal of Students as Partners* 2, no. 2 (2018): 57.
30 Ibid.
31 Ibid., 60. Not all partnership models evoke critical pedagogies and Freire in this way. See for example: Catherine Bovill, C., J. Jarvis and K. Smith, eds, *Co-creating Learning and Teaching: Towards Relational Pedagogy in Higher Education* (Critical Practice in Higher Education) (St. Albans, UK: Critical Publishing, 2020); Alison Cook-Sather, "Resisting the Impositional Potential of Student Voice Work: Lessons for Liberatory Educational Research from Poststructuralist Feminist Critiques of Critical Pedagogy," *Discourse: Studies in the Cultural Politics of Education* 28, no. 3 (2007): 389–403; Alison Cook-Sather, Catherine Bovill and Peter Felten, *Engaging Students as Partners in Learning and Teaching: A Guide for Faculty*, (San Francisco, CA: Jossey-Bass, 2014); Carmen Werder and Megan M. Otis, eds., *Engaging Student Voices in the Study of Teaching and Learning* (Sterling, VA: Stylus, 2010).

32 Paulo Freire, *Pedagogy of Freedom: Ethics, Democracy, and Civic Courage*, trans. Patrick Clarke (Lanham, PA: Rowman & Littlefield, 1998), 33ff.
33 Ibid., 101.
34 An example of this transgressive and justice-centered research is the work of the Myles Horton and the Highlander Center (now the Highlander Research and Education Center). Highlander was one of the few integrated places in the American South in the mid-twentieth century; participants in workshops made meals from start to clean up together. For an excellent overview of their historical context and scholarship of teaching and learning using popular education models, see Stephen Preskill, *Education in Black and White: Myles Horton and the Highlander Center's Vision for Justice* (Berkeley, CA: University of California Press, 2021).

Bibliography

Bishop-Clark, Cathy, and Beth Dietz-Uhler. *Engaging in the Scholarship of Teaching and Learning: A Guide to the Process, and How to Develop a Project from Start to Finish*. Sterling, VA: Stylus, 2012.

Bovill, Catherine, C. J. Jarvis and K. Smith, eds. *Co-creating Learning and Teaching: Towards Relational Pedagogy in Higher Education*. Critical Practice in Higher Education. St. Albans, UK: Critical Publishing, 2020.

Boyer, Ernest L., *Scholarship Reconsidered: Priorities of the Professoriate*. Princeton, N.J.: The Carnegie Foundation for the Advancement of Teaching. Carnegie Academy for the Scholarship of Teaching and Learning (CASTL) Higher Education (Stanford, CA: Carnegie Foundation, 2020). Available online: http://archive.carnegiefoundation.org/scholarship-teaching-learning.html, accessed August 25, 2021.

Charnas, Dan. *Work Clean: The Life-Changing Power of Mise-En-Place to Organize Your Life, Work, and Mind*. New York, NY: Rodale, 2016.

Charnas, Dan. "For a More Ordered Life, Organize Like a Chef," NPR Morning Edition, August 11, 2014. Available online: https://www.npr.org/sections/thesalt/2014/08/11/338850091/for-a-more-ordered-life-organize-like-a-chef, accessed August 26, 2021.

Chick, Nancy L., ed. *SoTL in Action: Illuminating Critical Moments of Practice*. Sterling, VA: Stylus, 2018.

Chick, Nancy L. "The SoTL Guide." Available online: https://nancychick.wordpress.com/sotl-guide/ accessed on September 1, 2021.

Cook-Sather, Alison. "Resisting the Impositional Potential of Student Voice Work: Lessons for Liberatory Educational Research from Poststructuralist Feminist Critiques of Critical Pedagogy." *Discourse: Studies in the Cultural Politics of Education* 28, no. 3 (2007): 389–403.

Cook-Sather, Alison, Catherine Bovill, and Peter Felten. *Engaging Students as Partners in Learning and Teaching: A Guide for Faculty*. San Francisco, CA: Jossey-Bass, 2014.

Freire, Paulo. *Pedagogy of Freedom: Ethics, Democracy, and Civic Courage*. trans. Patrick Clarke. Lanham, PA: Rowman & Littlefield, 1998.

Freire, Paulo. *Pedagogy of the Oppressed*. 30th Anniversary Edition. New York: Continuum, 2007.

Freire, Paulo, and Donald Macedo, *Literacy: Reading the Word and the World*. New York: Routledge, 2016.

Glassick, Charles E., Mary Taylor Huber, and Gene I. Maeroff. *Scholarship Assessed Evaluation of the Professoriate*. San Francisco, CA: Jossey-Bass, 1997.

Glennon, Fred. "Experiential Learning and Social Justice Action: An Experiment in the Scholarship of Teaching and Learning." *Teaching Theology & Religion* 7, no. 1 (2004): 30–7.

Grant, Suzanne, and Fiona Hurd, "Incorporating Critical Pedagogy into the Scholarship of Teaching and Learning: Making the Journey Alongside Our Students," *International Journal for the Scholarship of Teaching and Learning* 4, no. 2 (2010).

Gravett, Emily O. "The Scholarship of Teaching and Learning in Religious Studies," *Journal of the American Academy of Religion* 84, no. 3 (2016): 589–616.

Gurung, Regan A. R., and Beth M. Schwartz. *Optimizing Teaching and Learning: Practicing Pedagogical Research*. Malden, MA: Wiley-Blackwell, 2008.

Healey, Mick M. "Students as Partners in Learning and Teaching in Higher Education: A Selected Bibliography." (2018) https://www.healeyheconsultants.co.uk/resources, accessed on September 5, 2021.

Hutchings, Pat, Mary Taylor Huber, and Anthony Ciccone. *The Scholarship of Teaching and Learning Reconsidered: Institutional Integration and Impact*. San Francisco, CA: Jossey-Bass, 2011.

Killen, Patricia O'Connell, and Eugene V. Gallagher, "Sketching the Contours of the Scholarship of Teaching and Learning in Theology and Religion." *Teaching Theology & Religion* 16, no. 2 (2013): 107–24.

Killen, Patricia O'Connell. "Midrange Reflection: The Underlying Practice of Wabash Center Workshops, Colloquies, and Consultations." *Teaching Theology & Religion* 10 (2007): 143–9.

McKinney, Kathleen. *Enhancing Learning through the Scholarship of Teaching and Learning: The Challenges and Joys of Juggling*. Boston, MA: Anker, 2017.

Patterson, Barbara A. B. "Ethnography as Pedagogy: Learning and Teaching in a Religion Department Internship Class." *Teaching Theology & Religion* 6, no. 1 (2003): 24–36.

Pearson, Thomas, Kwok Pui-lan, and Eugene V. Gallagher. "Conversations on the Scholarship of Teaching and Learning." *Wabash Center Journal on Teaching* 1, no. 2 (2020).

Peters, John, and Leoarna Mathias. "Enacting Student Partnership as Though We Really Mean It: Some Freirean Principles for a Pedagogy of Partnership." *International Journal of Students as Partners* 2, no. 2 (2018).

Preskill, Stephen. *Education in Black and White: Myles Horton and the Highlander Center's Vision for Justice*. Berkeley, CA: University of California Press, 2021.

Rendón, Laura I. *Sentipensante (Sensing/Thinking) Pedagogy: Educating for Wholeness, Social Justice, and Liberation*. Sterling, VA: Stylus, 2009.

Servage, Laura. "The Scholarship of Teaching and Learning and the Neo-Liberalization of Higher Education: Constructing the 'Entrepreneurial Learner.'" *The Canadian Journal of Higher Education* 39, no. 2 (2009): 25–44.

Weisberg, D.S. et al., "Mise en Place: Setting the Stage for Thought and Action," *Trends in Cognitive Sciences* 18, no. 6 (2014): 276–8.

Werder, Carmen, and Megan M. Otis, eds. *Engaging Student Voices in the Study of Teaching and Learning*. Sterling, VA: Stylus, 2010.

Zara, J. "How to Organize Your Kitchen Like a Professional Chef." *The New York Times*, April 3, 2019. Available online: https://www.nytimes.com/2019/04/03/t-magazine/kitchen-organization.html, accessed on September 1, 2021.

17

Teaching about Religion and/at/as the Edge: From What to How to Why

Davina C. Lopez
Eckerd College

Over the last decade, and acutely since the Covid-19 pandemic and intensified social unrest have amplified the issue, I have found myself reflecting on the vocation of teaching religion with undergraduates at the small liberal arts college where I work. By vocational reflection, I mean engaging in a process of careful critical thinking about what exactly I do in my undergraduate classroom, how I do it, and why it matters. By what I do, I mean thinking more about process and practice than content and conscription. The shift in *what* precipitates the shift in *how*, and the *why* always lurks in the background. So, the question on my mind, for every class, concerns my own pedagogical choices and responsibilities as well as the reasoning behind those. And recently I have been thinking about the intersection of vocational reflection with the point of teaching about religion with undergraduates at our current historical and cultural moment, and what both trajectories have to do with the promise and prospects of teaching about religion in our current higher education landscape. Herein, I will briefly ruminate on this process, from *what* to *how* to *why*.

The *What*: Context before Content

What should constitute the central focus in a semester-long undergraduate religious studies course? What should I teach, or rather, where should my students' learning be concentrated? This question is not as easy to address as it might seem. My reflections on the *what* of teaching about religion with undergraduates are informed most recently by my work on what exactly students should learn in a religion course if it is the only religion course they will take during the course of their college program.[1] This suggests a reality in which students will not continue to explore the study of religion while in college, a reality that many undergraduate teachers at liberal arts colleges might share. If we cannot cram it all into fifteen weeks, as the various pivots precipitated by the coronavirus pandemic have underscored, then what?

My immediate teaching context informs these reflections. Eckerd College, where I have taught for nearly two decades, is Florida's only national liberal arts college. Situated on a waterfront campus in the city of St Petersburg, the College is historically related to the PC(USA) and has long been known for innovative liberal arts education and progressive values. Founded in 1958 as Florida Presbyterian College, Eckerd's academic program does not carry the same nineteenth-century baggage as other liberal arts colleges. On the cusp of the US civil rights movement, its founders were open to exploring what exactly a liberal arts education was and unsettling assumptions about what it meant to be(come) a "Christian college" in a rapidly changing modern world. Our curriculum in religious studies was initiated at a moment when religion departments were emerging at universities in the United States in the wake of the Supreme Court's 1963 Abington vs. Schempp decision. The first faculty hires in religious studies at Florida Presbyterian College came from teaching at state universities, and the program spanned the humanities and "comparative cultures" divisions, signifying an early commitment to comparison and cultural analysis.

Eckerd has no religion requirement for graduation, although many of our courses count toward a humanities requirement. Our religion courses are not sequenced, nor do most of them require prerequisites. Thus, I find myself in the pedagogical position of working with a variety of students in every religious studies course I teach, from (potential and declared) majors and minors, to the curious but apprehensive, to the devoutly certain, to the not quite committed. A further complication, undoubtedly a manifestation of American anti-intellectualism, is that my students tend to associate critical thinking about religion and the humanities with esoteric, and therefore irrelevant, academia, rather than with everyday situations. This pedagogical impasse impedes development of knowledge and awareness fostered through the study of religion.

Nevertheless, we soldier on. Our curriculum, the framework for the *what*, has long treated religion as a fundamental aspect of human experience that changes over time and across space. Learning about religion is a matter of cultural literacy and social importance for emerging citizens rather than advocacy for the would-be religious. For example, our introductory course, "Understanding Religion," is purposefully not world-religions focused. Instead, in that course we face a complex of questions: what exactly is religion, how do we decide and know what it is, who gets to decide, what categories do we use to identify religion, how do our assumptions about what religion is (and what it isn't) frame how we understand religion as a meaningful category in the world? So for me, at least, the *what* of teaching about religion with undergraduates entails staying with the basics: not the basics of asking what is inside religious institutions and what differentiates those (e.g., how are Jesus, Mohammed, and the Buddha similar to and different from each other?), or the basics of performing what I think our guild expects us to do (critics, caretakers, cultivators, cynics?), but the basics of asking what religion itself is and what difference such a classification makes with the people in front of me.

In reflecting on the *what*, I treat our local student population as a microcosm of larger social dynamics. My students come to college either open-mindedly curious or quietly judgmental about issues involving religion. They have little idea of how to approach religion if the goal is not affirmation or indoctrination. Many of these young adults have found it productive to fault religion for social problems, prejudice, and injustice. My students also resonate with the sentiment that religion is full of "hot-button" discussion topics that can get very personal very quickly, and they have significant apprehension about contributing to such conversations even as they see some value to participation. As in recent American public discourse, my students tend to treat religiosity as an identity marker that intersects with partisan and/or sectarian political interests. While some are open about a vaguely "spiritual" orientation, others, particularly Protestant and evangelical Christians, keep their religiousness to themselves out of fear that they will be labeled as closed-minded bigots by their peers (and, often, their professors). These students see their academic interests as a matter of identity and affinity, as if their major says something about what kind of people they are.

No one is neutral about religion, even as they might be underinformed about how to go about studying it in college as open-minded adults. This lack of neutrality is, for better or for worse, with us every day, no matter what kind of *what* happens to be on the syllabus. For me, then, the context matters more than the content. In my teaching context, clearly there is a need to implement strategies specific to courses in religious studies that would empower students across our curriculum, no matter the topic or level. Every course in our departmental offerings could theoretically be the only exposure to the study of religion our students will receive during their college experience. While this could lead to overwhelm on the part of teachers—one religion course, so much religion content to cover!—I contend that thinking about the *what* of teaching about religion through the lens of a "one-and-done" model can open some interesting doors for further reflection on *how* and *why*.

The *How*: One and Done, More than the Major

It seems to me that thinking about how best to conduct "one-and-done" pedagogies reveals a host of persistent issues in the undergraduate religious studies classroom. It is critical to clearly articulate the goals and principles of the study of religion for a variety of student audiences sitting in the same room at once. Teaching religion never occurs in a vacuum and is about more than the major. Everyone has feelings and assumptions about the subject and, in many cases, about the way the academic field of religious studies is constructed as a critical interlocutor in conversations about personal and communal faith commitments. For critically reflective teachers of religion, it is essential to attend to the intersections of world and classroom context, teaching persona, and local intellectual ecosystems. All these elements are at play in teaching about religion. I, for one, acutely feel the pressures and promises each brings to the table in liberal arts settings like the one in which I work.

So, if *any* given religious studies course could be "one-and-done," if any course might be the only religion course that a student will take, then what do we as teachers want them to take away from that course, and how will we get there? Does figuring this out involve developing a content strategy, a strategy that fronts skills and/or orientation to the field, or some combination? How can we integrate such pedagogies and assignments in such a way that accomplishes the "one-and-done" task while also reinforcing knowledge and skills for our repeat offenders (what I like to call students who take multiple religion courses), some of whom become majors and minors, and most of whom do not? I would hope that any "one-and-done" course experience would translate into a student taking more courses in the field, and yet this is not a guarantee in our local educational ecosystem (nor, I suspect, in many others). Moreover, I am not convinced that the future of teaching religion with undergraduates lies in our capacity to effectively evangelize for the major, even as the number of majors often serves to distribute resources between academic departments and divisions.[2] These questions are not just about putting students into our introductory course—they apply to all the courses in our curriculum. A student who does not plan to major in religious studies or in the humanities is as likely to enroll in a 300-level course in Religion and Cinema or Ecotheology as they are to take Understanding Religion.

Given my context, it makes sense to me to focus my pedagogical efforts on helping students understand, appreciate, and internalize the relevance of the study of religion, across the curriculum, from survey courses through our capstone experience, through teaching *how to handle differences without rendering judgments and reifying hierarchies.* Keeping the "one-and-done" orientation in mind, the *how* to me concerns what it would look like to help our students move, even if ever so slightly, out of apprehension into participation in difficult and unfamiliar conversations about real-world issues where religion plays a role, as well as develop and articulate a meaningful worldview of their own while understanding and embracing that all worldviews are ultimately partial, provisional, and located in space and time. I affirm that the undergraduate students I teach exhibit some measure of openness to learning about religion, even as they have presuppositions about what religion is. These students rather naturally react with suspicion when they learn that the study of religion is not primarily about established and eternal institutions, doctrines, and beliefs (what I call the "big R" issues). They additionally express dismay that their notions of religion and spirituality are tied to their latent conceptions of race, gender, sexuality, age, nationality, economic standing, and ability. This makes it difficult to negotiate a critically open discussion about religion, difference, judgment, and hierarchy.

My recent students, like many undergraduates,[3] desire tools to discuss difficult topics and to negotiate diverse questions of meaning in informed, respectful, and mature ways. They want to understand themselves as much as they want to encounter others. They perk up when they see that they could get the chance to engage in discussion about difference without judgment and hierarchy. And yet when it comes to religion, they approach conversation with a high degree of trepidation,[4] not to mention no shortage of unknowing and a lack of practice when it comes to evaluating information and relating to ambiguity. At the same time, I am sure I am not alone when I say that many students want and expect religion (humanities) courses to be "fun," which to them means that they do not have to think much or do a lot of work.

The idea that studying religion, no matter the level or entry point, requires some measure of attention and intellectual flexibility is something that can be difficult for undergraduates. That means, to me, that we need to emphasize the complexity of the study of religion further and in different ways. One of those ways might be through asking how the skills to self-reflectively negotiate differences without judgment and hierarchy will be cultivated before, during, and after every single class session, in every course, every time we teach. This kind of constant attention to the *how* makes a difference. My students struggle to articulate the relevance of their studies in religion and the humanities to themselves, their peers, and their parents. In other words, religion, for them, is something *other people do*. Students who take my introductory class may never be able to remember what Clifford Geertz meant by "thick description" or how Rudolf Otto's concept of the numinous is both wonderful and wonderfully traumatic. However, I am convinced that our daily focus on how to negotiate differences using the reading assignment at hand, regardless of what the reading is, makes the most difference for the widest variety of students over the long term. Students come as they are, with all their assumptions, traumas, and questions. It could very well be that my task is to help each of them become themselves through encountering, for however long, the study of religion.

To keep track of how the *how* is working out in a course, I occasionally ask students to identify one thing about studying religion they would want to tell someone who was not enrolled in the course. Usually, I ask them to identify the person they have in mind and write a letter to that person about what they are learning and why it matters. This proves to be a great writing and discussion exercise on account of the reality that students must think through how far they have come since the last time I asked them to reflect on this (I ask them several times throughout a semester). They also must think about how they say what they need to say to a person who is not steeped in the study of religion as they are. Often, my students talk about the skills they are acquiring, the new ways of thinking, the increased comfort around people who differ from them, their curiosity about how they make the judgments they do. They share their reflections with their colleagues, and there is a measure of humor and pain as they discuss their various audiences, from parents to presidents. Through facing up to the how early and often, we can articulate the ways in which religion is something that affects everyone—and that studying religion can help us understand and interact with humanity in robustly thoughtful ways.

The *Why*: Religion and/at/as the Edge

Inquiring about the *why* of teaching about religion with undergraduates as if every course were a one-and-done affair can be a revealing exercise. For me, the idea of one-and-done courses in religious studies rests on two curricular and pedagogical undercurrents that might conflict with one another. One undercurrent, embedded in our field, is that departmental courses are still structured somewhat cumulatively and involve information and knowledge collection toward a major. Despite our best intentions, we still tend to adhere to a model wherein we assume that there is some sort of progressive familiarity with "religion stuff" as the numerical level of the course increases. We accept the idea that there is a beginning, middle, and end to studying religion in college. We have tended to assume that a course will *not* be the only one students take, even if enrollments skew in that direction. Another undercurrent comes from our local curricular context, wherein students must take one course in the humanities for graduation. Many students assume that humanities courses are a) interchangeable, and b) a fun distraction. It seems to me taking seriously the why of teaching about religion necessitates challenging the first undercurrent, to be sure, and that deserves guild-wide conversation about what is at stake in how we structure undergraduate religious studies curricula. The second undercurrent can be addressed in the classroom on a regular basis. It is important to tell students about *why* religious studies is both an essential part of the humanities and different than other modes of humanistic inquiry. At the very least, I attempt to communicate early, often, and empathetically that the study of religion is a) fun, b) challenging but still fun, and c) useful.

Discussing the *why* can be empowering with students, no matter which course they take or whether they become majors or minors. To get at the *why* in my own teaching, I have tended to privilege what I call "the edge" of the study of religion. By the edge, I mean, of course, talking about weirdos, heretics, "cults," extremists, fringe individuals and groups, marginals, and other others. For me, the edge is a terrific window into a plethora of human differences, some of which persevere and many of which fall by the wayside. Hardly a day goes by in one of my courses without me mentioning something weird to get my students' attention. After all, isn't that where religion is at—the crossroads of the ordinary and extraordinary, the human and more-than-human, the center and the margins, affirmation and doubt, status affirmation and status rejection? How would a "big R" religion ever happen without a group of people at some point looking around at the world and saying "no thank you, we have other ideas" to the order of things? How does that work? Who gets to say? Why does it matter?

Considering the *why* suggests that I need to ask about the edge with students. If religion is about adherence to mainstream views, then why are there so many fringey and edgy ideas in religious discourses and practices? Where, and when, does the center stop and the edge begin? Once an extreme, always an extreme? What—who—makes an idea, person, group, or practice weird? What happens if and/or when the edge loses its, well, edge? What happens when we romanticize and/or idealize the margins—or the center? Could it be that every edge to one is a center to others, and vice versa? Why do we resist classifying some forms of knowing as religious, particularly ways of knowing at the social fringe? I do not ask these questions only in the special classes I teach about the edge, although I do teach plenty of those courses. If we take the intersection of *what*, *how*, and *why* of teaching religious studies with undergraduates seriously, then *every* class I teach needs to explore the dynamics and dialectics of the center and margins to help students explore what religion is, how it works, and why it matters as a cipher for human activity, agency, and articulations of power relations. In this respect, studying religion should bring the fullest possible range of human experiences to the table for description, comparison, analysis, and defamiliarizing interpretation. The edge is a good place to start.

Teaching about religion and/at/as the edge enables us to learn more about humanity. We can learn a lot about the center, or what counts as "normal," through looking at and understanding what and who is left out of that, by choice, by design, by accident, or some combination. The edge also pushes our capacity to resist the temptation to judge, to compartmentalize and dismiss the fringey edges as crazy, and to cultivate empathy. Perhaps some readers might be thinking that we live in "unprecedented" times, so now could be a good time to think about the edge. Teaching about religion as the edge reveals that a big reason to study religion lies in the notion that in doing so we might better understand how, if times are truly unprecedented, we got here. Studying religion as the edge might also help us see that our fringey, edgy time is not special at all. And if it is not special, and maybe not even crazy, how then should we understand our predicament, not to mention respond to it? Teaching about religion does not provide the answers, sadly, although it can provide a series of deliberative opportunities and methods for greater understanding and intervention.

Edge or no edge, I think that the evergreen quest for best practices in teaching about religion with undergraduates probably needs to start with a different set of questions. That is, instead of asking what students who may only take one course "need to know," we may be better served by asking what we must do to challenge *all* students' assumptions about what religion is, and then attempt to convince them that religion is a worthy object of analysis *no matter who they want to be or what they want to do in life.* I find that seeking clarity about the *what*, *how*, and *why* of teaching about religion and/at/as the edge matters a great deal, particularly given the ubiquity of edgy religion in the world and the religious dimensions of much of individual and social existence—central, marginal, and in-between. Despite occasional observations and predictions by social scientists,[5] religion is not disappearing from the American landscape, especially in its edgier manifestations. Teachers of religion are well-equipped to dwell at the edges. The question is whether we have the courage and stamina to do so.

Let me say, finally: this series of ruminations masquerading as an essay would not have been possible without the truly edgy pedagogical mentorship of Gene Gallagher and Patricia O'Connell Killen. Thank you for encouraging me to give voice to the fringey and crazy, to find unclarity in clarity, to question without trepidation, to compare without judgment, to ask the why question, to de-introduce and defamiliarize, to seek to expose the human hands at work. To this day, I make several drafts of detailed handwritten teaching plans, and yet I walk into every class prepared to discuss the three things I can fit on a Post-It note—and I consider myself lucky if I get to 2.5 of those. What I have learned alongside you, though: there is not a large enough notepad.

Notes

1 See also Bruce Forbes's contribution to this volume. Herein I should mention that some of my pedagogical reflection on the potential of one-and-done pedagogies in religious studies was catalyzed by a small departmental grant from the Wabash Center for Teaching and Learning in Theology and Religion (2019–20). While the scope and activities of this grant's plan were fundamentally altered by the advent of the Covid-19 pandemic, my reflection on the various pedagogical questions and conundrums raised by the reality that most of the students we teach will not major in religious studies persists.

2 Here I agree with Eric Hayot's cogent call to disentangle humanist pedagogy and program planning from material resource allotment. See Hayot, *Humanist Reason: A History, An Argument, A Plan* (New York: Columbia University Press, 2020).

3 For recent data and reporting on the characteristics of Gen Z, see Kim Parker and Ruth Igielnik, "On the Cusp of Adulthood and Facing an Uncertain Future: What We Know about Gen Z So Far," *Pew Research Center* (May 14, 2020), https://www.pewresearch.org/social-trends/2020/05/14/on-the-cusp-of-adulthood-and-facing-an-uncertain-future-what-we-know-about-gen-z-so-far-2/, accessed: July 11, 2022.

4 This trepidation has been exacerbated by the pandemic's necessary pedagogical shifts and practices. For a brief discussion of how student fear played out in a fall 2020 religious studies classroom, see Davina C. Lopez, "(Un)Masking Fear and

Power: A 2020 Teaching Reflection," *Journal of Feminist Studies in Religion* 37, no. 2 (2021): 187–90.
5   I usually read such claims to indicate a decline in religious affiliation, not in religious activity or affinity. For a data-informed argument, see Ronald Inglehart, *Religion's Sudden Decline: What's Causing It, and What Comes Next?* (New York: Oxford University Press, 2021).

Bibliography

Hayot, Eric. *Humanist Reason: A History, An Argument, A Plan*. New York: Columbia University Press, 2020.

Inglehart, Ronald. *Religion's Sudden Decline: What's Causing It, and What Comes Next?* New York: Oxford University Press, 2021.

Lopez, Davina C. "(Un)Masking Fear and Power: A 2020 Teaching Reflection." *Journal of Feminist Studies in Religion* 37, no. 2 (2021): 187–90.

Parker, Kim, and Ruth Igielnik, "On the Cusp of Adulthood and Facing an Uncertain Future: What We Know about Gen Z So Far." Pew Research Center, May 2020, https://www.pewresearch.org/social-trends/2020/05/14/on-the-cusp-of-adulthood-and-facing-an-uncertain-future-what-we-know-about-gen-z-so-far-2/.

Contributors

Richard S. Ascough, Queen's University

Molly H. Bassett, Georgia State University

Alicia J. Batten, Conrad Grebel University College

Kathryn D. Blanchard, Alma College (*emerita*)

Mara Brecht, Loyola University Chicago

Andrea Nicole Carandang, St. Michael's College, University of Toronto

Bruce David Forbes, Morningside University

Anita Houck, St. Mary's College

Rebekka King, Middle Tennessee State University

Reid B. Locklin, St. Michael's College, University of Toronto

Davina C. Lopez, Eckerd College

Joanne Maguire, University of North Carolina, Charlotte

Susan Marks, New College of Florida

Kevin J. O'Brien, Pacific Lutheran University

Thomas Pearson, Nielsen Center for the Liberal Arts at Eckerd College

Tina Pippin, Agnes Scott College

Kwok Pui-lan, Candler School of Theology

Arthur M. Sutherland, Loyola University Maryland

Lydia Willsky-Ciollo, Fairfield University

Index

assessment (*see also* grading) 76, 87, 111–13, 118–24, 153–61

classroom and race 17, 43, 45, 86, 105–13, 145, 213
classroom and silence 34–5, 58, 83–5, 181
classroom as safe space 80 n. 37, 107, 111, 157
community based learning 98, 138–48, 200–3
constructivism 59, 75, 84, 201
course content 76–77, 86, 104, 105–7, 130, 139–41, 209–17
critical pedagogy 199
critical thinking 16, 20, 27–28, 32–34, 50, 54, 57, 96, 98, 121, 192–3, 200–1, 210
curriculum 5, 86–7, 91–9, 129, 192–4, 180, 210–17

design
    active learning 15, 45, 71, 73, 75–6, 83–5, 200
    of assignments and activities 3, 29–30, 54–7, 74–6, 83–6, 89, 98–9, 108–9, 130, 132–5, 139, 141, 143, 155, 157, 170–1, 179, 214
    backward 30–4, 42–3, 76, 87
    of courses 19–22, 31–2, 34, 40–1, 57, 86–8, 91–9, 130–5, 139–40, 155
    focused teaching 28–29, 41
    letting go of 30, 49, 71–2, 76, 83, 86, 88–9
    and Post-It note 3, 76, 83–5, 88–9, 171, 217
    universal 17
discussion 41, 85–6, 91, 93, 107–8, 211, 213–14
    and silence 34–5, 58, 84–5
diversifying the syllabus 41, 43, 103–13

embodied pedagogy 103–13, 140, 144
empowerment 72, 83, 137, 202, 211, 215

festschrift 1, 2, 10
Freire, Paulo 4, 141, 145–6, 148, 166, 199, 201–3

Gallagher, Eugene V. 1–10
    context 5–6
    general education 5, 193
    mentor 2, 8, 9, 15, 77, 83, 84, 89, 129, 132, 134, 138, 179, 194, 217
    persona 7–10
    plan 3–4
    play 8, 73–4
    post-it notes 3, 83–4, 88–9, 171, 217
    SoTL 4, 7, 16, 104, 120–2, 153, 189, 197–8, 202
    students 1, 3, 42, 73, 84–5, 87–8, 193–4
    vocation 6, 8
    workshop design 1–10, 15, 21, 72, 77, 130, 191–2, 199
general education curriculum 5, 86–7, 91–9, 155, 180, 192–4, 210–17
grading (see also, assessment) 111, 119, 153–61

hooks, bell 55, 141, 145–6, 148
hospitality 2, 42, 72, 124, 179, 182–5, 189, 199
humanities 5, 18–21, 54, 84, 87, 97, 107, 111, 168, 209–17

institutional context (*see also* place) 2, 5–6, 9, 18, 30–1, 93, 96–8, 112, 118, 121–4, 129–30, 133–4, 159, 168–9, 171, 188, 192–3, 209–13, 215
introductory course 56, 87, 91–9, 117–18, 177–18, 156, 184, 193–4, 209–17

Index

Killen, Patricia O'Connell 1–10
  Catholicism 27–35
  context 5–6
  mentor 2, 15, 27–9, 35, 77, 129, 134, 138, 179, 189, 194, 217
  mid-range reflection 3–4, 9, 15–16, 19–23, 117–18, 121–4, 198–9
  persona 7–10
  plan 3–4, 76
  play 8, 72, 189
  SoTL 4, 7, 16, 19, 21, 104, 120–2, 153, 189, 197–8, 202
  students 1, 5, 19–20, 42, 54, 73, 190–1, 194
  vocation 189–91
  workshop design 1–10, 15, 21, 27, 29, 59, 72, 77, 118, 130, 199

learning 3, 15, 18–21, 29–30, 74
  and action 18–21
  and design 30–4
  experiential 40, 139, 199
  goals 40–1, 31, 39, 86–9, 91–9, 123–4, 129, 179, 184, 193, 200–2, 210–17
  and grading 118–19, 121, 153–61
  and humor 49–60
  lifelong 40–1, 46
  and play 72–7
  student resistance to 42, 180–1
  transformative 107, 19, 72, 104, 107–8, 111, 113, 151, 148, 182, 185, 189–90, 201–2
lecture 41–4, 76, 84, 92, 117, 158, 179, 182
liberal arts 5, 91–2, 97, 118, 130, 180, 209–17, 212

metaphor for teaching 3, 7, 19–23, 165–72, 187, 197
midrange reflection 3–4, 9, 15–16, 21–2, 117–18, 121–4, 198–9

neoliberal 4, 199, 202

Palmer, Parker 6–8, 168
persona 2, 6–10, 104–13, 137–8, 144, 148, 153, 159–61, 179

place (*see also* institutional context) 2, 5–6, 9–10, 40, 133, 145, 153, 185, 187–91, 201, 197–8, 203
plan (*see also* design) 2–5, 9–10, 30–1, 76, 84–5, 88–9, 146–7, 179, 184, 197, 202, 217
postcolonial 103–11, 118

religious literacy 87–8, 97–9, 123, 192

"Sketching the Contours of the Scholarship of Teaching and Learning in Theology and Religion" (by Patricia O'Connell Killen and Eugene V. Gallagher) 4, 16, 104, 120–2, 153, 197–8, 202
skills 40, 71, 75, 86–7, 93, 97, 108, 111–12, 121, 123, 157, 187, 192–4, 212–14
students 5, 16, 17, 20–3, 29–30, 73, 179–85
  and anxiety 16–17, 33–4, 42, 45–6, 52, 62 n.21, 73–4, 86, 211
  and complaining 156–60
  demographics 40–1
  disillusionment 17–18
  diversity of 40, 85, 93, 96, 103–4, 109–13, 143, 180–5
  engagement 18, 83–5, 88, 92, 131, 166, 169, 182, 184–5, 200–1, 213
  humor 49–60, 53
  importance of understanding them 85, 95–6, 180–5, 190–4, 210–17
  motivation 18, 62 n.21, 154–5, 160, 180–5
  play 73–7
  and religion 41–2, 45–6, 49, 54, 56, 57, 95–6, 103–4, 131, 141, 181, 182, 187, 193, 210–12
  professor's relationship to 156, 170, 180, 182–5, 202

teaching
  Bible 39–46, 74–7, 184
  Christianity 27–35, 39–46, 74–7, 93, 99, 103–13, 131–2, 138–48, 179–85
  justice 15–23, 40, 98, 103–13, 137–48, 199–203, 211

online 41, 43, 157
religion, arguments for 16, 19–21, 54, 59, 86–7, 97–8, 122–3, 131, 133–4, 184–5, 187, 193–4, 211–17
student centered 30, 41, 73, 83–9, 99, 201, 203
theology 29, 45, 49, 53, 54, 103–13, 137–48, 181–5
topics and theories of religion 86–9, 91–9, 117–18, 122–3, 192–4, 209–17

vocation of teaching 6, 8, 165, 166–9, 189, 209

Wabash Center for Teaching and Learning in Theology and Religion 1–10, 21, 27–9, 53, 59, 87, 72, 77, 105, 108, 118, 129–32, 132, 134, 179, 191–2, 197–9
writing the scholarship of teaching 3–4, 16, 19, 104, 118–22, 153, 197–203

www.ingramcontent.com/pod-product-compliance
Lightning Source LLC
Chambersburg PA
CBHW052107300426
44116CB00010B/1569